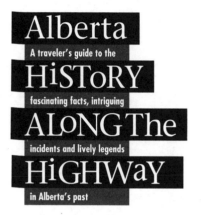

Alberta

A traveler's guide to the

HiSToRY

fascinating facts, intriguing

ALoNG The

incidents and lively legends

HiGHWaY

in Alberta's past

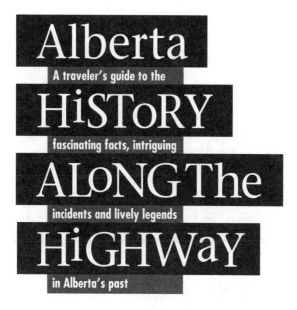

Alberta
A traveler's guide to the

HiSToRY
fascinating facts, intriguing

ALONG The
incidents and lively legends

HiGHWaY
in Alberta's past

Ted Stone

Red Deer College Press

The Publishers
Red Deer College Press
56 Avenue & 32 Street Box 5005
Red Deer Alberta Canada T4N 5H5

Acknowledgments
Cover photograph courtesy of Tony Stone Images
Cover design by Kunz + Associates
Text design by Dennis Johnson
Printed and bound in Canada by Quality Color Press for
Red Deer College Press

Financial support provided by the Alberta Foundation for the Arts, a
beneficiary of the Lottery Fund of the Government of Alberta, and by
the Canada Council, the Department of Canadian Heritage and Red
Deer College.

COMMITTED TO THE DEVELOPMENT OF CULTURE AND THE ARTS

Canadian Cataloguing in Publication Data
Stone, Ted. 1947–
Alberta history along the highway
Includes index.
ISBN 0-88995-133-0
1. Alberta—History, Local. 2. Historic sites—Alberta. 3. Automobile trav-
el—Alberta I. Title.
FC3661.S76 1996   971.23   C94-910903-7
F1078.S76   1996

Photograph Acknowledgments

The Publishers gratefully acknowledge the Provincial Archives of Alberta for each of the photographs appearing in this book:

"A" COLLECTION
A.3887 Macleod Hotel, pages 26-27
A.2275 Charles S. Noble, page 58
A.2658 The "Big Four," pages 96-97
A.12,116 Calgary Stampede, page 98
A.2235 Main Street Markerville, pages 130-131
A.453 NWMP Fort Saskatchewan, pages 154-55
A.2198 Drumheller, page 160
A.1685 Fort Edmonton, pages 190-191
A.12,151 Louis Riel, page 196
A.2263 Whyte Avenue, page 198
A.1967 Alexander Mackenzie, page 218
A.2245 Old Hudson Bay Company Buildings, page 228
A.2287 Day After Frank Slide, pages 238-239
A.11,289 The Bungalows, pages 252-253

ERNEST BROWN COLLECTION
B.1960 J.F. Macleod, page 22
B.2428 Fort Macleod, page 28
B.105 Round-up Branding, page 35
B.1835 Jerry Potts, page 48
B.2409 Fort Benton, page 53
B.2020 James Walsh, page 67
B.2411 I.G. Baker Store, page 91
B.3175 Fort Calgary, page 92
B.7131 John Rowand, page 192
B.5170 Klondikers, page 202

B.2967 Fort Chipewyan, page 167
B.5683 HBC's Transport, page 120
B.69 Ranching Scene, pages 104-105
B.1684 Scene of the Frog Lake Massacre, page 176
B.5243 First Woman Klondiker over Edmonton Route, page 203
B.9527 Father Lacombe, page 208
B.2396 Banff, pages 244-245

NICHOLAS GAVINCHUK COLLECTION
G.2182 George McDougall, page 108

O.M.I. COLLECTION
OB.1023 Grey Nuns, page 128
OB.820 Monument to the Frog Lake Massacre, page 177

HARRY POLLARD COLLECTION
P.3414 Fort Whoop-up, pages 38-39
P.197 Big Bear, page 51
P.215 Fort Walsh, page 73
P.129 Crowfoot, page 82
P.3430 Old Fort Calgary, pages 88-89
P.453 Barr Colonists, page 173
P.200 Father Lacombe, page 181

PUBLIC AFFAIRS BUREAU COLLECTION
PA.196⅔ Twelve-Foot Davis, page 221
PA.6899½ Kootenai Brown, page 236

For Heather Ann Stone

Contents

Chapter 9
Mountain Country
Land of Parks and Peaks / 233

Chronology of Alberta History / 258

Directory of Alberta Museums / 262

Useful Further Reading / 292

Name Index / 294

Subject Index / 297

Preface

THE IDEA FOR THIS BOOK came one day after speeding past an historical marker on Highway 16 west of Edmonton. Almost immediately, I regretted not stopping. I'd done this sort of thing before. Sometimes I'd be in a hurry. Sometimes I would just avoid the stop because I had a long way to go and didn't want to interrupt the rhythm of my travel. Always, though, for a long time afterward I would wonder what the sign had said.

But west of Edmonton that day, it occurred to me that other people must sometimes pass by roadside historical markers and then wish they had stopped. What we all needed, I thought, was a book of Alberta history written especially for travelers. It would be a book not just for looking up information about the road signs, but also for finding additional information and anecdotes about Alberta's past.

Compared to most places, even on this continent, Alberta's historical record is short. But few places in North America offer a more interesting and varied record. For those who think Canada lacked a Wild West, let them come to Alberta. From the days of the fur trade to the coming of the North-West Mounted Police, and for some time afterward, Alberta's history was as wild and woolly as any place's.

It was here, after all, that American desperadoes and plainsmen came when the law got too oppressive south of the border. American and Canadian traders peddled whiskey to Alberta Indians partly because the law forbade such practices across the line in Montana. And it was here that there was no law, at least no European-style law.

All this changed in 1874, when the North-West Mounted Police came west. By the time the Mounties got here, the fur and whiskey trades had already started to decline. Fur-bearing animals had been decimated by decades of overtrapping and the buffalo were nearly gone. The independent life of Alberta's Indians was almost over. European settlement and the new Province of Alberta were right around the corner. And authors would soon begin writing books about Alberta's history.

This is one of those books but one written especially for travelers. For the most part, I've followed the provincial tourist zones when dividing *Alberta History Along the Highway* into chapters. The only exceptions occur where reason seems to dictate another demarcation. Cochrane and Highway 1A, for instance, are included in the "Calgary to the Mountains" chapter instead of "David Thompson and Evergreen Country." All of Peace River country west of Lesser Slave Lake is included in "Game Country and the Mighty Peace," even though a small portion of it falls in the Land of the Midnight Twilight tourist zone. The Rocky Mountains, including the three mountain national parks, are in a chapter of their own.

Although the chapters of *Alberta History Along the Highway* reflect the provincial tourist zones, and much of the book can be classified as local history, I have made no attempt to write a community-by-community record of the past. Nor is this a step-by-step guide to Alberta highways. Rather, *Alberta History Along the Highway* is an overview of the history of the province based on the chronicles of each region, the highway historical markers and the stories that came to mind as I traveled Alberta's roadways.

No single book can possibly provide a full accounting of Alberta's history. A writer has to choose which stories to include from thousands of fascinating tales. It is my hope that for readers fortunate enough to travel Alberta's highways the present volume will encourage them to begin their own exploration of Alberta's past. At the very least, I would like everyone who's ever whizzed by an historical marker to still be able to find out what it was about.

For their help in the preparation of this book, I'd like to thank Alberta Tourism, especially the many local tourist information representatives across the province who helped me find historical points of interest in each region, the Alberta Museums Association, Chris Robinson of Community Heritage Services, Brock Silversides at the Provincial Archives, Camille Duesener at Fort George/Buckingham House Interpretive Centre, Michael Gormley at the Wainwright Museum, staffs at the Glenbow Archives and the Local History Room of the Calgary Public Library, Dennis Johnson and Carolyn Dearden for their tireless editorial assistance, and Bob and Marge Walde for the chokecherry syrup.

Introduction
On the Trail of Alberta History

A LTHOUGH A WELL-DOCUMENTED ACCOUNT of Alberta's past is only possible for something like the last 150 years, the human history of the province began thousands of years earlier. At least 20,000 years ago, people who became the first North Americans crossed a land bridge between Siberia and Alaska. Despite excellent hunting grounds in ice-free areas of what is today Alaska and the Yukon Territory, the way south was almost completely blocked by glaciers. From the east and west, the Cordilleran and Laurentide ice sheets converged along the eastern slopes of the Rocky Mountains. As the climate warmed, however, a narrow ice-free corridor opened from the far north to the southern edge of the glaciers in present-day Montana. Archaeologists believe the ancestors of all the original peoples of the Americas migrated along this corridor.

As the glaciers retreated northward, the first Albertans began to settle the area east of the mountains. As the climate became drier, the coniferous forests that had developed first in southern Alberta gave way to grasslands. Here aboriginal people lived for several thousand years before any European set foot on the continent.

Once Europeans began to arrive on the eastern shores of North America, Plains Indians started to hear stories about them. Metal tools, coins and other articles of European origin showed up in prairie camps long before traders arrived in the Canadian West. By the end of the seventeenth century, half a century before any white people would come to what is today Alberta, the tribes of the Blackfoot Confederacy began to trade regularly for European goods from both Montreal and Hudson Bay.

The Blackfoot obtained most of these goods from the Cree, who lived closer to Europeans and were the first western Indians to obtain firearms. With guns, the Cree expanded their territory at the expense of most other Alberta tribes. Cree warriors drove the Blackfoot southwest toward the mountains. About the same time, the Shoshoni (or Snakes), who had come into southern Alberta after they obtained horses, began to put pressure on the Blackfoot by pushing them north again toward the Cree.

By 1730, the fortunes of the Blackfoot people improved. With horses obtained from the south and guns from the north, the Blackfoot soon began to reclaim and then expand their territory. Initially, this came at the expense of the Shoshoni and others who lacked firearms, but the Cree—still without horses—began to lose ground, too.

For Plains Indians, the acquisition of guns and especially horses transformed their lives. Before horses, people were forced to travel almost constantly. They had to stay close to the buffalo, walking in small family groups with dogs to help carry their possessions. An entire day's journey would seldom cover more than a few miles.

After the arrival of horses, buffalo were almost always within a few hours ride. Carrying household possessions became easier. Instead of hunting in small groups, dozens of families banded together to hunt on horseback. With buffalo closer and easier to kill, more leisure time could be devoted to spiritual and artistic matters. There was also more time to raid neighboring tribes to steal horses or occupy hunting grounds.

It's possible that French fur traders entered what we now call Alberta as early as 1750, but Anthony Henday was the earliest known European visitor. He arrived in the employ of the Hudson's Bay Company on September 11, 1754. Henday had been sent south from York Factory, the great fur post on Hudson Bay, because the English company had been losing furs to French competitors. Instead of waiting for Indians to come to them, the French had established trading posts inland on Lake Winnipeg and along the North Saskatchewan River. These posts diverted furs that would otherwise have gone to the English on Hudson Bay.

Henday's mission was to get the Blackfoot to come to York Factory to trade with the English. Although he failed, Henday's journey to the place we now call Alberta taught Hudson's Bay traders the true nature of the fur trade in western Canada. Henday discovered that the Cree he traveled with were not trappers as had been supposed but entrepreneurial middlemen who traveled south every year from the Hudson's Bay Company post at York Factory to trade with the Indians of the prairies.

In 1763, the Treaty of Paris ended the French fur trade in the northwest, but soon new, independent, mostly Scottish traders were sending voyageurs west from Montreal. Alberta furs were once more diverted from the English company at York Factory to Quebec. By the late 1770s, when Montreal traders combined forces to form the North West Company, Hudson's Bay traders finally abandoned their idea of trading from a fortress on the northern sea.

For the next 40 years, the two companies penetrated the heart of the continent in fierce competition. In 1778, Peter Pond became the first white resident of Alberta when he built a fur post on the Athabasca River. Within the decade, another post had been established at present-day Fort McMurray. In 1788, Alexander Mackenzie built Fort Chipewyan, which is today the province's oldest continuously occupied settlement. In the spring of 1789, Mackenzie set out for Great Slave Lake. From there, he followed the river we know today by his name until he reached the Arctic Ocean. In 1793, he traveled from a spot near today's town of Peace River to the Pacific, beating the Americans Lewis and Clark across the continent by more than a decade.

Competition between the North West and Hudson's Bay companies was especially fierce along the North Saskatchewan River. By 1785, both companies had established fur posts almost as far upriver as today's Alberta–Saskatchewan border. In 1792, they built the first fur posts on the North Saskatchewan inside Alberta's present boundaries.

In the summer of 1795, the North West Company built Fort Augustus near present-day Fort Saskatchewan. The Hudson's Bay Company built Edmonton House nearby in October. Although Hudson's Bay traders would change the location of this post several times, Edmonton has been a name on Alberta maps ever since.

Four years later, Rocky Mountain House and Acton House were constructed near the present town of Rocky Mountain House. From here, in 1807, David Thompson began his explorations west of the mountains, opening areas of trade in present-day British Columbia, Washington, Oregon, Idaho and Montana.

In 1821, with competition severely straining the resources of both, the two companies merged under the charter of the old Hudson's Bay Company. For the next half-century, the Hudson's Bay Company operated a virtual monopoly through most of its territory, and Edmonton became the most important fur post in the northwest.

By 1870, when Canada took over Rupert's Land, the heyday of the fur trade had passed and the glory days of the Plains Indian were already over. In the south, whiskey traders moved into the country in ever-increasing numbers. In 1869, Alexander Hamilton and John J. Healy built what became the best known of the whiskey forts. It was located at the confluence of the St. Mary and Oldman rivers near present-day Lethbridge and quickly became known as Fort Whoop-Up.

Whiskey contributed to the other problems already faced by Indians. The fur trade was disintegrating after decades of overtrapping. Buffalo were disappearing across the plains, so the Cree, Assiniboine and other tribes, invaded traditional Blackfoot hunting grounds to compete for the last remaining buffalo.

White encroachment into Blackfoot and other Indian lands also increased. By 1870, Blackfoot power on the North American prairies had gone into steep decline. Smallpox and other white diseases, along with whiskey, had done what white rifles could not. The demise of the Blackfoot Confederacy left the road open for white settlement of the future province of Alberta.

The North-West Mounted Police brought European law to the region in 1874. By 1880, after treaties had been signed with the Indians, ranchers began to move into the area. In 1881, the Canadian government began leasing huge tracts of western grasslands to eastern and foreign syndicates for a pittance.

The railroad, in its relentless drive to the Pacific, arrived in Alberta in 1883. Along its tracks came increasing numbers of homesteaders. They would take a place beside Alberta's ranchers to form the backbone of the new white society. Soon, settlement reached a point where Alberta's new citizens demanded self-government, and the Province of Alberta became part of Canada in 1905. Alberta's rapid development from 1905 to the present has been characterized by dramatic changes in the social, political and economic fabric of the region. Today, as we look at some of Alberta's historical characters and intriguing events, we find a province rich not only in resources but in a colorful past as wild and interesting as any ever recorded.

Chapter 1

Chinook Country

The Land Under the Arch

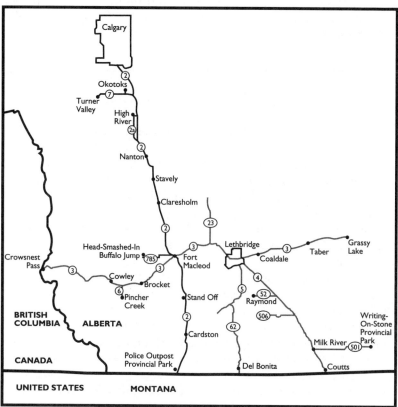

IF YOU'RE YEARNING TO GO OUT WEST, go to Alberta's Chinook Country. Here big blue skies, shortgrass prairies, foothills and coulees evoke familiar scenes of the Old West. Chinook Country is where the first whiskey traders came to plunder Indian wealth. It's where the cattle industry flourished in the days of the open range and where homesteaders began to take up land even before the big range leases expired. Chinook Country is where the North-West Mounted Police journeyed to bring European law to the Canadian West. It's where Alberta's oil industry began.

But Chinook Country is home to an even older history. Aboriginal people have lived here for thousands of years. Head-Smashed-In Buffalo Jump is older than the Egyptian pyramids, and the ancient chronicles at Writing-On-Stone Provincial Park make up the largest body of Indian petroglyphs and pictographs on the North American continent. The Old North Trail, which is this area's first highway, is the oldest Indian trail in the Americas.

The Old North Trail
(roughly) Highway 2 between the Montana border and Calgary

The Old North Trail began at least as far north as the North Saskatchewan River, which flows through Edmonton. From there, the trail followed the eastern side of the Rocky Mountains all the way to present-day Mexico. In Alberta and Montana, according to the North Peigan chief Brings-Down the Sun, the trail stayed on the open prairie, keeping a relatively uniform distance from the mountains. It deviated from this pattern only as it wound its way around the eastern stretches of forests and foothills.

Like most aboriginal trails in North America, the Old North was used by Europeans once they arrived here. Parts of today's Highway 2 south of Calgary follow portions of the Old North. In Alberta's extreme southwest, the Old North probably lies somewhere between highways 2 and 6. In Montana, U.S. Highway 89 loosely follows the old trail as it winds its way south from the Alberta border.

In all likelihood, the Old North Trail developed from an even more important north–south route that aboriginal people once traveled. Perhaps 20,000 years ago or more, people who became the first North Americans crossed a land bridge between Alaska and Siberia. Their descendants worked their way south over the only route open between the glaciers—the route along the eastern side of Alberta's mountains. When the glaciers retreated, the trail continued to be used, first by the native people of the area and later by whites. Eventually, it evolved into today's Highway 2.

Highway 2 from the Montana Border to Calgary

North-West Mounted Police Move In on Smugglers
Highway 2, access road 9 miles (15 km) north of Montana border, then southwest 9 miles (15 km) to Police Outpost Provincial Park

Police Outpost Provincial Park lies west of Highway 2, just north of the Alberta–Montana border, 15.5 miles (25 kilometers) southwest of Cardston. This small park and campground on Outpost Lake is the site of an early Mounted Police outpost.

In the 1890s, smugglers from Montana often crossed into Canada along nearby Boundary Creek. The Mounted Police established a small post here as a base for two or three men to patrol the border. These days, smugglers are more likely to take alternate routes. Visitors to the park, though, can slip quietly past the boundary marker for a brief visit to the south side of what Indian people once called the Medicine Line because of the almost magical powers the border between the United States and Canada appeared to have on white people.

Mormons Establish Cardston in Southern Alberta
Highway 2, 15.5 miles (25 km) north of the Montana border

Cardston is named for Charles Ora Card, the charismatic son-in-law of Brigham Young. Card led his Mormon followers into southern Alberta in order to escape what he felt were persecutory laws in the United States. Legend has it that on the settlers' first morning in Canada, June 2, 1887, the new immigrants came out of their tents to discover 6 inches (15 centimeters) of snow on the ground. "Brother Card," someone asked, "what kind of a place have you brought us to?" Card smiled and answered, "Isn't it beautiful?"

When cowboys at the nearby Cochrane Ranch told William Cochrane, son of ranch founder, Senator Matthew Cochrane, that the Mormons were tearing up the good grasslands, Cochrane told the cowboys to leave the settlers alone. "They'll winter kill," he said. But the Mormons thrived in Alberta. In fact, within a few years, the new settlers bought out the huge Cochrane Ranch holdings and opened the land for settlement to members of their church.

Unlike many later settlers who homesteaded in the province, the Mormons were experienced farmers. Soon after their arrival, they began the first of the irrigation projects that today water some of the richest agricultural lands in Alberta.

Points of historical interest in Cardston include the C.O. Card House, the log home that Card built in 1887, when he first arrived. Cardston's Mormon Temple is also open to visitors. So is the Courthouse Museum, which includes an old jail cell in its basement. The Fay Wray Fountain honors local girl Fay Wray, who grew up on a nearby ranch and then left for Hollywood. In 1933, Wray played leading lady to the tallest, darkest leading man in the history of movies—King Kong.

One of Alberta's newest and best museums is also in Cardston. The Remington–Alberta Carriage Centre features one of North America's largest and most diverse collections of horse-drawn vehicles. Audio-visual displays at the museum include a wide-screen video theater and smaller displays that, among other things, take visitors on simulated carriage rides and provide instructions for how to drive a horse and buggy. The more than 200 coaches in the collection range from fancy carriages to stagecoaches and carts. Visitors can see many of the carriages in action, pulled by horses from the center's stable of Clydesdales, Quarter Horses and Canadians. They can even arrange a ride in some of the carriages.

Cobblestone Manor, now a Cardston restaurant, was built by Henry Hoet, a Belgian immigrant who should qualify as one of the great romantics of western history. Hoet built the stone house for his sweetheart, who was back in the old country. He hauled nearly 200 metric tons of rock to the site, load after load in a wheelbarrow pulled by his dog.

Inside, Hoet built rooms of hard woods scavenged from

leftover materials from the Mormon Temple. He designed and built elaborate mosaic ceilings, and he imported stained glass from Europe. Construction took 16 years. When he finished, Hoet wrote to his sweetheart only to find she had married someone else years earlier. After he got the news, Hoet went insane. The house was sold for a fraction of its value to pay his bills at Alberta Hospital in Ponoka.

Blood Indians Choose Reserve
Highway 2, Cardston's northern boundary

As you drive north past the Cardston village limits, you enter the Blood Indian Reserve, the largest Indian reservation in Canada. This land was chosen by the Blood people after their chiefs signed Treaty No. 7 with the Canadian government in September 1877. The Bloods were part of the Blackfoot Confederacy, which also included the Peigan and Blackfoot.

Through principal interpreters, Jerry Potts and Jimmy Bird, chiefs of the Blackfoot Confederacy joined with those of the Stoney and Sarcee to negotiate the treaty with the Canadian government. It took more than a year to reach an agreement, but on September 17, 1877, when everyone arrived to sign the treaty at Blackfoot Crossing—about 60 miles (97 kilometers) from present-day Calgary—the Bloods were absent.

Red Crow was head chief of the Bloods at the time, and he kept government officials wondering about whether he would sign the treaty until the last possible moment. He had several reasons for hesitating. Part of his reluctance stemmed from what he considered a snub by the Mounted Police. Colonel Macleod, one of the principal commissioners of this treaty, seemed to favor Crowfoot, the Blackfoot chief. Crowfoot favored signing the treaty, but Macleod didn't realize that Crowfoot, though a prominent and respected chief, was not the head of the entire Blackfoot Confederacy. He was only one chief among many.

Red Crow, who led a larger band of Bloods than Crowfoot's Blackfoot, resented the Mounties for their apparent favoritism. When all was said and done, however, Red Crow, like the other chiefs, knew the glory days of the once powerful Blackfoot Confederacy had come to an end, and its tribes were left with no real alternative. Their land would be taken from them no matter what they did.

Still, Red Crow wavered for several days before he made his decision. For two days in September 1877, he kept government officials waiting. Finally, a deeply troubled Red Crow rode into the camp at Blackfoot Crossing with his band of Bloods. The next day he signed the treaty.

Along with the other chiefs, Red Crow turned over 50,000 square miles (130,000 square kilometers) of land to the Canadian government. In exchange, the government gave each band member twelve dollars, an additional five dollars yearly, the freedom to hunt throughout surrendered lands and an annual supply of ammunition. The treaty also promised that "each Chief and each minor Chief, and each Chief and Councillor duly recognized as such, shall, every three years, receive a suitable suit of clothing and each Chief and minor Chief, a suitable medal and flag, and, the next year, each Chief and minor Chief shall receive a Winchester rifle." But perhaps the strongest inducement for signing the treaty was that the Blood people were allowed to keep their land in the Belly Buttes along the Oldman, Belly and St. Mary rivers. For the Bloods, land near the Oldman River was sacred ground. The river was named for Napi, the Old Man trickster hero of Blackfoot legend.

Desperadoes Stand Off Montana Sheriff
Highway 2, 18.5 miles (30 km) north of Cardston at Standoff

Stand Off, the largest community on the Blood reserve, is named after an early whiskey post located near here on the Belly River. The post was founded after metis trader Joseph Kipp and his partner, Charles Thomas, successfully avoided arrest by Montana Sheriff Charles D. Hard south of the present town near the United States border.

Sheriff Hard was known for his unusually vigorous stance against the whiskey trade, which was illegal in Montana. Learning that Kipp and Thomas were carrying a load of whiskey, Hard doggedly tracked the pair up the trail from Fort Benton. By the time Hard caught up to the desperadoes, Kipp gleefully pointed out that they'd already crossed the north fork of the

Milk River, erroneously thought to be the U.S.–Canada boundary at that time. This put the traders, by their reckoning, beyond the reach of American justice. There was nothing for the Montana lawman to do but concede defeat.

The victorious whiskey traders then set themselves up in business on the Belly River and named their new post in honor of their successful standoff. Stories of their encounter with Sheriff Hard became even more sensational when, in 1874, the International Boundary Commission completed its report on the border and it was discovered that Kipp and Thomas had been 300 yards (274 meters) south of the U.S. border at the time of their encounter with Sheriff Hard. Other notoriously named forts of the era included Slide-out, Robbers' Roost and Whoop-Up, the largest of the Alberta whiskey posts.

An historical marker on the edge of Highway 2 in Stand Off commemorates Red Crow, the great Blood chief who signed Treaty No. 7 in 1877 and chose the land of the Belly Buttes for the Blood reserve. It was an act that would eventually drive the Bloods to poverty and dependency. But by the time of this treaty, Red Crow had witnessed the demise of the buffalo, the ravages of smallpox, the death of many Bloods in intertribal conflicts over remaining land and food, and the fatal effects of the whiskey trade. He, himself, had killed his brother and two other Bloods in a drunken fight. Red Crow knew that his people's land would be lost either peacefully through treaties or in bloody battles with whites. Though he kept the other signatories of Treaty No. 7 waiting for two days before signing, Red Crow saw no alternative. His once strong people, who had freely ranged the Great Plains for centuries, were in no position to fight. Once on the reserve, members of the Blood band became the first Alberta aboriginals to make the difficult transition to farming. Red Crow remained a leader of the Blood people during the following years of white settlement in the West. He died in 1900.

Missionaries Come to Big Island
Highway 2, 8.5 miles (14 km) north of Stand Off

An historical marker on the east side of the highway tells of Reverend Samuel Trivett, an Anglican missionary who came to this area from England in 1880. Reverend Trivett established a church, Omoksene (or Big Island), on the Belly River at the edge of the Blood reserve. Later, he opened a residential school. He served at the mission until 1891.

Mounties Name First Fort After Macleod
Highway 2, 18.5 miles (30 km) north of Stand Off at Fort Macleod

Lieutenant Colonel James F. Macleod, c. 1877.

Fort Macleod was named after Colonel James F. Macleod of the North-West Mounted Police. In 1874, Macleod was second in command during the long police trek to establish Canadian law in the West. Soon after the Mounties arrived here, though, Police Commissioner George Arthur French left to establish North-West Mounted Police headquarters at Swan River in northwestern Manitoba. This left Colonel Macleod in charge of the force in present-day southern Alberta. Macleod ordered a fort built on an island in the Oldman River, then christened it with his own name, which was standard practice at the time.

At Fort Macleod the real work of the Mounties in Alberta began. Despite the hardships the troops encountered on their trek west, the march had marshaled the force into a cohesive, well-disciplined unit. The generally high caliber of recruits, their persistence and camaraderie, and their notion of bringing British legal tradition to Indians and whites alike all went into developing the unique characteristics of the North-West Mounted Police.

Initially, Macleod and his police force faced two important tasks: ridding the country of whiskey traders and making friends, and eventually treaties, with the Indians. Perhaps the Mounties didn't realize it, but the success of the former had a lot to do with the success of the latter.

The Blackfoot and their allies waited several weeks before making contact with the police after they arrived at Fort Macleod. Finally, Crowfoot, the main chief of the Blackfoot, sent his foster brother, Three Bulls, to investigate Macleod and the new lawmen. During the course of his visit, Three Bulls casually announced that he had been sold three bottles of bad whiskey by traders camped at Pine Coulee, 50 miles (80 kilometers) north.

Immediately, Macleod sent 10 troopers guided by Three Bulls and the well-known metis scout Jerry Potts to arrest the traders. The police surprised the five men and not only made their first arrests but confiscated the traders' whiskey, wagons and other goods. These included more than 100 buffalo skins, which were turned over to the men at Fort Macleod for use as sleeping robes once the whiskey traders were found guilty as charged.

Macleod had enough evidence to convict the traders in most any court, but at Fort Macleod, conviction was easier to get than back in the East. Macleod, in addition to his role as the chief police officer for the region, was also the only Justice of the Peace in the area. Thus, in one man was vested the authority of policeman and court. In effect, Macleod arrested anyone he thought guilty of a crime, then held a trial to decide if he had arrested the right person.

Faced with law enforcement that amounted to nothing less than military occupation, all but a sorry few of the old-time whiskey traders packed up and fled or immediately switched to legitimate businesses. By the first of December 1874, before Mounted Police officers had even moved into permanent quarters, Assistant Commissioner Macleod was able to write to his superior that the Mounties had caused the "complete stoppage of the whiskey trade throughout the whole of this section of the country." It was a somewhat optimistic claim but not far from true.

In the coming months, the Mounties earned the admiration of the Indians. Not only did the officers quash the whiskey trade, which had devastated traditional native society, but they brought a measure of equality before the law that the Blackfoot had not known south of the border. In the frontier settlement that grew up around Fort Macleod, the Mounties were as quick to punish a white man for a transgression against an Indian as they were an Indian when the situation was reversed.

As a commander, Macleod was tough but popular. One day, while he and two of his men were on liquor patrol, they discovered a keg of Montana whiskey hidden along the trail. It was a hot day. All three of the men thought longingly of the liquid inside the barrel, but standing orders were to destroy any whiskey they found. "Should I knock the bottom out of the keg, Sir?" the corporal asked Colonel Macleod. There seemed only one answer.

"Wait a minute," said Macleod. "We don't really know what's in there. Bring it here and let me taste it first." The corporal brought the barrel forward, and the colonel scooped out a cupful of whiskey. After one taste, he downed the whole cup. Then he turned to the sergeant with a perplexed look on his face. "I can't say as I know what this is," the colonel said. "Maybe you'd better taste it."

The sergeant dutifully downed a full cup of the liquid.

"Well," said Colonel Macleod, "do you know what it is?"

"No, Sir, can't say as I do," the sergeant replied.

"Well, then, give the corporal a taste," said the colonel. "Maybe he'll know what it is."

But the corporal didn't know what it was either, so they all tried it again, and again. After the third round, Colonel Macleod said, "Boys, I'm not sure, but I think that's whiskey." The remainder of the barrel's contents was used to water the prairie grass.

Today in downtown Fort Macleod, a North-West Mounted Police post has been reconstructed. It operates as a museum. An historical marker on the fort palisade tells of Fort Macleod's history as a North-West Mounted Police post and the most important commercial center in southern Alberta during the early years of white settlement.

Macleod Hotel Built
Highway 2, Fort Macleod

Although the old Macleod Hotel is no longer standing, it is still one of the town's most famous buildings. Harry "Kamoose" Taylor, an ex-wolfer, hide hunter, gold prospector and former member of the Spitzee Cavalry, opened the original Macleod Hotel in 1882. In keeping with the spirit of the times, Taylor posted the following set of rules, among others, in the hotel lobby.

1. Guests will be provided with breakfast and dinner, but must rustle their own lunch.
2. Spiked boots and spurs must be removed at night before retiring.
3. Dogs are not allowed in bunks, but may sleep underneath.
4. Towels are changed weekly; insect powder is for sale at the bar.
5. Special rates for Gospel Grinders and the Gambling Profession.
6. A deposit must be made before towels, soap, or candles can be carried to rooms. When boarders are leaving, a rebate will be made on all the candles, or parts of candles, not burned or eaten.
7. The bar will be open day and night. All Day drinks, 50 cents each; night drinks, $1.00 each. Every known fluid except water for sale. No mixed drinks will be served except in case of a death in the family. Only registered guests allowed the privilege of sleeping on the barroom floor.
8. No kicking regarding the food. Assaults on the cook are strictly prohibited. Those who do not like the provender will be put out. When guests find themselves or their baggage thrown over the fence, they may consider they have received notice to leave.
9. Baths furnished free down at the river, but bathers must provide their own soap and towels.
10. Guests without baggage must sleep in the vacant lot next door or board elsewhere until their baggage arrives.
11. Valuables will not be locked in the hotel safe, as the hotel possesses no such ornament.
12. Guests are expected to rise at 6:00 A.M. This is imperative since the sheets are needed for tablecloths.
13. Quarrelsome or boisterous persons, also those who shoot off without provocation guns or other explosive weapons, and all boarders who get killed, will not be allowed to remain on the premises.
14. To attract the attention of waiters or bell boys, shoot through the door panel. Two shots for ice water, three for a new deck of cards, etc.
15. No jawbone. In God we trust. All others pay cash.

It was said that guests fresh from England would sometimes leave their boots outside their doors at the Macleod Hotel,

*The Macleod Hotel, shown here in 1890, was built by the colorful
Harry "Kamoose" Taylor, who, prior to going into the hotel
business, had been a whiskey trader put out of business
by the arrival of the North-West Mounted Police in 1874.*

expecting their footwear to be shined overnight. At Taylor's hotel, though, the boots were promptly hurled back through the transom accompanied with a barrage of oaths normally reserved for oxen on the bull trains coming up the trail from Fort Benton.

A notorious practical joker named Jim Collins ran the dining room at the Macleod. One day for dinner, Collins passed out bowls to the waiting patrons, then emerged from the kitchen with a huge garden syringe loaded with tomato soup. Collins then proceeded to squirt soup into each bowl. When a patron protested that he didn't want the soup, Collins just backed up a step, plunged the end of the syringe into the bowl and sucked up the fare before going on to the next diner.

Many of Fort Macleod's original buildings have been refurbished. A pamphlet for a self-directed walking tour is available at the tourist information center on the south side of town.

Dave Cochrane Milks Government, Ranchers and Mounties
Highway 2, Fort Macleod

Fort Macleod two years after Harry "Kamoose" Taylor built the Macleod Hotel in 1882.

Dave Cochrane was another of Fort Macleod's favorite, though slightly disreputable, characters. He originally came west as a Mountie but stayed after his tour of duty ended. Despite his police experience and affable ways, Cochrane lived on the fringes of the law in Fort Macleod.

His first homesteading venture took him to a place on the Blood Reserve. When the Indians complained of Cochrane's encroachment, the ex-Mountie left his homestead but put in a claim to the government for the improvements he'd made. His ramshackle one-room cabin netted him $3,500 from the Indian Department—an amount equal to about $25,000 today. Knowing a good thing when he saw it, Cochrane proceeded to build a new "homestead" on the Walrond Ranch lease. Here, too, he was finally persuaded to leave after suitable compensation was offered.

One famous story about Cochrane came about after Ed Maunsell, an early rancher in the area, came to Cochrane looking for a wheel nut for a buggy. Cochrane was known for his large collection of junk and old parts, but in all his holdings, he was unable to find the right size wheel nut. Cochrane hated anyone to leave empty-handed, though, so he told Maunsell that if he'd wait a few minutes he'd be back with a wheel nut.

True to his word, Cochrane returned 15 minutes later, brandishing a nut just the right size. Maunsell paid Cochrane a dollar for it and left. A short distance away, however, Maunsell came across a broken-down buckboard stuck in the mud with one of its wheels lying on the ground nearby. The rig's driver, the mail carrier, was searching through the mud for a missing wheel nut.

Maunsell put two and two together. A man of conscience, he returned to tell Cochrane that the nut hadn't fit his buggy. Then he made his way back to the mail carrier, who was still mucking through the prairie gumbo. When Maunsell suggested that Dave Cochrane might have a nut the size he needed, the mail carrier abandoned his search and headed for Cochrane's cabin. There, he was delighted to find that Cochrane not only had the nut he needed but was willing to part with it for just a dollar.

Cochrane's most ingenious stunt came after he noticed a new cook stove behind the Mounted Police barracks for the summer. It was in an out-of-the-way spot, and Cochrane made a point of passing by the stove on his way home in the evenings. Whenever he could, he'd fetch a bucket of water from the river to throw over the stove as he passed. Occasionally, he'd swipe a lid or grate.

By autumn, the stove had been stripped of parts and the frame was covered in rust. The wily Cochrane then went to the post commander to see if he could haul away the "junk" at the back of the barracks. The junk, of course, included the rusted "old" stove. Given Cochrane's well-known penchant for collecting odds and ends, permission was readily granted.

Early the following winter, the post's commanding officer paid a visit to Cochrane's cabin and remarked on the fine stove sitting in the kitchen. "Where'd you get it, Dave?" asked the Mountie.

"Isn't it a beauty," said Cochrane. "It's that old stove that was out back of the barracks, the one you gave me. All I had to do was fix it up a bit and put some polish on it."

Napi Makes People Rich from the Buffalo
Highway 2, 2.5 miles (4 km) north of Fort Macleod at the Oldman River

---

The Oldman is a sacred river in Blackfoot legend. It's named for the trickster hero, Napi, the Old Man. It was Napi who created the world, and Napi who taught the Blackfoot how to hunt buffalo. It has been almost forgotten today, but at one time, according to Blackfoot legend, buffalo used to eat people. At that time, everyone was afraid of the buffalo.

When Napi found out about this, he became angry. Napi thought it was wrong for buffalo to eat people, so he changed everything. He made the buffalo eat grass, and he taught people how to hunt buffalo and eat buffalo meat. He showed them how to make lodges and clothing from buffalo skins. He showed them how to make cups and eating utensils from buffalo horns and how to make other tools from buffalo bones. The Old Man made the Blackfoot people rich from the buffalo.

Head-Smashed-In Buffalo Jump Saved from Bone Pickers
Highway 2, 11 miles (18 km) northwest of Fort Macleod on Secondary Road 785

Head-Smashed-In Buffalo Jump is one of the oldest, largest and best preserved buffalo jumps in North America. Most of the hundreds of known buffalo jump sites on this continent were at least partially destroyed in the late nineteenth and early twentieth centuries. At that time, buffalo bones were used for making fertilizer, gun powder, processed sugar and other products. Everyone, from recently arrived homesteaders to ex-buffalo hunters, stripped the sites and sold the bones at the railroad to be shipped east. Sometimes bones at shipping points were piled higher than houses and stretched in rows longer than the trains.

Head-Smashed-In was saved from bone pickers because the site had not been used for many years and was partially buried. The few bones whites could see appeared to be of little value.

Because it was an old site that represented an important part of aboriginal history, Indians left it alone, too. Their legends taught them that hunting at a buffalo jump meant more than driving a herd of animals over a cliff. Buffalo jumps were first used in the days before prairie Indians had horses. Hunting buffalo on horseback required skills almost unimaginable for today's urbanites, but on foot, buffalo hunters required an even keener understanding of the way the animals lived. Organizing a hunt at a jump site meant several days of spiritual preparation and practical planning.

When everything was ready, runners were sent out to find the buffalo grazing in the grasslands of the Porcupine Hills above the cliff at Head-Smashed-In. Hunters, who had to remain downwind from the buffalo to avoid detection, would disguise themselves in the skins of wolves and antelopes. By following and carefully observing the herd as it grazed, they devised strategies to manipulate the buffalo closer to the jump site. Sometimes a hunter would even cover himself in the skin of a calf and attempt to lure the herd in the right direction by mimicking the cries of a young animal looking for its mother.

As the hunters deceived the herd into grazing closer to the jump area, previously placed cairns of stone, dung and brush would begin to mark a funnel-shaped drive lane ending at the cliff. Other hunters would join the hunt, continually manipulating the animals in the right direction. Still others would take up positions between the cairns to keep the herd from escaping as it moved at an increasingly quicker pace toward the jump site.

Finally, the hunters would panic the animals and drive them full speed over the cliff.

According to legend, Head-Smashed-In takes its unusual name from the actions of a young brave who wanted to watch the melee of buffalo as they tumbled over the jump. The foolish young man crawled under a ledge in the sandstone cliff. On this hunt, however, the herd was unusually large. As the carcasses piled higher and higher at the bottom of the cliff, some rolled toward the young brave, pinning him to the cliff wall. Later, he was discovered with his skull crushed against the rocks.

Town Established at Clare's Home
Highway 2, 20 miles (32 km) north of the Oldman River bridge at Claresholm

The town of Claresholm is named after settler Clare Amundsen. The Amundsen home was a popular meeting place near the railroad in the early days. A settlement developed near the siding around what became known as Clare's Home, and the name stuck.

A number of the town's early buildings are still in use, and a brochure outlining a walking tour of the village is available at the local museum, located in the old Canadian Pacific Railway (CPR) Station. The Claresholm Museum was built in 1900 with sandstone saved when a larger CPR station in Calgary was dismantled. The museum focuses on the ranching and homesteading history of the area. The Appaloosa Horse Club of Canada Museum is also in Claresholm. This small museum is one of only two in the world dedicated to the Appaloosa horse.

"The Leavings" Abandoned
Highway 2, 2 miles (3 km) north of Claresholm

An historical marker on the east side of the highway here tells of a prominent stop on the old Fort Macleod-to-Calgary trail. In the 1870s, four miles (six kilometers) west of today's Highway 2, Henry Kountz, an old buffalo hunter and trader, built a stopping house where the trail crossed Willow Creek.

From this spot, the trail struck out cross-country toward Calgary. Because the stopping house was located where the trail left the shelter of the valley for the open prairie to the north, it became known as The Leavings. In 1886, the North-West Mounted Police established a detachment at The Leavings, but when the railroad came, the old trail fell into disuse. In 1903, the police outpost was abandoned.

Town of Stavely Named After Rancher
Highway 2, 10.5 miles (17 km) north of Claresholm at Stavely

An historical marker on the east side of the road at Stavely gives a short account of some of the community's history. It explains, for instance, how the town was named for the chairman of the Oxley Ranching Company, Alexander Staveley Hill. It fails to mention, however, how the town's founders happened to misspell Staveley's name.

The Oxley, which was west of present-day Stavely, was one of the huge ranches leased from the Canadian government in southern Alberta in the 1880s. When the railroad was built between Calgary and Fort Macleod in 1891, homesteaders began to come to the region in increasing numbers. Towns such as Stavely were established along the railroad, and the government started canceling the old ranch leases.

In the following years, grain growing and cattle ranching provided the foundation for the area's economy. For a time, the Alberta Farmers' Cooperative grain elevator in Stavely was the largest country elevator between Winnipeg and Vancouver. The town was incorporated as a village in 1912. Additional history of the area can be discovered at the Stavely Museum.

Spitzee Whiskey Post Established
Highway 2, 17 miles (27 km) north of Nanton

On the east side of the highway an historical marker tells of Spitzee Post, an early whiskey fort. The fort was built near here about 1869 by two notorious Alberta pioneers, Dave Akers and Liver-eating Johnston. The Blackfoot destroyed Spitzee Post almost as soon as it was built. Akers and Johnston went on to other pursuits. Later, another whiskey fort was built on the site, but by 1874, when the Mounties came to southern Alberta, Spitzee Post had already been abandoned a second time.

In addition to establishing Spitzee Post, Dave Akers and Liver-eating Johnston became famous in southern Alberta for a number of notorious activities. Johnston received his moniker after allegedly eating human liver near the Yellowstone River—a charge he always denied.

According to a rumor spread among the Blackfoot, it was Johnston who started the great smallpox epidemic of 1869, which eventually killed nearly half of Alberta's Indian population. The legend holds that after a few Blood Indians stole some of his horses, Johnston, in revenge, sold infected blankets to other members of the tribe. Soon the disease spread to the Peigan, Sarcee, northern Blackfoot and other Indian and metis bands.

The story of Liver-eating Johnston's role in the tragedy is almost surely apocryphal. But it's not surprising that the Blackfoot, observing white behavior at that time, would suspect Johnston of intentionally spreading the disease. After all, he, and other whites, had intentionally spread alcoholism, which in the long term was even more deadly.

Liver-eating Johnston's cohort, Dave Akers, was an occasional whiskey trader until the coming of the North-West Mounted Police in 1874. It was Akers, in fact, who was in charge of Fort Whoop-Up the day Colonel Macleod and his new force of Mounties arrived to put a stop to the whiskey trade there. Macleod's guide, Jerry Potts, assured him that the traders would put up no fight. To prove his point, Potts rode nonchalantly through the fort's open front gate. Macleod followed cautiously after marshaling his troops in front of the post, ready for battle.

Inside, however, Macleod found only a few Indian women and the white-bearded Dave Akers tending his garden. The Mounties searched the post but found nothing. Any whiskey that might have been there had obviously been packed out. But Akers proved an amiable sort and he invited Macleod to stay for dinner. Macleod accepted and, according to his report, feasted on an excellent meal of buffalo steaks and garden vegetables.

With the arrival of the Mounties, Akers abandoned the whiskey trade and went into a cattle ranching partnership on land near the old post. A few years later, he shot and killed his partner, which netted him three years in the Fort Macleod jail. While he was there, Akers worked in the jail's harness shop. Periodically, he slipped new leather straps or brass fittings to visiting friends, asking that they be kept for him until his release. When he got out, Akers had the makings of a full set of harnesses waiting for him.

Cattle Brands Come to Alberta
Highway 2, 7.5 miles (12 km) north of High River

Branding calves near Calgary in 1883.

An historical marker on the east side of the highway displays a few of the early cattle brands in the High River area. Branding domestic animals has been practiced since the days of the Egyptians. In the Canadian West, the first branding ordinance was passed by the government of the North-West Territories in 1878. Its purpose was to provide a means of establishing ownership of cattle intermingling on the open ranges of the West. A brands registry office was opened, and the first brand registered under the new ordinance, the letters *NWMP*, was issued to North-West Mounted Policeman Sam Steele. Other early brands in the High River area included the North West Cattle Company's Bar U, Fred Ing's OH, John Ware's 9999 and George Lane's Flying E.

Oil Discovered at Turner Valley
Highway 2, 7.5 miles (12 km) north of High River

Across Highway 2 from the cattle brands' marker, an historical sign tells about the discovery of the first major oil and gas field in Alberta in 1914. William Herron's Calgary Petroleum Products Company made the discovery near Turner Valley, 18.5 miles (30 kilometers) east of the sign. Herron, a rancher from Ontario, had a keen interest in petroleum geology, so when he saw oil seepages in the Turner Valley area, he began exploration drilling. It took a few years of determined effort, but he was finally successful on May 14, 1914. A flurry of speculation in oil and gas stocks followed, and more than 500 companies formed within months of Herron's strike. Most quickly went bust, and World War I soon brought drilling operations in the area to a standstill. After the war, however, exploration resumed and, by the late 1930s, Turner Valley had become the most profitable oil field in Canada.

Big Rock at Okotoks Once Chased Napi
Highway 7, 5 miles (8 km) west of Okotoks turnoff

Evidence of the convergence of the Cordilleran and Laurentide glaciers can be seen by the frequent appearance of large boulders, called glacial erratics, scattered in southern Alberta far from their places of origin. The best known Alberta erratic can be seen from Highway 7 west of Okotoks. This rock, weighing 16 metric tons and standing nearly 33 feet (10 meters) high, is one of the largest erratics found in North America. It originated in the Rocky Mountains to the northwest, near Jasper, and was dropped by glaciers in its current location at the eastern extent of the Cordilleran Ice Sheet approximately 10,000 years ago. Other well-known glacial erratics in southern Alberta include the Hetherington erratics fields, 13 miles (21 kilometers) southeast of Fort Macleod, and the Airdrie erratic, which has Indian pictographs on its side and is located 2 miles (3 kilometers) east of Airdrie.

Erratics also appear in native legends. According to one story, there was once an even larger boulder than the big rock at Okotoks. Napi, the trickster hero of the Blackfoot, took pity on the great rock because it had nothing to protect itself from the prairie wind, rain and cold. Napi covered the boulder with a large buffalo robe. But with the coming of winter, Napi got cold and took back his gift. This so angered the boulder that it broke into smaller rocks that chased Napi all over the prairie. According to legend, this single enormous boulder, not glaciers, was the source of all the strange rocks and boulders that now dot the prairie landscape.

ALTERNATE ROUTES THROUGH CHINOOK COUNTRY
Highway 4 from the Border to Lethbridge

Whiskey Traders Travel Whoop-Up Trail
Highway 4, at the Montana Border

Alberta Highway 4, which begins at Coutts on the Montana border and runs north to Lethbridge, follows the approximate path of the infamous Whoop-Up Trail. The old trail was the main artery of travel for goods and settlers coming into southern Alberta in the 1860s and 1870s. It ran from the Missouri River at Fort Benton, Montana, to Fort Whoop-Up, near present-day Lethbridge. Branch trails off the main route provided access to other areas.

Anybody who says there was no Wild West in Canada knows nothing about the early days of the Whoop-Up Trail. In the 1860s and early 1870s, the country around Fort Whoop-Up was a sparsely settled land with the majority of the population, by far, native Indians. There were also a few metis and a scattering of white wolfers, buffalo hunters and Indian traders. The latter came to Alberta mostly because of the absence of law enforcement here.

Until the 1860s, there was little in the way of law enforcement on either side of the Canada–U.S. line. Then, scattered

An early photo of Fort Whoop-Up, the largest of several southern Alberta fur posts where American traders competed for business that might otherwise have gone to the Hudson's Bay Company post at Edmonton.

attempts at more vigorous policing in the territory of Montana, where trade in guns and alcohol was illegal, encouraged traders to move their operations north. Until 1870, the Canadian side of the boundary was nominally under the control of the Hudson's Bay Company. In short, there was no European law.

Even after 1870, when the area became part of Canada's North-West Territories, there was no attempt at law enforcement. It was, according to W.F. Butler, whom the government sent to investigate the area, a region "without law, order, or security for life or property; robbery and murder for years have gone unpunished; Indian massacres are unchecked; and all civil and legal institutions are entirely unknown." It was a perfect place for free traders and whiskey peddlers to carry on illegal commerce, and their numbers increased year after year.

Supporters of the Hudson's Bay Company, as well as Canadian nationalists, were outraged at this incursion of mostly American traders into what the company saw as its territory. They soon denounced the invading Americans as unscrupulous whiskey traders. The Hudson's Bay Company, of course, never stooped to trading whiskey to native people. It preferred to sell them rum, which was cheaper.

Despite such moral posturing by Canadian patriots and Hudson's Bay Company supporters, exchanging alcohol for furs had been a part of the Indian trade since its beginnings. In the early days of intense competition between the Hudson's Bay and North West companies, commerce in guns and alcohol was a primary ingredient of the trade—though each company accused the other of being the more unconscionable in its use of spirits. After the Hudson's Bay and North West companies amalgamated in 1821, trade in alcohol declined somewhat in Canada. As a monopoly, the Hudson's Bay didn't need liquor to stimulate trade as much as it had when the competition was fierce.

But whiskey traders who moved in from Montana renewed the competition. They also sent their profits south to the United States, which was the primary concern of Hudson's Bay Company traders, not the trade in whiskey itself. Although whiskey trading was morally reprehensible, it wasn't considered contemptible by many westerners at the time. Profits, especially for a trader working alone or in small partnerships, could be huge.

Many of the early whiskey traders were prominent members of the frontier community and later went on to lead otherwise respectable lives.

John J. Healy, one of the earliest of these traders, later became a Montana sheriff known for his vigorous pursuit of lawbreakers—including whiskey traders. D.W. Davis, a Vermont native who worked for Healy in the whiskey trade, later became the province of Alberta's first elected Member of Parliament.

The first traders in southern Alberta worked from wagons, exchanging goods with the three tribes of the Blackfoot Confederacy—the Bloods, Peigans and Blackfoot—as well as their allies the Sarcee. There was also occasional trade with the Kootenay, Assiniboine, Cree, Gros Ventre and Flathead Indians, who were sometimes encountered along the trails.

Traders with less than honorable intentions, however, soon found drawbacks to fur trading from the back of a wagon. A band of cheated Indians could sometimes be unpleasant to deal with. Safer quarters were called for, and soon trading posts, built as much like fortresses as their owners could afford, came into use.

Alfred Hamilton and John J. Healy built Fort Whoop-Up, the best known of the whiskey forts, in 1869. Located at the confluence of the St. Mary and Oldman rivers, it quickly became the center of Indian trade in southern Alberta. Initially, the traders called their post Fort Hamilton, but for reasons lost to history, it became known as Fort Whoop-Up. Probably the title was simply a descriptive name for the kind of behavior that went on there after a lively day of trading firewater whiskey.

Several recipes were commonly used to create the terrible alcoholic concoctions usually sold to Indians. All included cheap whiskey. Liberal amounts of water were added to dilute the liquor and lower costs. Most formulas also included chewing tobacco. Jamaica ginger, red peppers and other ingredients were added to set the resulting liquid on "fire." Red ink was often added for coloring.

In addition to whiskey and rifles, all manner of goods—from blankets and beads to food staples such as sugar, flour, salt and tea—were traded at Fort Whoop-Up and the other posts in the area. The greatest profits, though, were made from whiskey, so many of the independent, poorly financed traders relied on it almost exclusively.

North-West Mounted Police Arrive in Alberta
Highway 4, 13 miles (21 km) north of Coutts

On the east side of the highway, an historical marker commemorates the nearly 1,000-mile (1,600-kilometer) trek made by the North-West Mounted Police in the summer of 1874. Their route is commemorated by today's Red Coat Trail, which follows several roads and highways from southern Manitoba to southern Alberta. The journey was made to bring European law enforcement to the Canadian West. The Mounties started from Fort Dufferin on the Manitoba–North Dakota border amidst rumors of war with the armies of whiskey traders said to be on the southern plains. Indian rebellions, too, it was said, would be waiting for the Mounties when they arrived in the land of the Blackfoot.

The Canadian government had neglected matters in the West since Confederation, but by 1873, even John A. Macdonald, the country's first prime minister, knew it was time to bring some sort of law to the region. In the spring of that year, Macdonald, who was known by the nickname Old Tomorrow because of his propensity to procrastinate, introduced a bill in Parliament to create the North-West Mounted Police. In September, the call went out for volunteers. No western recruits were sought. The new Mounties were to receive a paltry 75 cents a day as salary, but the prospect of an adventure in the West was enough to induce 1,500 applicants to apply for the 300 positions within a few weeks.

George Arthur French, a 32-year-old ex-lieutenant colonel in the British Royal Artillery, was named commissioner of the new force. The first 150 recruits—including Samuel Benfield Steele, whose long and distinguished career with the Mounties would eventually win him fame—were sent almost immediately by steamer from Toronto. The new Mounties traveled through the Great Lakes region to the head of Lake Superior. From there, the recruits marched the last 450 miles (724 kilometers) across the western end of the Canadian Shield to Lower Fort Gary on the Red River north of Winnipeg.

At the old fur post, it was soon discovered that, although horsemanship had supposedly been a prerequisite for recruitment, the majority of new Mounties had exaggerated their abilities in the saddle. Sergeant Major Steele spent the winter drilling his recruits and training them to ride. Whenever a man complained of saddle sores, he was given salt to rub in his wounds. This, after a suitable interval, replaced blisters with calluses. One recruit claimed that after the treatment, he could sit on a prickly pear cactus without pain.

The second contingent of troops remained in Ontario, where they trained over the winter. In the spring, after making arrangements with the American government, these recruits, dressed in civilian clothing with their weapons stowed from view, went by train across the American Midwest to Fargo, North Dakota. From there, the new Mounties marched about 120 miles (193 kilometers) north to Fort Dufferin, just across the Manitoba border. Here, they were met by Steele and the first contingent of troops.

In the late afternoon of July 8, 1874, the long journey west began. The new Mounties, now clothed in their scarlet tunics, made an impressive sight as they paraded from the small fort. Each of the six divisions rode distinctively colored horses. Behind them came 73 large wagons and more than 100 Red River carts. These were followed by an assortment of animals and support goods, including extra horses, 142 oxen, 93 head of cattle, two nine-pounder field guns, two brass mortars, portable forges and several mowing machines for cutting hay.

In some ways, the 1,000-mile (1,600-kilometer) ride across the prairies should have been relatively uneventful. Contrary to the legend that grew up since the journey, the Mounties were not the first to forge a trail across the northern plains—or even along the particular route they traveled.

Indian trails through the area were hundreds of years old, and metis and white explorers, traders and buffalo hunters had roamed the area for decades. A joint Canada–U.S. boundary survey team, who would finish marking the 49th parallel across the prairies that year, had followed essentially the same route the Mounties planned to take. In theory, the recruits would have to go only where the surveyors had already been.

But what might have looked simple on paper proved to be more difficult in reality. In the first place, the new Mounties were easterners, not plainsmen used to traveling the trails of the West. In addition, there was a staggering number of men, livestock and equipment to move. Almost immediately, the contingent began to flounder from the prairie heat and the recruits' inexperience. Even the metis guides who had been chosen to lead the troops seemed unequal to the task.

The horses, thoroughbreds chosen in the East for their impressive stature and color, lacked the stamina and endurance required of saddle animals in the West. Soon, horse after horse weakened under the prairie sun. Even before their handsome eastern mounts began to die, it was obvious the new Mounties would have been better served with the meager-looking western ponies common to the area.

After only 16 days, French called his troops to a halt at La Roche Percee on the Souris River not far from the present-day border between Manitoba, Saskatchewan and North Dakota. French hoped a few day's rest would give the troops some respite from the heat, dust and swarms of mosquitoes that had plagued them since they left Dufferin. Many of the men already suffered from dysentery. After four days, French sent one division, along with the weakest of the men and horses, and most of the cattle, on the well-worn 900-mile (1,450-kilometer) trail to Fort Edmonton. This contingent's horses continued to die, and many of the cattle and oxen the Mounties were obliged to take north with them also succumbed to the rigors of the journey. French had hoped this trail would be easier on the men and animals. Clearly, it wasn't.

More troubles came to the main body of the force before they even started west again. News from Ottawa warned of American army troops chasing Sioux just south of the border. The Mounties were ordered to move away from the boundary to avoid conflict with the Indians and the pursuing Americans. French took his troops northwest on a more rugged route through the Dirt Hills before resuming the westward march again.

A few days later, despite their northerly route, the Mounties ran into a band of the feared Sioux. The Indians were hardly the fierce tribe the recruits expected, however. There were only about 30 of them, predominately women and children, and all were nearly starving.

Commissioner French met the Indians in a spirit that

would characterize Canadian–Indian relations on the prairies. The Indians were invited to parley, given food and gifts, and told of the Mounties' intentions. Red men and white, French said, would be equal in the Canadian West, bound and protected by the same laws, and punished the same for similar transgressions. The Indians, perhaps because they were familiar with American laws, which for the most part protected only whites, seemed to think the Canadian policy funny. They laughed heartily when French's words were translated by a metis scout.

After their meeting with the Sioux, the Mounties continued west, but their troubles remained. By September, horses were collapsing regularly, sometimes as many as 8 or 10 dying in a night. Temperatures became cooler, a foretaste of the approaching prairie winter. Then, when the soldiers finally reached the confluence of the Bow and Belly rivers, where their maps said they would find Fort Whoop-Up, no trace of the notorious whiskey post could be found.

The Mounties knew they were either lost or misinformed. The area lacked feed for their horses, and supplies for the men were short, so French led his troops south across the border to the Sweet Grass Hills in Montana. Game and grass were plentiful there. Leaving his men in the hills, the commissioner, along with Assistant Commissioner James Macleod, rode another 60 miles (97 kilometers) south to Fort Benton. There, they arranged for provisions and learned the correct location of Fort Whoop-Up.

It was in Benton that French received a more realistic appraisal of what lay in store for the Mounted Police in the West. After arranging for supplies, French left immediately with a contingent of 98 men for Swan River, near the present-day Manitoba–Saskatchewan border, to set up the headquarters detachment of the Mounted Police in western Canada.

Macleod, meanwhile, took the remainder of the force, led by Jerry Potts, a scout recommended to him in Fort Benton, and marched north again. This time they went directly to Fort Whoop-Up. Encountering no resistance at the old whiskey fort (and after inquiring about the possibility of buying the post to use for their new headquarters) Macleod moved to a spot Potts had suggested on an island in the Oldman River 31 miles (50 kilometers) away. The area could furnish good pasture for horses, plenty of cottonwoods along the river for timber and a ready supply of game. Macleod ordered stables for the horses to be built first, then barracks for the men and, finally, officers quarters. This last building wasn't completed until mid-December.

Eight Flags Unfurled at Milk River
Highway 4, 25 miles (40 km) north of the U.S. border

A cairn in the town of Milk River notes that eight flags have, at least figuratively, flown over this region of Alberta since Europeans first claimed ownership of North America. In 1682, La Salle claimed the entire Missouri and Mississippi watershed, including the Milk River area, for France. He named the huge territory Louisiana in honor of Louis XIV.

From 1762–1800, Louisiana was ruled by Spain; from 1800–1803, France once again claimed ownership. In 1803, the Milk River area was included in the Louisiana Purchase and became part of the United States. In 1818, however, a treaty with Great Britain established the border at the 49th parallel. From that year until 1869, the Milk River above the American border became part of Rupert's Land, under the flag of the Hudson's Bay Company. In 1870, Rupert's Land became part of Canada, and the British flag flew until 1945, when it was replaced by the Canadian Red Ensign. In 1965, the new Canadian flag, the Maple Leaf, replaced the Red Ensign.

Writing-On-Stone Discovered
Provincial Road 501, 22 miles (35 km) east of the town of Milk River

In 1855, American James Doty discovered one of the continent's greatest collections of ancient Indian pictographs and petroglyphs in the sandstone cliffs and hoodoos of this short stretch of the Milk River Valley, some dating as far back as 3,000 years. In the years before the border was marked, Doty, here as a representative of the American government, attempted to make treaties with members of the Blackfoot Confederacy.

In 1887, a North-West Mounted Police outpost was established in the valley. It became one of several posts along the Canada–U.S. border created to prevent whiskey and other smuggled goods from entering the country. Ironically, it was the Mounties themselves who often slipped across the border. In 1892 five of the six officers assigned to the once busy post on the Milk River deserted to the United States, lured by a gold rush then underway in Montana. The prohibition of liquor in southern Alberta was revoked in 1891, and the police outpost at Writing-On-Stone was officially closed in 1918.

Today, Writing-On-Stone is a provincial park that offers visitors a chance to hike through a spectacular river valley and examine the province's oldest form of historical chronicling. Some of the images here are over 3,000 years old. There's also a reconstructed police outpost at the mouth of Police Coulee. Tours of the area can be arranged at the tourist information booth in Milk River.

Milk River Ridge
Highway 4, 2 miles (3 km) north of Milk River

On the east side of the highway an historical marker notes some of the unique characteristics of the Milk River Ridge. This elevated, dome-shaped area, stretching nearly 18.5 miles (30 kilometers) north and south by nearly 25 miles (40 kilometers) east and west, rises approximately 4,000 feet (1,200 meters) in elevation and forms the height of land between the drainage systems of the Saskatchewan and Missouri rivers. Water falling on the ridge's north slope flows into the South Saskatchewan River and eventually into Hudson Bay. On the south slope, water drains into the Milk River, where it finds its way to the Missouri and Mississippi rivers and finally to the Gulf of Mexico. Historically, the northern watershed was British territory, and the southern was French, Spanish and finally American. In 1818, the United States ceded the area north of the 49th parallel to Britain. Administration of the region was given to the Hudson's Bay Company. In 1870, the area became part of Canada when it purchased Rupert's Land from the English company.

Jerry Potts Joins the Mounties
Highway 4, 3.5 miles (6 km) north of Secondary Road 506

An 1877 photo of North-West Mounted Police guide Jerry Potts. Potts and a friend used to entertain themselves by standing 25 feet (8 meters) apart and trimming each other's mustaches with six-shooters.

An historical marker here recounts the life of the legendary Mounted Police scout Jerry Potts. In 1874, when the North-West Mounted Police arrived in southern Alberta, they couldn't find Fort Whoop-Up, the notorious whiskey post they had come west to close. Retreating south of the border into Montana, where they could buy supplies and find feed for their horses, the Mounties hired Jerry Potts to guide them on their return trip north. Over the next 20 years, Potts became the most famous police scout in the history of the Mounted Police.

It was said that Potts could lead the Mounties swiftly over trails where no other scout could discern even a single track. His ability to find his way through ferocious prairie blizzards was described as uncanny. Though Potts could speak French and several Indian dialects, he kept his use of English to a minimum. Once, on a long trail, when asked by an impatient Mountie what lay over the next hill, Potts replied, "'Nudder hill."

His sparing use of the language often irritated Blackfoot chiefs. Acting as an interpreter, Potts would usually reduce their longest orations to half a dozen words. One time, when the chief of a band of hungry Indians arrived at the Mountie post to speak with Assistant Commissioner Macleod, Potts reduced the chief's long, apparently eloquent speech to three words. After listening to the chief for several minutes, he turned to Macleod and said, "He wants grub."

Known to the Blackfoot as Ky-yo-kosi, or Bear Child, Jerry Potts was the son of a Scots trader and a Blood Indian mother. Before the Mounties arrived in the West, he had been a buffalo skinner, a freighter and an all-round plainsman. For a time, Potts had been a hunter employed at the notorious Fort Whoop-Up. It was said that Potts and a friend in Fort Benton used to stand 25 feet (8 meters) apart and trim each other's mustaches with their six-shooters.

Potts claimed to have taken 16 scalps at the famous 1870 Indian battle where Blood and Peigan warriors routed a band of Cree and Assiniboine at today's Lethbridge. It was also about this time that Potts' mother and half-brother were killed by another Indian. Potts tracked him down and shot him dead.

Japanese Settle in Alberta
Highway 52, 1 mile (1.5 km) west of Raymond

Japanese immigration to Canada began after 1885, when a ban against their immigration was lifted. They first settled in British Columbia and were initially welcomed as they met local industries' needs for additional labor. However, it was not long before anti-Chinese sentiment, already raging at the time, developed into a hatred for all Orientals. As tensions increased, unjust allegations about the Japanese became commonplace. Many whites, including those represented by the Asiatic Exclusion League and the White Canada Association, said Japanese workers lowered the standard of living and increased unemployment among whites. Japanese personal habits and their high birth rate were also attacked. With little money or opportunity to go elsewhere, most Japanese Canadians remained along the shores of British Columbia until well into the twentieth century, although a small group of forty did arrive in Alberta in 1903, when a sugar beet factory opened at Raymond.

Agitating locally, provincially and nationally to prevent further Japanese immigration, and to restrict the rights of Japanese already in Canada, whites in British Columbia were successful by degrees over many years. Japanese immigration was restricted unofficially in 1907, and in the early 1920s, Japanese were banned from employment in certain industries. By the time World War II arrived and the bombing of Pearl Harbor occurred, Japanese Canadians had faced a long and bitter legacy of white prejudice. When, in February 1942, the Canadian government forcibly relocated more than 2,500 Japanese Canadians from British Columbia to southern Alberta, it opened one of the darkest chapters in Canadian history. Most of the evacuees were made to work the fields around Raymond and Taber, and all suffered the indignities of travel restrictions, bans against buying or selling property and prohibitions against living in cities. In 1947, Japanese Canadians' pre-war rights were returned, but not until 1949 were they granted all rights of Canadian citizenship. Most evacuees to the area around Raymond chose to stay in Alberta. Today, they and their children continue to farm in the region, or they have moved on to larger centers like Lethbridge, Calgary and Edmonton.

Large-Scale Irrigation Comes to the Prairies
Highway 4, 5 miles (8 km) south of Lethbridge

An historical marker on the west side of the highway tells about the development of irrigation in southern Alberta. The first irrigated land in the province was a short ditch used to water a field in present-day Calgary in the 1870s. Larger irrigation projects came after the immigration of Mormon settlers in the nineteenth century.

In 1890, Richard Pilling dug an irrigation ditch from the St. Mary River to water a vegetable field at Cardston. Within two years, this ditch was extended to water other land in the community, and by the turn of the century, a comparatively large-scale irrigation project was diverting water to farmland throughout the district. In 1901, the Alberta Railway and Irrigation Company began irrigating 600 acres (243 hectares) of land near Lethbridge and 3,000 acres (1,214 hectares) near Magrath. Today, there are nearly 1,000,000 acres (404,700 hectares) of irrigated land in southern Alberta.

Indian Battle at Lethbridge
Highway 4, Indian Battle Park in Lethbridge

*Chief Big Bear, Cree leader during one of the last major battles
fought between Indian combatants on the Canadian prairies.*

Indian Battle Park is named for what turned out to be one of the last major battles between Indian combatants fought on the Canadian prairies. An historical marker in the park tells of the battle, which was fought late in the autumn of 1870. The battle began when Cree and Assiniboine warriors, led by Big Bear, Piapot and Little Pine, decided to attack a band of Blood camped nearby. The night before the attack, Big Bear dreamed of a Cree defeat. The next morning he tried to convince the others to abandon their plans for battle.

Only a few of the Indians followed Big Bear's advice and retreated to the Cypress Hills. The others, nearly 800 warriors, swooped down on the sleeping camp of the Blood. At first, it looked as if the Cree would land a crushing defeat on their traditional enemies, but the noise of the battle reached a band of Peigan camped a short distance away near Fort Whoop-Up. Soon, the Peigan, along with Jerry Potts, came to the rescue of their Blood allies. Now, not only did the Blackfoot tribes outnumber the Cree and Assiniboine, but they were better armed because many of the Peigan had recently traded for the latest model repeating rifles at Fort Whoop-Up. Potts later said a brave could shoot anywhere and hit an enemy. Between 200 and 300 Cree and Assiniboine were killed that day, many as they tried to escape across the river.

Today, Indian Battle Park is home to a replica of Fort Whoop-Up. The original whiskey post was only a few log huts built in a crude semicircle and connected by a picket fence. This first fort, however, was burned to the ground—perhaps accidentally—by rowdy customers. The fort's owners, John J. Healy and Alfred Hamilton, had already made $50,000 from the Indians in six months of operation, so they soon rebuilt a more substantial post.

By anyone's standards, the new Fort Whoop-Up, which became the model of today's replica, was a true fortress. Canons were mounted in square bastions set at opposite corners of the rectangular structure. Slits for rifles were strategically placed in the heavy, square-timbered exterior walls. Indians were seldom allowed inside. Instead, they were forced to do their trading through barred wickets beside the front gate. Buildings inside the walls were roofed with sod for fire protection, and iron bars in chimney holes prevented uninvited guests from gaining entry from above.

As with almost all trade in the area, goods were brought to Fort Whoop-Up from Fort Benton, at the western terminus of steamboat traffic on the Missouri River. From there, freight was usually hauled north in wagon trains pulled by teams of oxen. Sometimes mules were used, which was faster but more expensive.

Fort Benton, at the head of navigation on the Missouri River in Montana, was the supply point for early Alberta whiskey forts, like the notorious Fort Whoop-Up.

The 210-mile (338-kilometer) road between Fort Benton and Fort Whoop-Up became known as the Whoop-Up Trail. It served as a trunk road for the whole region. Throughout the 1870s, it was one of the busiest transportation routes in both the American and Canadian West.

A large reddish rock, called *Mek-kio-towaghs* by Blackfoot tribes, rests near today's replica of Fort Whoop-Up. It's said that long ago, even before the original fort was built, a hunter on the opposite side of the river saw a medicine-pipe man in a traditional red robe descending the hill above this rock. In order to speak to the holy man, the hunter crossed the river at a nearby ford.

By the time he arrived on the opposite bank, the medicine-pipe man had disappeared. Only this large rock, gleaming red in the sun, was visible on the spot where the holy man had stood. That night a medicine-pipe man came to the hunter in a dream. He told the hunter that he was the rock and that the hunter and his children should leave offerings for him. The hunter, his children and his children's children did as the medicine-pipe man said. For many years after the coming of white settlers, gifts of clothing, tobacco and food were regularly seen lying at the painted rock.

Other points of interest in Lethbridge include the Alexander Galt Museum—which has an excellent collection of local history displays—the Nikka Yuko Japanese Garden, the Helen Schuler Coulee Centre and the High Level Railway Bridge, which can be seen from Indian Battle Park.

Highways 5 and 62 south of Lethbridge

Fairfield Farm Established
Highway 5, .5 mile (1 km) south of Lethbridge

An historical marker on the west side of Highway 5 commemorates the efforts of William Fairfield in the development of agriculture in southern Alberta. Fairfield was an agriculture professor from Wyoming who came to Alberta to farm soon after the turn of the century. At the time, farmers in southern Alberta were perplexed because alfalfa, an important livestock feed that enriched the soil with nitrogen, did not grow in Alberta. The problem was significant enough that Charles Ora Card contemplated taking his Mormon followers back to Utah.

Fairfield, though, had experimented with alfalfa at the University of Wyoming, and he remembered that the legume seemed to grow only in soils that had previously grown alfalfa. Fairfield arranged to have a bag of Wyoming dirt sent to him from an alfalfa field in Laramie. When it arrived, he sprinkled it around the spindly alfalfa plants he'd been trying to grow. The next year, the field produced the first healthy alfalfa crop grown in Alberta. Soil from Fairfield's farm was then used to inoculate other alfalfa fields in the area.

When the Alberta Railway and Irrigation Company learned of Fairfield's work with alfalfa and other crops, they hired him to set up an experimental station to encourage and improve irrigated farming techniques. Later, the farm became the Agriculture Canada Research Station at Lethbridge.

Fort Whoop-Up Built
Highway 5, 5 miles (8 km) south of Lethbridge

Built by two whiskey traders, Alfred Hamilton and John J. Healy, the original Fort Whoop-Up was located near here at the forks of the Oldman and St. Mary rivers. During the five years of its operation, from 1869–74, Fort Whoop-Up became one of the most notorious whiskey posts in the West. The original fort consisted of log buildings and a picket fence, but when this burned to the ground, Healy and Hamilton used the $50,000 they made in their first six months of operation to build a fortress. The Whoop-Up Trail—the main artery supplying the fort—ran from Fort Benton, Montana, to Fort Whoop-Up. Although the whiskey trade ended at Fort Whoop-Up when the North-West Mounted Police came to southern Alberta in 1874, the trail continued to be used until the railroad reached Lethbridge in 1885. Even today, oxcart ruts in the prairie sod can be found along the route of the old whiskey trail.

Last Great Land Rush in Southern Alberta Draws Homesteaders
Highway 62, 48 miles (77 km) south of Lethbridge

An historical marker just north of Del Bonita tells of "the last great land rush of southern Alberta." This occurred after more than 90,000 acres (36,400 hectares) of land that had been leased from the Canadian government by the McIntyre Ranching Company was thrown open to homesteaders in 1912. There was so much interest in this so-called the "lease country" between the United States border and the north branch of the Milk River that 40 people were already camped at the door of the Land Titles office in Lethbridge a month before homestead applications could be filed. All during April 1912, land seekers pitched tents and fashioned improvised shelters with blankets fastened to fences and buildings.

On May 1, the land office began accepting applications, and 350 applicants filed for land. In succeeding years, communities of homesteaders developed around the original school districts at Twin River, Del Bonita, Lens, Rinard, Shanks Lake and Hillmer. As the years went on, it became clear there were too many farms for the land to support. Most of the homesteads became parts of bigger farms and ranches. The McIntyre Ranching Company, which eventually acquired many of the land-rush homesteads, survives after more than 100 years of operation in southern Alberta. Ranch headquarters is on the Milk River a few miles north of the historical marker.

Highway 3 Between Grassy Lake and the Crowsnest Pass

Laying the Turkey Track Railway
Highway 3, Taber

On the north side of the highway, an historical marker gives a brief account of the Turkey Track Railway. This small railroad was built to haul coal from the mines at Lethbridge to the main line of the Canadian Pacific Railway (CPR) near Medicine Hat. The North West Coal and Navigation Company constructed the Turkey Track after a disastrous attempt to run a steamship line on the South Saskatchewan River. The company built three steamboats and tried to haul coal, but the river was closed to shipping while iced over in the winter, and water levels in summer were too shallow for navigation during all but a few of the warmest months.

Undaunted, the company decided to go into the railroad business. Unfortunately, the new line was built with the 36-inch (91-centimeter) narrow-gauge track, which was popular in the western United States and cheaper to build. When Turkey Track trains got to Dunmore near Medicine Hat, coal had to be unloaded into CPR cars because the Turkey Track cars wouldn't run on the CPR's standard-gauge line. Despite this difficulty, the

Turkey Track won favor among isolated settlers, who received mail and news of the rest of the world along its line. The track was extended south to Great Falls, Montana, and many new immigrants from the United States arrived in Alberta on a Turkey Track rail car. Eventually, the Turkey Track was sold to the CPR, then extended west to the Crowsnest Pass and into British Columbia. By 1909, the narrow-gauge railway was changed to standard.

Mennonites Settle in Southern Alberta
Highway 3, 2 miles (3 km) east of Coaldale

On the north side of the highway, an historical marker is dedicated to the memory of Mennonite settlers in Alberta. Mennonites are a German-based Anabaptist religious group united by pacifism and a simple life but divided by many other issues of faith. Those moving to Alberta before World War I represented four Mennonite sects from Ontario, Manitoba and the United States. They were initially welcomed as industrious and trustworthy newcomers, but World War I saw the rise of anti-German sentiments leveled at the German-speaking Mennonites. Additional antagonism developed because many of them refused military service as conscientious objectors to the war. Despite these difficulties, Mennonites continued to make a living for themselves in Alberta.

A second major wave of Mennonite immigration came from Communist Russia after World War I, when anti-German sentiments there became more widespread. Mennonite families, fleeing persecution in their Russian homeland, began arriving in Alberta in 1925. By 1936, more than 1,000 Mennonites owned 20,700 acres (8,377 hectares) of land in this area.

During World War II, Mennonite persecution in Canada peaked again, which lead to the closure of German-language schools and libraries, and even the burning of two Mennonite churches. Turning the other cheek, as their faith directed, Mennonites continued to farm the area and make significant contributions to their communities. Today, Mennonites make up a significant proportion of the population in this part of Alberta.

C.S. Noble Develops Dryland Farming Techniques
Highway 23, 6 miles (10 km) north of Highway 3 and Highway 23 junction

Charles S. Noble invented the Noble Blade in the 1930s and contributed other advances in the development of dryland farming.

Just past Nobleford, an historical marker tells of innovative farming tools and techniques developed by local farmers. Farming in this unique region of the prairies often requires specialized farming methods and machinery. In the 1930s farming here was virtually impossible. Not only was southern Alberta suffering from a severe drought, but dust storms and soil erosion could make even travel unbearable. Dust sometimes drifted 10 feet (3 meters) high. These conditions, along with the Great Depression, turned the 1930s into a decade of torment and bad fortune. Farmers left southern Alberta in droves.

A few determined pioneers stayed and worked hard to improve conditions. Experiments in shallow cultivation led to the development of the blade cultivator. One of the most successful was the Noble Blade, which was developed by Charles S. Noble of Nobleford in the mid-1930s.

Southern Alberta Opens for Ranching
Highway 23, 23.5 miles (38 km) north of Highway 3 and Highway 23 junction

An historical marker commemorates the days of the great ranches on the open range of southern Alberta. In order to stimulate settlement, the Government of Canada began leasing huge tracts of land in 1880 for just under one cent an acre (half a cent a hectare). The excellent prairie grasses, readily available water and sheltered coulees made conditions here almost ideal for cattle ranching. In fact, large cattle herds were already being brought into Alberta when the government set out terms for leasing government land.

Almost all the early cattle were from Montana and Idaho, and most of these were only a generation or two removed from the lean, long-legged, short-tempered Longhorns that had come up the trails from Texas after the Civil War in the United States. Thus, the pattern of early ranching in Alberta—with Texas cattle and to a large extent Texas cowboys—was virtually the same as it had been everywhere else on the northern ranges of the continent. In a sense, early ranching in Alberta and on the plains in the United States was an extension of a cattle-raising culture that had its roots not only in Texas but in Spanish America, too.

Ranching was firmly established in Spanish America before 1800. By 1800, several million cattle ranged from South America to northern Mexico, many of them unbranded and virtually wild. Thousands of these long-horned, semiwild Spanish cattle ranged as far north as Texas.

Even before the Civil War began, enterprising Texans had begun to round up some of them to drive to markets in California and New Orleans. Most of these animals came from areas close to the Mexican border, and early Texas cowboys learned the tricks of their trade from the Spanish-speaking vaqueros of the region.

After the Civil War, Texas cowboys, both English- and Spanish-speaking, spread this ranching culture northward when they brought Texas cattle up the trails to stock the new ranges. Today, throughout North America, the influence of these early Texas cowboys and vaqueros can still be seen in many of the standard methods of handling cattle. Even the language of the cowboy can be traced to the vaquero. *Ranch, lariat, lasso, dally, buckaroo, bronco, chaps* and *rodeo* are only a few of the dozens of words that have come down to modern cowboys from their Spanish-speaking predecessors.

As the first railroads began to extend west of the Mississippi after the Civil War, huge markets in the American northeast were opened to any Texas drover who could get his cattle to a shipping point along the rail lines in Kansas. Hundreds of Texans rose to the challenge. In 1867, 35,000 head of cattle were driven north to towns along the railroad; in 1868, 75,000; in 1869, 350,000; in 1871, 600,000.

In succeeding years, as the northern prairies were cleared of buffalo and the native inhabitants starved into submission, huge new areas of public land were suddenly made available for grazing. At first, cattlemen thought northern winters would be too cold for cattle. It didn't take long to notice, though, that Texas Longhorns not only survived in the north, but they seemed to do better. Some people said this was also true of Texas cowboys.

Before long, Texas steers were being trailed north to fatten on grass in Nebraska, Wyoming, Montana and the Dakotas. Once fattened, animals could be shipped to eastern markets on the new northern railroads. As western cattle ranges in the northern United States filled, it was only natural that ranching would continue to spread farther north across the Canadian line. After the North-West Mounted Police signed treaties with the Indians, forcing them onto reserves and out of the way of white settlement, Alberta was ready for large-scale ranching.

Although M.H. Cochrane's was the first of the huge ranches, others soon followed. Some of the best known of the early ranches were the Oxley, the Quorn and the Walrond. The most famous was the North West Cattle Company near the present town of Longview. Known familiarly by its cattle brand, the Bar U, the ranch was started by Fred Stinson, with Montreal backers. The first cattle were brought in from Idaho by Tom Lynch and John Ware in late September 1882.

Over the years, some of the province's most famous cowboys, including Lynch and Ware, George Lane and Herb Miller, rode for the brand. So did Harry Longbaugh, a young fellow from south of the border known as the Sun Dance Kid. In 1992, the federal government named the Bar U, which was still a working ranch at the time, a National Historic Site.

Pincher Creek Named

Highway 6, 1 mile (1.5 km) south of the Highway 3 and Highway 6 junction at Pincher Creek

An historical marker here tells how Pincher Creek got its name. It came about in 1868, when two prospectors found a pair of hoof pincers in the creek. They named the creek for the pincers, and later the town took its name from the creek. In 1878, the North-West Mounted Police, attracted by the rich grazing land of the area, established a horse and cattle ranch here to supply the force. By the 1880s several other large cattle ranches had been established.

The Pincher Creek Museum features displays based on the history of the region. Exhibits include household items, saddles, clothing and tools. John George "Kootenai" Brown's cabin is located on the museum grounds. The Lebel Mansion, built in 1909 by local merchant Timothee Lebel and now used as a community cultural center, overlooks the business district of the town. Lebel designed the house to combine French Canadian and New Orleans styles of architecture. The Old Man Antique

Equipment and Threshing Club also displays historic farm equipment at Heritage Acres in Pincher Creek.

Charcoal Murders Sergeant Wilde
Highway 6, 2.5 miles (4 km) south of Pincher Creek

On the east side of the highway an historical marker recounts the death of North-West Mounted Police Sergeant W.B. Wilde. Wilde was shot and killed by a Blood Indian known as Charcoal in 1896. The trouble began when Charcoal killed a young Indian he caught with one of his two wives. After the killing, Charcoal fled the reserve with his wives, his two young sons, a grown daughter and one of his mothers-in-law. Before he left, he also shot and wounded a former Mountie named McNeil for no apparent reason.

No trace of Charcoal could be found until the snow came. Then tracks were discovered near Chief Mountain on the Montana border. Soon Charcoal's camp was discovered, and his daughter, one son and the mother-in-law were caught. But Charcoal escaped with his two wives and the other son. This time they fled north to the Porcupine Hills. Eventually, Charcoal's wives ran away from him, and his son, too, escaped. Charcoal was forced to move on.

Later, he tried to get food on the nearby Peigan Reserve but failed. The Peigans formed a posse and gave chase. They also sent word to Sergeant Wilde at Pincher Creek that they were on Charcoal's trail. Wilde caught up with the Indians just as they were closing in on Charcoal. He overtook the fugitive a few miles east of the present-day highway sign. As Wilde yelled for Charcoal to stop, the Indian whirled and shot. The Mountie fell from his horse. Charcoal returned and shot Wilde a second time. Then he took the dead Mountie's horse and, leaving his own tired mount behind, rode toward Waterton River.

The Mounted Police scout Tail Feathers continued the pursuit while the other Indians took Wilde's body to Pincher Creek. By evening, Charcoal had outpaced the Mountie scout and ridden to the home of his brother, Left Hand, on the Blood Reserve. While he was there, one of Left Hand's wives, a woman weighing nearly 300 pounds (136 kilograms), grabbed Charcoal and held him down while another wife ran for help. The police took Charcoal to Fort Macleod, where he was executed on March 16, 1897.

Wagon Train Surrounded: Settlers Massacred
Highway 3, 2.5 miles (4 km) north of Cowley

At a place known today as Massacre Butte, a Government of Alberta cairn marks the spot where in 1867 a dozen American settlers were killed by a war party of Blood Indians. The settlers had come from Minnesota in a wagon train led by Captain James L. Fisk. Along the Missouri River in present-day Montana, the Cowley settlers decided to leave Fisk and the main party to travel north to the reputed gold fields along the North Saskatchewan River.

Traveling through the heart of Blood Indian territory at night, when they thought they would be safer, this group of men, women and children was overtaken by a band of Bloods at Massacre Butte. Led by Medicine Calf, the Indians attacked, and the settlers drew their wagons into a circle, western-movie-style. But no movie-star heroes arrived to save the day. When the ammunition gave out, the settlers were slaughtered. In later years, a blond scalp reported to have belonged to one of the victims decorated a Pincher Creek liquor store.

Doukhobors Settle in Alberta
Highway 3, .5 miles (1 km) west of Cowley

An historical marker here is dedicated to the memory of Doukhobor settlers in Alberta. Formally known as the Christian Community of Universal Brotherhood, more than 300 Doukhobors, guided by their motto "Toil and Peaceful Life," settled near Cowley in 1915. A second colony started near Shouldice in 1926.

Although Doukhobor settlers came relatively late to Alberta, when Canada's original Doukhobors fled persecution in Russia in 1898, they intended to settle here. Ironically, the new immigrants encountered persecution in Canada, too. Frank Oliver, the Liberal Member of Parliament from Edmonton at the time, stepped in to keep the Doukhobors out of Alberta. He persuaded the federal government to give them land in Saskatchewan instead.

Oliver's meddling in Doukhobor affairs did not end there, however. After he became Minister of the Interior in the federal cabinet, he went after them again. One of the tenets of Doukhobor faith stipulates that its members swear allegiance only to God. Oliver required them to swear allegiance to the Crown before he would grant them title to their homesteads. This effectively kept the Doukhobors from ever gaining ownership of their Saskatchewan farms. Faced with this disappointment, most abandoned their homesteads and moved to British Columbia. A few years later, some of these British Columbia families established the first Doukhobor settlements in Alberta.

Chapter 2

Gateway Country

Land
of Open
Spaces

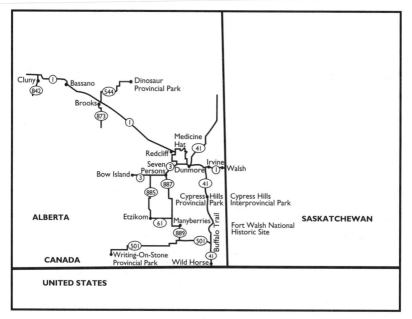

THE ROADS OF GATEWAY COUNTRY crisscross the arid plains and wide-open spaces of southeastern Alberta. Along the way, they travel through a surprisingly diverse countryside. Here you can drive from the forests and meadows of the Cypress Hills into gently rolling grasslands. You can travel past huge fields of prairie wheat, lush irrigated farms and desert badlands.

History in Gateway Country is the history of the railroad and the thousands of homesteaders it brought to a new land. It's the history of cattle ranching, dryland farming and irrigation. It's the history of natural gas and industrial development. In Gateway Country, history goes back as far as the dinosaurs. It includes Indian battles, whiskey traders, Mounties and buffalo herds so large they blackened the prairie for as far as the eye could see.

The Buffalo Trail

Described on maps as the Buffalo Trail, Highway 41 stretches along the eastern edge of Alberta from Wild Horse on the Montana border north across the Trans–Canada Highway to the Red Deer River and beyond. The road was named to commemorate the huge herds of buffalo that once roamed these plains before white settlement.

At one time, more than 60,000,000 buffalo lived on the prairies of North America. The land around the Cypress Hills, through which today's Highway 41 extends, lay in the heart of that country, and it provided the last refuge for the great buffalo herds of the nineteenth century.

As late as 1874, a Mountie estimated 80,000 animals in one herd. The year before, riders on the south side of the Cypress Hills reported an even bigger herd. For seven days, averaging 25 miles (40 kilometers) a day, the riders traveled continuously through one placidly grazing herd of buffalo. But even in Gateway Country, buffalo hunters finally took their toll. By 1879, the great herds of North American buffalo were gone from the Canadian prairies.

Points of Interest Near Highway 1 from the Saskatchewan border to Bassano

Village of Walsh Named for Friend of Sitting Bull
Highway 1, at the Saskatchewan border

Inspector James Walsh became such a good friend of the Sioux chief Sitting Bull that many criticized him for not pursuing Canadian government policy and forcing the famous Indian back to the United States.

The village of Walsh is named for James Walsh, the North-West Mounted Police inspector who established a post in the Cypress Hills south of here in 1875. Walsh was not a native of the West, but he became a westerner and preferred buckskins to the Mounted Police uniform.

Around this time, Sitting Bull and his Sioux killed Custer and the 265 soldiers under his command. Fearing retaliation, Sitting Bull and several thousand American Sioux fled Montana for Canada. Their arrival at Fort Walsh, and Wood Mountain in Saskatchewan, occurred when the Canadian government was attempting to keep the lid on Indian discontent. With the buffalo almost gone and Indians afraid of the future, the government felt the only option was to sign treaties that would leave the Indians enough land to learn an agricultural way of life. Sitting Bull and his Sioux, however, complicated an already difficult situation. Many Canadian Indians resented the Sioux for coming into their territory, and the Canadian government worried that the United States Army would pursue Sitting Bull into Canada and thereby challenge the legitimacy of the Canada–U.S. border. Into this volatile situation rode James Walsh, charged with persuading the Sioux to return to the United States and ordered to keep the peace while negotiations with Canadian Indians continued.

Walsh and Sitting Bull soon became friends. Unhappily, Walsh's friendship with the great Sioux chief was tested by his official duty. Their conflicting loyalties sometimes led the two leaders into fierce arguments. During one heated exchange, Walsh literally threw Sitting Bull out of the tent serving as his headquarters. Following close behind, the Mountie kicked him squarely in the seat of his pants. The proud Sioux warrior, who had defeated Custer and endured three years of misfortune and hunger in Canada, was forced to put up with this humiliation in front of his men because his people desperately needed to stay in this country. Sitting Bull could not afford to have his nation at war with both the United States Army and the Canadian Mounties.

Despite their disagreements, Walsh and Sitting Bull eventually became such close friends that Walsh began to be criticized for his reluctance to pursue government policy. Eventually, Walsh was transferred from the Cypress Hills. After he left, Sitting Bull was finally convinced to return to the United States. Nine years later he was killed.

Town of Irvine Named
Highway 1, 10 miles (16 km) west of Walsh

The town of Irvine is named for North-West Mounted Police Commissioner A. G. Irvine, who was in command of the Mounties at the time the Canadian Pacific Railway reached Alberta. He had first come west with the Quebec Rifles on the Wolseley Expedition during the Red River Rebellion of 1870. Afterward, he stayed in the West, joining the North-West Mounted Police in 1875. Ten years later, Irvine led a column of police to Prince Albert during the second Riel Rebellion. He was widely criticized for not taking more decisive action during the conflict, and the following year he resigned from the force.

Constable Graburn Murdered
Highway 1, 17 miles (27 km) west of the Saskatchewan border

On the south side of the highway, an historical marker recounts the first murder of a North-West Mounted Policeman in the Canadian West. Constable Marmaduke Graburn was found at a police horse camp in the Cypress Hills with two bullet wounds in his back on November 18, 1879.

In 1881, the police arrested a Blood Indian named Star Child for the murder. Although Star Child confessed to the crime, an all-white jury found him innocent. Jury members were reportedly afraid a guilty verdict would incite Blackfoot reprisals. Today, the old horse camp where Graburn was killed is called Graburn's Coulee. A commemorative cairn has been built near the spot where he died.

The Hills That Shouldn't Be
Highway 41, 18.5 miles (30 km) south of Highway 1

Visitors passing through this area for the first time are sometimes startled by the tree-covered Cypress Hills, which stand out from the surrounding countryside like an oasis. As the highest point of land between Canada's east coast and the Rocky Mountains, the Cypress Hills receive more moisture than anywhere else in Gateway Country. Stands of poplar, spruce and lodgepole pine grow here in sharp contrast to the arid, tree-less plains below.

With a view from the north or west, you can see the hills climb rather steeply from the surrounding prairie. From the south or east, they rise gently as the countryside changes from flat plains to undulating hills. A long plateau running east to west lies like a spine through the middle of the hills. At its highest point, the land rises 4,800 feet (1,463 meters) above sea level and 1,500 feet (457 meters) above the surrounding prairie.

During the Pleistocene Ice Age, the Cypress Hills escaped glaciation. Few places in the prairie West boast such a fascinating variety of plants and animals concentrated in such a small area. Perhaps that's one reason the Blackfoot called this area *Ketewius Netumoo,* "the hills that shouldn't be."

Metis and French Canadians working for fur companies named the hills when they came to the area in the early 1800s. They called them the *Montagnes de Cypres,* or Pine Mountains, because the lodgepole pine of the hills reminded them of the more familiar jack pines farther east. English-speaking visitors in the area mistranslated the French words for the region. As a consequence, though no cypress trees grow here, we continue to call the area the Cypress Hills.

Cypress Hills Massacre Sparks Deployment of Mounted Police
Highway 1, 6 miles (10 km) from the Alberta border in the Cypress Hills of Saskatchewan

---

For native people, the Cypress Hills were a sacred place. All the tribes of the prairies knew of them, but no tribe ever controlled them, so the area was often the scene of fierce battles.

When whites first settled here, they came as fur traders. and soon several whiskey posts were located in the hills. It was a battle between whites and Assiniboine near one of these posts in 1873 that sparked the deployment west of the first troop of North-West Mounted Police.

Before the formation of the Mounted Police, Alberta was a lawless land. Until 1870, it was nominally under control of the Hudson's Bay Company. After that, it was ignored by the Canadian government until 1873. Then Prime Minister Macdonald, whose tendency to procrastinate had won him the title "Old

Tomorrow," decided it was time to bring Canadian law to the region.

On April 28, Macdonald introduced a bill in Parliament to create a force of Mounted Police for the West. Originally conceived as the North-West Mounted Rifles, Macdonald changed the name at the last minute. He did this to avoid antagonizing public opinion in the United States, where politicians sometimes had trouble distinguishing between Canadian nationalism and British imperialism. The bill passed Parliament without opposition.

Macdonald intended to postpone the actual formation of the police force for at least a year. Soon after the bill passed, however, the gun battle in the Cypress Hills changed his plans. The fray, which became known as the Cypress Hills Massacre, aroused anti-American opinion in the East. To help diffuse the situation, Old Tomorrow assembled his new police force immediately.

That the tragedy was so swiftly called a massacre in the East had more to do with making events serve personal and national purposes than anything known to have happened in the hills. According to the tale that surfaced in eastern Canada, a gang of lawless American whiskey traders ambushed and murdered 30 friendly Assiniboine Indians camped peacefully in their own territory. What actually happened was something equally terrible but with the villains less clearly defined.

The trouble began when unidentified Indians stole a few horses from a group of white and metis traders and wolf hunters camped near Fort Benton. Angry over their loss, the men, who were about equally divided between Canadians and Americans, gave chase. They were rough men intent on teaching the horse thieves a lesson. A few days later, they stopped to camp near Abe Farwell's trading post in the Cypress Hills. A band of Assiniboine were camped nearby, but these Indians didn't have the missing horses. In fact, one of the Assiniboine even returned a previously stolen horse to a Canadian named George Hammond.

The Indians, too, were in a hostile mood. They were upset at the shoddy treatment they had received from an American whiskey trader named Mose Solomon at another nearby trading post. On Sunday, June 1, after both the Assiniboine and the whites had spent the previous night nursing their grudges in separate, extended bouts of drinking, George Hammond went to check on his horse. When he discovered the animal missing again, he grabbed his rifle and started for the Assiniboine camp. His comrades, coming to his aid, followed close behind.

Like so many incidents of this kind, it's not known who fired the first shot. In all likelihood, both Indians and whites were still feeling the effects of the previous night's whiskey. Some witnesses from a metis camp nearby said the initial volleys seemed to come from both groups at the same time. Others blamed the Indians. Once the shooting began, the whites took cover in a gully where they could fire down on the Indian camp.

Despite this natural fortress, the Assiniboine, under Chief Little Soldier, continued the battle. Three times, the Indians attacked and were beaten back under a shower of bullets. Once, they tried to outflank the whites from the shelter of a nearby bluff. When they finally withdrew, between 15 and 30 of them had lost their lives. Only one white, Canadian Ed Grace, suffered the same fate.

Abe Farwell brought the first reports of the incident back to Fort Benton, Montana. Farwell, who operated his trading post as a representative of the T.C. Power Company, told a story that pinned the bulk of the blame on the white wolfers and traders. Most of these men were connected with the I.G. Baker Company, a rival Fort Benton transportation and merchandising business. Since both the Power and Baker interests were anxious to discredit each other and thus obtain a larger share of the trade, Farwell's initial report was suspect.

When Canadian nationalists and supporters of the Hudson's Bay Company got wind of the story, the events were easily adapted to their purposes, too. It was the same kind of tactic the Hudson's Bay and North West companies had used against each other in the days before their amalgamation.

In no time, the story circulated in eastern Canada that a gang of American murderers had massacred a band of friendly Canadian Indians. Not surprisingly, people were outraged and demanded action from the government. Prime Minister Macdonald was forced to move. He ordered the recruitment of 300 men for his new Mounted Police. The following year, the force traveled through the region of the Cypress Hills on their way west. Their first order of business was to shut down the whiskey trade.

Sitting Bull Comes to the Hills

Secondary Road 271, Fort Walsh National Historic Park, 6 miles (10 km) east of the Saskatchewan border on the south side of Cypress Hills Provincial Park

The North-West Mounted Police established Fort Walsh in 1875. The following year Sioux warriors defeated General George Custer on the Little Big Horn River, killing all 265 of Custer's soldiers. Within days, Sioux refugees began to cross the border to look for safety in Canada.

In the summer of 1875, police scout Jerry Potts led 30 Mounties under the command of Inspector Walsh from Fort Macleod to the Cypress Hills. The Mounties came to establish a new post. Fort Walsh, as it became known, lay just across the present Alberta border in Saskatchewan. Today, the fort has been rebuilt in its former location at the Fort Walsh National Historic Park.

A year after the original fort was established, Sioux Indians led by Crazy Horse and Sitting Bull killed General George Custer and all 265 men under his command at the Battle of Little Big Horn. Afterward, as many as 5,000 of the Sioux, including Sitting Bull, fled to the Canadian side of the 49th parallel, which prevented the U.S. Long Knives from following them. During the next five years, the North-West Mounted Police had the worrisome duty of keeping Sioux warriors under control.

In Canada, the Sioux usually camped between the Cypress Hills and Wood Mountain in present-day Saskatchewan. Here they competed with Blackfoot, Cree and Assiniboine hunters for the dwindling supply of buffalo. This added to Blackfoot and Cree unrest. After 1879, when the buffalo were effectively gone, Canadian government policy was directed at starving the Sioux until they returned to the United States. Despite the Sioux's long history of ranging back and forth across the 49th parallel, the Canadian government maintained they were "American" Indians.

The government refused to sign treaties with Sitting Bull, thus denying his people land and the opportunity to make a living. When the landless Sioux began to starve, the government refused them food. Finally, in 1881, Sitting Bull and his followers moved south. Nine years later, once more resisting U.S. Army efforts to arrest him, Sitting Bull was killed along with eight of his followers. This action precipitated the massacre of 350 more Sioux two weeks later at Wounded Knee, South Dakota. By this time, Fort Walsh had been abandoned, and the Cypress Hills were policed from Maple Creek, 50 miles (80 kilometers) north on the main line of the new Canadian Pacific Railway.

Turkey Track Railway Comes to Dunmore
Highway 1, 26 miles (42 km) west of the Saskatchewan border

When the Canadian Pacific Railway (CPR) arrived in Alberta, business interests in Medicine Hat saw that the new railroad provided a ready market for coal from the Galt Mines at present-day Lethbridge. The problem was getting the coal to the railroad.

Initially, the businessmen thought they could float it down the South Saskatchewan River. Three steamboats were built and the North West Coal and Navigation Company was born. Backers knew that no coal would move in winter, when the river was frozen, but the following summer they were disappointed to learn that the South Saskatchewan also was often too dry to navigate in the warm months.

Undaunted, the company went into the railroad business. The first plan was to lay track from Lethbridge to Medicine Hat, but when they found the grade too steep at Medicine Hat, they continued to the main line of the CPR at nearby Dunmore. Dubbed the Turkey Track Railway, the new line started to haul coal. But the company's problems weren't over.

The Turkey Track had been built with the narrow-gauge track popular with small railroads in the western United States. When the coal company's trains reached Dunmore, they couldn't continue on the CPR's standard-gauge track. To compensate, the Turkey Track was built close enough to the CPR for coal to be transferred between cars. Finally, in 1893, the CPR bought the Turkey Track and widened the line to accept standard-gauge equipment.

Ghost Trains Foretell Crash
Highway 1, 3 miles (5 km) west of Dunmore

In the spring of 1908, along a dangerous section of the Canadian Pacific Railway (CPR) near here, engineer Robert Twohey rounded a curve and saw another train coming toward him on the same track. Twohey pulled the brakes, but the train he'd seen disappeared. Fireman Gus Day confirmed that he, too, had seen the phantom train.

Perhaps the incident would have been forgotten, but four years earlier a palm reader had told Twohey that he would be killed in a train accident on May 10, 1908. Twohey hadn't paid much attention to the prediction when it happened, but when he saw the phantom train, he began to worry.

A few days after Twohey had seen the ghost train, James Nicholson, engineering another CPR train, saw what appeared to be the same train speeding toward him around the same curve in the tracks. He applied the brakes, but again the phantom train disappeared. Once more Gus Day was the fireman on board. When Twohey heard the news, he became so worried that he booked off for the entire month of May.

By June, both Nicholson and Twohey were back on the job. On July 9, Nicholson filled in to take someone else's normal run from Medicine Hat to Dunmore. He was scheduled to hook up with the Spokane Flyer when it arrived over the old Turkey

Track Railway from British Columbia. It was Nicholson's first day back on the job since booking off sick a few days before, and he neglected to look at the bulletin board listing incoming trains. Likewise, clerk H.B. Ritchie forgot to tell Nicholson that Train #17 from Maple Creek was two hours late.

About 8:20 A.M. as Engineer Nicholson took his train over the same section of track where he'd seen the ghost train, he looked up to see another train coming toward him. This time, though, it was not a phantom. It was Engineer Twohey in Train #17. Both engineers could have jumped, but they tried to save their trains instead. Because they took the time to brake, only nine people died in the collision. Nicholson and Twohey, however, were both killed. According to some reports, a phantom train still occasionally whistles through this section of track between Medicine Hat and Dunmore.

Medicine Hat Named
Highway 1, Medicine Hat

The city of Medicine Hat owes its birth to the Canadian Pacific Railway (CPR), which reached here in 1883. But this spot on the South Saskatchewan River was known as Medicine Hat many years before. Several stories circulate about the origin of the name. One of the most common tells of a Cree medicine man who dropped his headgear as he crossed the river during a battle with a band of Blackfoot. The Cree took the lost hat of their spiritual leader as an omen and fled rather than chance a fight on a bad day. The Blackfoot later found the medicine man's hat at the edge of the river and afterward called the place Medicine Hat Crossing.

Medicine Hat and nearby Redcliff were two of Alberta's first industrial communities. Railroad construction crews discovered gas near here while drilling for water in 1883. By the 1890s, natural gas was being piped to the city to heat homes and businesses.

Rudyard Kipling called Medicine Hat "the city with all hell for a basement," but natural gas brought added wealth to the community. Some of that wealth can still be seen in the early architecture that remains. A guide is available at the tourist information center on Highway 1 for a self-directed walking tour of historic buildings in the downtown area. Included are the old Provincial Court House and St. Patrick's Roman Catholic Church, which overlooks much of the city.

The Medicine Hat Museum and Art Gallery features exhibits of local and area history. The Clay Products Interpretative Centre at Medalta Potteries near Strathcona Island Park is a Provincial and National Historic Site that focuses on the local pottery industry, which developed here because of the area's rich clay deposits and the availability of natural gas for heating kilns. Other points of historical interest in the Medicine Hat area include Echo Dale Farm and the Ajax Coal Mine, both in Echo Dale Park off Highway 3. The Saamis Archaeological Site (next to the big teepee near the tourist information center on Highway 1) and the interpretive displays at Police Point Park are also of interest.

North of Medicine Hat on the southeast corner of the Suffield Military Base is the Cactus Flower Archaeological Site—one of the largest on the prairies. Artifacts found here date back 8,000 years.

Kaye Property Located Near Present Town of Redcliff
Highway 1, west of Medicine Hat

In 1887, an Englishman named Sir John Lister Kaye organized the Canadian Agricultural, Coal, and Colonization Company. He secured 10 separate blocks of land of 10,000 acres (4,047 hectares) each along the Canadian Pacific Railway (CPR). Redcliff is on the eastern side of one of the Kaye land holdings.

Kaye had a lot of money, but little in the way of farming experience. That combination is often fatal in agricultural enterprises. Kaye proved no exception. His ranches became known as the 76 after he bought large herds of cattle with that brand from the Powder River Cattle Company in Wyoming. Kaye also brought in large numbers of sheep.

More than anything else, it was the cultivation of wheat and grains that proved Kaye's undoing. All of his money couldn't buy rain. His most inept attempt at compensating for lack of moisture occurred in 1890, a particularly dry year. To make up for the lack of rain, Kaye built large water carts with holes for sprinklers, similar to the water wagons used to sprinkle city streets in England. Kaye then had the carts filled with water from the South Saskatchewan River and driven over the parched fields. His sprinklers, unfortunately, were like spitting at a dust storm. In short order, the Canadian Agricultural, Coal and Colonization Company became one of the fascinating footnotes of Alberta history.

Hatfield the Rainmaker Comes to Chappice Lake
22 miles (35 km) north of Redcliff (inaccessible today)

By 1920, summer droughts were already demonstrating that many of the arid regions in southern Alberta were more suitable for livestock than grain growing. Several farmers in the area started talking about hiring a rainmaker. The idea began after Charles Mallory Hatfield gained some measure of notoriety in southern California by claiming credit for recent rains there. In the spring of 1921, a group from Medicine Hat arranged for Hatfield to come north. He set up shop near an alkali slough known as Chappice Lake.

Hatfield built a cabin complete with eaves troughs to handle the expected deluge and a pair of towers, where some mysterious chemical concoctions were to create ample rainfall over the course of the summer. Before the month of May was out, rain began to fall. True, it wasn't much more than a drizzle, but it lasted several days. Local farmers went to town to buy boots and raincoats. Nearly 1.5 inches (4 centimeters) of rain fell during the month, and crops got off to a good start. Hatfield was hailed as a hero. No one seemed to notice that areas somewhat removed from Chappice Lake received similar amounts of moisture that spring.

A bit more rain came in June, but by July, with Hatfield working away at his chemical shenanigans in his towers, the prairie had dried out again. The embarrassment was particularly galling because surrounding areas were now getting rain while the farmers around Chappice Lake were looking at parched fields. Bowing to mounting criticism, Hatfield accepted a reduced payment of $2,500 and left for home. He assured everyone he would be back the following spring, but no one around Medicine Hat has seen a professional rainmaker since.

Natural Gas Discovered
Highway 1, 30 miles (48 km) west of Medicine Hat

On the south side of the highway, an historical marker commemorates the first gas well drilled in Alberta. In 1883, nobody
was looking for natural gas, but two miles (three kilometers)
southwest of here, the Canadian Pacific Railway was looking for
water for its trains. The company sank a deep well and, at a depth
of 10,662 feet (3,250 meters), struck natural gas. Within a few
years, several more gas wells had been drilled, and gas was being
piped to Medicine Hat to heat homes, stores and factories. From
this small beginning, the Alberta natural gas industry developed.

Gathering Wood Beside Highway Prohibited
Highway 1, west of Medicine Hat (sign no longer exists)

The highway between Medicine Hat and Brooks has long
been a lonely one. In the early years of the century, only two
ranches could be seen on the south side of the railroad for the
entire distance. One ranch belonged to George Lane, the other to
the company of Gordon, Ironsides and Fares, which had bought
Sir John Lister Kaye's 76 ranch.

Especially after irrigation came to the area near Brooks, travel from there to Medicine Hat became known for its wide-open,
treeless spaces. In the 1950s, after the route became part of the
new Trans–Canada Highway, a local wag placed a small sign
along the road advising: Gathering Wood Beside the Highway is
Strictly Prohibited.

Aqueduct Constructed at Brooks
Secondary Road 873, 5 miles (8 km) southeast of Brooks

The Brooks Aqueduct National and Provincial Historic Site
preserves a remnant of Alberta's monumental, turn-of-the-century irrigation projects. The Canadian Pacific Railway (CPR)
began many of these early undertakings. In order to stimulate
settlement in this area, it built a dam on the Bow River at Bassano west of Brooks on Highway 1. An extensive canal system,
including the Brooks Aqueduct, soon irrigated thousands of

acres of prairie soil. When the aqueduct was completed in 1915, it was the largest concrete structure of its kind in the world.

Promises of irrigation brought settlers, but not all the CPR's promises were fulfilled. In 1935, local farmers took over and managed what is now known as the Eastern Irrigation District. As a result, the irrigated area east and south of Brooks, though situated in one of the most arid regions of the prairies, is also one of the most agriculturally rich areas of the continent.

More of the history of this region can be discovered in Brooks at the Brooks Museum and in Scandia, south of Brooks on Highway 36, at the Scandia Museum and the Eastern Irrigation District Historical Park.

Dinosaur Provincial Park Named World Heritage Site

Off Secondary Road 544 at Patricia, 30 miles (48 km) northeast of Brooks

One hundred million years ago, the land of this arid region of Canada was a tropical jungle with shallow deltas flowing into the Bear Paw Sea. Dinosaurs roamed here, and flying reptiles ruled the skies. Then 65,000,000 years ago, for reasons no one really understands, the dinosaurs became extinct. Evidence of their life, though, can still be found in the fossils of southern Alberta. One of the richest fossil sites in the world can be found along the Red Deer River in Dinosaur Provincial Park.

Camping and picnic grounds are available in the park. Guided hikes and tours are also available through the designated nature preserves, where some of the most spectacular fossil finds have been made. Be aware, however, that no bone collecting is allowed. Visitors discovering a significant fossil location will be awarded special fossil-finder certificates by park officials.

At its field station in the park, the Royal Tyrrell Museum of Palaeontology features many fascinating exhibits and multimedia presentations focusing on its research in the park. Over the years, museum paleontologists have made many significant contributions to the world's understanding of Cretaceous dinosaurs. In 1979, Dinosaur Provincial Park was named a United Nations World Heritage Site.

John Ware Ranches in Red Deer River Valley
Dinosaur Provincial Park
Off Secondary Road 544 at Patricia, 30 miles (48 km) northeast of Brooks

The home of one of the provinces's most famous early ranchers can be found in Dinosaur Provincial Park. John Ware's cabin was originally located on the Red Deer River north of Duchess, but it was moved to the park for preservation in 1955.

Ware was born a slave in South Carolina but made his way to Texas after the Civil War. In the Lone Star State, he became a cowpuncher and an excellent horseman. In 1879, he helped deliver a huge herd of Texas cattle to a ranch in Montana.

The next year and a half, Ware spent prospecting for gold in the mountains of Montana and Idaho. When he failed to find his fortune, he decided to go back to Texas with a cowboy buddy named Bill Moodie. Before they got around to leaving Idaho, however, they were offered a job by an Alberta trail driver named Tom Lynch. Lynch needed help delivering a herd to the newly formed North West Cattle Company in southwestern Alberta.

On the way north, near the Marias River just south of the border, cattle thieves ran off with a few head of North West trail stock. Ware volunteered to track them down. He set out alone but returned before another night passed, driving the missing cattle in front of him and towing two rustlers at the end of his lariat.

After the herd was delivered, Ware was hired on as one of the regular ranch hands. He soon developed a reputation as the best bronc rider and all-round horseman in the province. In 1885, the *Macleod Gazette* reported that "the horse is not running on the prairie which John Ware cannot ride, sitting with his face either to the head or tail, and even if the animal chooses to stand on its head or lie on its back, John always appears on top when the horse gets up, and he smiles as if he enjoyed it— and he probably does."

Later, Ware took up ranching on his own, first in the Rocky Mountain foothills and then on the banks of the Red Deer River north of Brooks. In 1905, he was killed when his horse stumbled in a badger hole and fell on him.

Majorville Cairn
Secondary Road 847, approximately 9 miles (15 km) south of Bassano

South of Bassano near the Bow River, a large cairn stands in the middle of a medicine wheel approximately 5,000 years old. Alberta is home to more than forty medicine wheels, but little is known about the Majorville one. It may have played an important role in the spiritual life of ancient Albertans or it may have served as a monument to important people or events.

Blackfoot Sign Treaty No. 7
Secondary Road 842, 1.2 miles (2 km) south of Highway 1

Lieutenant Colonel James Macleod of the North-West Mounted Police mistakenly thought Crowfoot, the Blackfoot chief, could speak for the entire Blackfoot Confederacy.

On the Bow River south of Cluny, at a place called Blackfoot Crossing, Treaty No. 7 was signed on September 22, 1877. Five thousand Indians of the Blackfoot Confederacy assembled that day to meet with federal government officials. They traded 50,000 square miles (129,490 square kilometers) of what is today western Canada for $53,000 and what must have seemed vague promises of future help. The Blackfoot, under Crowfoot, chose the land around Blackfoot Crossing for their reserve.

Crowfoot promised peace that day, and since that time, his word has been kept. Even during the Riel Rebellion of 1885, when white officials feared the Blackfoot would join the metis and Cree rebels, Crowfoot kept his promise, so the rebellion was quickly crushed. But the government still worried about Blackfoot discontent. The following year, Prime Minister John A. Macdonald invited Crowfoot and other chiefs to Ottawa so they could see the extent of white civilization. Ottawa officials hoped that after a tour of the East the Blackfoot would be impressed with white society and less likely to cause problems.

The Blackfoot chiefs agreed to travel east on the Canadian Pacific Railway for a guided tour of Canada's big cities. While in the East, they met the Prime Minister. They reviewed a military parade. They rode in open carriages through the streets of Ottawa, Montreal and Toronto. On the way home, the train stopped in Winnipeg, where a reporter asked Crowfoot what had impressed him most about the East. Was it the crowded cities? The Prime Minister? Parliament? Crowfoot gave the matter some thought. No, he said, what impressed him most were the monkeys at the Toronto Zoo, and in his own way, he passed comment on the glory of white civilization.

Today, the Siksika Nation Museum near Blackfoot Crossing highlights the culture and heritage of the Blackfoot people.

ALTERNATE ROUTES THROUGH GATEWAY COUNTRY
Highway 3 Between Medicine Hat and Burdett

Seven Bodies Found at Seven Persons
Highway 3, Seven Persons

On the south side of the highway, an historical marker tells how the town, which took its name from a nearby creek, began in the 1880s as a siding on the old Turkey Track Railway, a narrow-gauge railway built by the North West Coal and Navigation Company. After a wave of homestead settlement in the early 1900s, Seven Persons flourished as a service center for the surrounding agricultural community. It boasted five grain elevators, a stockyard, a creamery, lumberyards, stores, churches, a community hall and a hotel. By the 1920s, after the region's arid climate forced many dryland farmers out of business, the town's population began to dwindle.

At least two stories account for the name of the town. Some say the name dates from when a band of Blood Indians led by Calf Shirt killed seven Cree in a battle on the banks of the creek. Another account claims that a band of Blackfoot came upon the long-dead but undecayed bodies of seven hairless men. Bewildered, the Blackfoot watched over the bodies for five days before concluding that the men had been struck down by the Great Spirit. The following spring when the Blackfoot returned to the creek, no trace of the "seven persons" could be found.

In 1865, John George "Kootenai" Brown and three companions lost their way while traveling to Edmonton. They ended up camping near Seven Persons Creek, where they were attacked by a small party of Blackfoot. Brown was shot in the back, although some accounts place the arrow slightly lower on his anatomy. The four men managed to escape, however, and in later years, Brown maintained that had he and his friends been killed, the town and the creek would have been called Eleven Persons.

Etzikom Museum and Canadian National Historic Windpower Centre
Secondary Road 885, 37 miles (60 km) south of Highway 3 at Etzikom

---

Exhibits at this location include a pioneer general store, hotel, school, blacksmith shop and post office, plus a collection of windmills. The nearby Fletcher Archaeological Site—35 miles (56 kilometers) west of town and 5 miles (8 kilometers) north of Highway 61—is one of the oldest in Alberta. Some of the artifacts and bones found here are more than 7,000 years old.

If you don't mind back roads and would like to spend some time in the extreme southeastern part of Alberta, I'd recommend a side trip to Manyberries after a visit in Etzikom. Stop at the local café for a piece of pie and a cup of coffee. Then drive south to the Canadian Customs station at Wild Horse before turning west to Writing-On-Stone Provincial Park. You won't pass an historical marker or museum on the entire route, but history, and probably pronghorn antelope, will be all around you.

Bow Island Gas Field Discovered
Highway 3, Bow Island

At the Bow Island Tourist Information Centre on Highway 3, an historical marker commemorates the drilling of the first successful gas well in the Bow Island field in 1909. Soon afterward, the Bow Island field became Alberta's first gas field with sufficient reserves to supply distant markets. In 1912, a pipeline was laid from the Bow Island field to Lethbridge and Calgary. Later, when reserves declined, Bow Island became the first major storage field in Canada.

Bow Island Ferry Carries Politician
Highway 3, Bow Island

Although named for an island, the Bow Island community is several miles from the river and surrounded by dry land. Despite this, according to one old story, every time a former provincial politician visited the community he would claim the price of tickets for the Bow Island Ferry on his government expense account.

Chapter 3

Calgary to the Mountains

**From
Prairies to
Foothills**

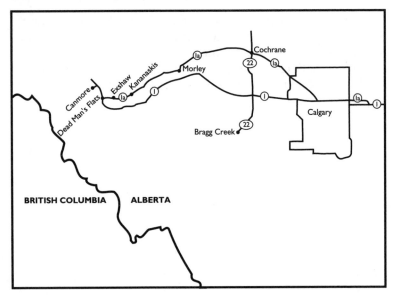

DEPENDING ON WHAT DIRECTION you come from, Calgary can be either a city of the prairies or the foothills. From the east, travelers enter from the plains. Drive the Trans–Canada Highway out of town to the west, and the landscape suddenly changes. Now the foothills and the jagged barrier of the Rocky Mountains loom ahead.

Somewhat surprisingly, the first white men to forge a trail between what became Calgary and Banff traveled east. The Palliser Expedition, sent by the British government to report on western Canada's potential for settlement, covered part of this route in 1858, but it wasn't until 1864 or 1865 that white men traveled the entire route. This feat was accomplished by a group of British Columbia prospectors that included John J. Healy and Sam Livingston.

Healy later became known in Alberta as a whiskey trader and mine promoter. Livingston, after prospecting for a time on the North Saskatchewan River and then trading whiskey, would settle down to become Calgary's first farmer. These trail-blazing prospectors came into Alberta over the treacherous Kicking Horse Pass, then wandered south to the Bow River. Here they picked up another Indian trail to the east and followed it as far as the forks of the Bow and Elbow rivers at modern Calgary. After camping on the Bow for several days, the party split up.

Livingston and a few others headed north to prospect for gold on the North Saskatchewan. Somewhere near modern Sundre, however, the men ran into a hostile band of Blackfoot. Instead of killing the white men, the Indians took their horses and some of their clothes, then left them to walk the 30 to 37 miles (50 to 60 kilometers) to Rocky Mountain House.

After prospecting along the North Saskatchewan, Livingston returned to the Bow River around 1870. At first, he ran a small trading post near present-day Cochrane. By 1873, he had moved back to the area that would become the city of Calgary. He traded here until the arrival of the Mounties, then started a small farm along the Elbow River.

Old Fort Calgary was the scene of a North-West Mounted Police meeting and an Indian siege.

Points of Interest In and About Calgary

Early Settlers Come to the Elbow and Bow Rivers
Fort Calgary Historic Park
750 – 9th Avenue S.E.

Calgary's earliest known residents were the Blackfoot Indians who camped in the shelter of the Bow and Elbow rivers, and made weapons from the wood of the Douglas Fir that grew there. The larger stream became known as the Bow River.

David Thompson wintered with Indians at the confluence of the Bow and Elbow in 1787, but attempts at permanent white settlement didn't occur for nearly 100 years. For most of the intervening decades, the Blackfoot did not tolerate either Canadian or American trading posts in the area. The only exception was the short-lived Peigan Post established by the Hudson's Bay Company some distance up the Bow, west of present-day Morley. It operated for parts of two seasons in 1832 and 1833 until traders, fearing for their lives, retreated to Rocky Mountain House. Blood Indians evidently burned the post to the ground almost as soon as the traders left.

It was nearly 40 years before any white man attempted to live near the Bow River again. In 1871, whiskey trader Fred Kanouse arrived and set up a small trading post on the banks of the Elbow in what is today the city of Calgary. The following year, Kanouse was wounded during a skirmish with Blood Indians and withdrew to a deputy sheriff's job in Choteau County, Montana. Later, Kanouse joined John George "Kootenai" Brown, another early southwestern Alberta resident, in a trading venture in the Kootenay Lakes district of Alberta.

Sam Livingston moved to the Elbow in 1873. John Glenn settled on Fish Creek soon afterward. Within a few years, Glenn was irrigating 20 acres (8 hectares) of his land with Fish Creek water, making his the first irrigated crops grown in Alberta. Several Roman Catholic priests also came early to the Calgary area, establishing a mission along the Elbow in 1873. They moved their mission closer to the confluence of the two rivers just before the Mounted Police established Fort Calgary in 1875.

North-West Mounted Police Establish Fort Calgary
Fort Calgary Historic Park
750 – 9th Avenue SE

In the summer of 1875, Inspector Ephram Brisebois led "F" Troop of the North-West Mounted Police to the Bow River. Here he chose a spot for a new post that eventually became the city of Calgary. Fort Calgary was built in what is today the downtown area.

Brisebois intended to name the new post Fort Brisebois, but this aroused resentment among his troops, and from Colonel Macleod and Assistant Commissioner Irvine. Macleod recommended changing the name to Fort Calgary in honor of a castle belonging to members of his mother's family back in Scotland.

The contract for constructing Fort Calgary went to the I.G. Baker Company of Fort Benton, Montana. The work took place between September and December 1875. As soon as the Baker people finished building the fort, they built a trading post nearby. A village sprang up around the new post almost immediately.

Until the coming of the railroad in 1883, Calgary and most of southern Alberta were supplied by merchants like the I.G. Baker Company from Fort Benton, Montana. The I.G. Baker Store was one of the first buildings in Calgary.

By the summer of 1876, Calgary was already a frontier town. Sam Livingston, John Glenn and the Catholic mission had been in the area before the police fort was built. A number of metis freighters moved in from the Edmonton region before the fort was completed. A cluster of Indian teepees soon materialized. Harry Taylor, who later ran the Macleod Hotel, built a dance hall and billiard room. Perhaps partly to counteract Taylor's dance hall, the Reverend George McDougall built a church.

When the CPR built its station across the Elbow River west of Fort Calgary, the new city took shape around the railway depot, not the old fort that had been the center town until that time.

Mutiny at Fort Calgary
Fort Calgary Historic Park
750 – 9th Avenue SE

Soon after the Mounties built Fort Calgary, it was the scene of the only mutiny in the history of the North-West Mounted Police. It happened when the men of "F" Troop refused to follow the orders of Inspector Brisebois, their commanding officer. Brisebois was from a prominent Conservative family in Quebec, and his appointment to the force was in large part due to political influence. By most accounts, Brisebois was an easy-going, good-humored fellow, but he was young and discipline at his fort was lax.

Despite his good nature, or, perhaps partly because of it, the men of "F" Troop had little respect for him. Brisebois' attempt to name the fort after himself was met with derision. Several times in the early winter, men or groups of men, refused to follow orders. In each case, the matters under contention were of little consequence, but punishments were minimal or nonexistent and precedents were set.

Then in December, Brisebois took a metis woman to his quarters. This in itself would not have created resentment, except the hospitable inspector also ordered the frigid fort's only iron stove put in his room. With animosity already running high, the men of "F" Troop rebelled. They took over the fort. Three of them rode south to present their case at Fort Macleod, but on arrival, they were promptly arrested. Officers Macleod and Irvine left for Fort Calgary immediately. Soon, they settled the mutineers' grievances, but Brisebois' days with the Mounted Police were numbered. The following July, amidst the continued antagonism of his men and fellow officers, he submitted his resignation.

Today, the site of old Fort Calgary is home to a 40-acre (16-hectare) riverside park and historical interpretive center. A self-guided tour offers displays, artifacts and an audio-visual presentation of the early days of Calgary.

Sarcee Indians Demand Recognition
Tsuu T'ina Museum
Sarcee Reserve, 3700 Anderson Road SW

For a short time in 1880, Fort Calgary was the scene of a near siege. The trouble started when Sarcee Indians, also known as Tsuu T'ina, led by Chief Bull Head, arrived from the Blackfoot Reserve and surrounded the fort. Bull Head demanded winter provisions and a separate reserve for his people, who were a distinct tribe though loosely affiliated with the Blackfoot.

Originally, the Sarcee were part of the Beaver tribe from the far north. In the late 1700s, a family feud started over the shooting of a dog. Soon the rift developed into a major schism among the

Beaver people. Then, in one battle, 80 members of the tribe were killed. Afterward, a tribal council was convened, and it was decided that some 60 people—friends and family of the chief who had killed the dog—should go into exile. They left before morning and apparently vanished from their northern hunting grounds.

It was nearly 100 years before the Beaver people heard of the exiles again. A Beaver trapper traveling with a white trader to Fort Edmonton discovered among the Blackfoot a group of Indians who spoke his language. On investigation, he learned that they were the descendants of the legendary exiles. The original band had worked its way south, where they allied themselves with the Blackfoot against the Cree, who were long-time enemies of the Beaver people.

The Sarcee exiles took up the ways of the Plains Indians, and the tribe grew steadily during its initial years in the south. With the coming of the whites, life changed for the Sarcee, as it did for all Plains tribes. By 1877, when the Indians of southern Alberta signed treaties with the Canadian government, the Sarcee had been so decimated by disease that only 250 of them remained.

Instead of giving them a reserve of their own, the government assigned them a place on a corner of the Blackfoot reserve. Here, for the most part, they were ignored. When Bull Head took his warriors to Fort Calgary in 1880, however, things changed. To prevent the Sarcee insurgents from burning the fort, wagons of provisions were sent from Fort Macleod for Bull Head and his people. The government also promised the tribe a reserve. In 1883, the Sarcee were given land bordering the southwest side of today's city of Calgary.

Today, the Sarcee operate the Tsuu T'ina Museum on the Sarcee Reserve. The museum focuses on Plains Indian culture and the history of the Sarcee people. Displays range from clothing to teepees.

Canadian Pacific Railway Comes to Calgary

In 1883, the Canadian Pacific Railway (CPR) reached Calgary. Originally, the company had intended to cross Alberta farther north through Edmonton but in the end decided on a southern route to bring areas closer to the American border into the Canadian rail system. The southern route through the mountains was more difficult, but when the decision was made to go that way, Calgary's future was secure. Until the CPR arrived in Calgary, Edmonton and Fort Macleod were the major settlements in the province. But with the arrival of the railroad, Calgary seemed poised to become Alberta's dominant city.

Settlement in the province proceeded somewhat more slowly than in the neighboring provinces of Manitoba and Saskatchewan. Calgary's population increased only gradually during the days of the big cattle spreads and through the agricultural depression of the 1890s. In 1894, with a population of 2,500, it incorporated as a city. In 1905, when Alberta became a province, residents of Calgary, now with a population of 13,000, were sure their city would be the new provincial capital. But Edmonton, with a population only slightly larger (when combined with Strathcona), got the nod from the legislature.

Calgary's Big Four Finance Calgary Stampede
Stampede Park and Exhibition Grounds
1410 Olympic Way SE

In 1905, Edmonton became the seat of government in Alberta, but Calgary had already established itself as the province's main cattle ranching center. Because it was on the main line of the Canadian Pacific Railway (CPR), it soon out-paced earlier ranching communities like Fort Macleod, High River and Pincher Creek.

Ranchers of all stripes played an active role in Calgary's community life, but in the early years of the twentieth century four men from the ranching community—George Lane, Pat Burns, Alfred E. Cross and Archie J. McLean—became especially prominent. George Lane was a Montana cowboy when he was hired as foreman on the famous Bar U Ranch in 1884. It was Lane, in fact, who chose the Bar U brand. After a time, Lane began ranching on his own, and in 1902 he even bought out the Bar U to add to his own extensive holdings.

Alfred E. Cross ran the a7 Ranch and later a brewery in Calgary. He and Lane became good friends after they ran some cattle together on the Bar U. According to Cross, when he wanted to separate the herds, Lane told him he'd have to wait for his a7 cattle because Bar U cowboys were too busy with other jobs at

The "Big Four" were (L–R, excluding center): Patrick Burns, George Lane, Archie McLean and Alfred Cross. They appear here with the Duke of Windsor (center) at the Duke's EP Ranch a decade after the four men organized the first Calgary Stampede.

the time. Cross didn't complain. He simply went to the Bar U cowboys and offered them five dollars a month more in wages to work for him. The cowboys promptly quit and went to work for the a7, separating Cross's cows from the Bar U's. Despite these antics, Lane was impressed by Cross's spunk, and the two men remained good friends.

In 1912, Guy Weadick and Southern Alberta's "Big Four" staged the first Calgary Stampede. The Stampede was not held again until after World War I in August 1919. In 1923, it became an annual event and remains so to this day.

Pat Burns was born in Ontario and came west as a young man to homestead in Manitoba, where he began raising cattle. Soon, Burns began supplying meat on contract to railroad camps. By the turn of the century, he was selling wholesale meat across the West. He also owned several ranches, including his huge Bow Valley Ranch south of Calgary. Southern Alberta cattle could be driven to the Burns ranch, released inside the fence, then, after feeding on the ranch's grass, turned out at Burns' abattoir on the other side of the ranch in Calgary. Eventually, Burns owned 450,000 acres (182,115 hectares) of land. It was said that he could ride from the international boundary near the Milk River all the way to Calgary without ever having to leave his property.

Archie Maclean was another Ontario native who came west, first raising horses on a ranch in Manitoba and then moving to Alberta, where he became a partner in the Cypress Cattle Company (the CY) northwest of Taber. In 1909, Maclean entered provincial politics and represented the Lethbridge district until 1921.

In 1912, Lane, Cross, Burns and Maclean, who collectively became known as the Big Four, backed a young American cowboy showman by the name of Guy Weadick. According to the legend, which might be true, they gave Weadick a check for $100,000 and told him to put on the greatest outdoor show in the world. The Calgary Stampede was born late that summer.

Although the first Weadick Stampede was a success, another one didn't occur until 1916, when it was staged in Winnipeg. In 1919, the Stampede returned to Calgary, and in 1923 it became an annual event.

Calgary Eye-Opener Raises Eyebrows

Capping a remarkable career, Bob Edwards, the legendary editor of the *Calgary Eye-Opener*, was elected to the provincial legislature in 1921. Edwards had first come to Alberta in 1895. He started newspapers in several Alberta towns—including Wetaskiwin, Leduc, Edmonton and High River—before he brought his *Eye-Opener* to Calgary.

Edwards said he moved to Calgary from High River because he'd offended the Methodists there. According to one story, Edwards met a traveling salesman at a High River watering hole one Saturday night. The salesmen sold gramophone records and told Edwards he planned to take a sample of choir music to the local church the following morning. Later in the evening, Edwards learned that, in addition to church music, the salesman sold recordings of a somewhat risqué nature. At his first opportunity, Edwards secretly removed the choir music from its cover and replaced it with songs no Methodist wants to hear on Sunday morning.

Soon after, Edwards moved his paper to Calgary. Subscriptions to the *Eye-Opener* were five dollars a year, but Edwards gave a four-dollar discount because of what he called "irregularity." This probably referred to missed publication days due to his not infrequent hangovers. Despite such antics, Bob Edwards' satirical, irreverent paper was a success in Calgary.

Some of Edwards' musings over the years included such memorable lines as "Some men spoil a good story by sticking to the truth"; "A little learning is a dangerous thing, but a lot of ignorance is just as bad"; and "All good people don't die young. Lots of them live to a ripe old age and die poor." When Calgary's new city hall was built, the *Calgary Eye-Opener* observed, "We hate to say anything about it, but how in thunder did the new city hall of Calgary come to cost $350,000 when Pat Burns' splendid residence, which everybody knows well by sight, was erected for less than $25,000? This is a profound mystery—one of the seven mysteries of the world, in fact."

Edwards raged against politicians for his entire newspaper career. When he was elected to the provincial legislature, it was as an independent and with no campaigning. His political career was short-lived, however. After the legislature's first session, Edwards fell ill and died. His friends buried him with the last issue of the *Calgary Eye-Opener* and a bottle of whiskey tucked in the coffin beside him.

The Dirtiest Leg in Canada

In the early twentieth century, a woman known as Mother Fulham ran a pig farm on the edge of Calgary. Fulham used to collect Calgary garbage to feed to her pigs, and she'd often end up in verbal shouting matches with local citizens while collecting her pig feed from behind hotels and saloons.

Sometimes conflicts would escalate to near brawls. More than once, Fulham was brought before Calgary courts. On one occasion, it was necessary for a doctor to examine her ankle in order to testify on the extent of an injury she'd suffered. Fulham removed her sock, and the doctor, somewhat taken aback, said, "Why I'll bet a dollar there's not another leg as dirty as this one in all of Canada."

Fulham grinned. She told the doctor she'd take him up on that bet and then immediately removed her remaining stocking so he could see her other leg.

Points of Interest Near Highway 1
Between Calgary and Canmore

Since Calgary's earliest days, two roads have led to the mountains along the Bow River. The earliest trail on the north side crossed the river at the police fort and followed the Bow River west to Morley, roughly along today's Highway 1A. The southern route approximately followed the path of Highway 1. Although the two roads joined at Morley, they quickly split again. One took a northern route into the mountains along the Ghost River and Lake Minnewanka. The other continued along the Bow. Weather seems to have been the primary criterion for people debating which road to take. As is the case today, the southern route was faster, but at the turn of the century, in the spring, it was often clogged with mud.

The first automobile to travel the route between Calgary and Banff literally followed the railroad tracks. It was 1904 and Charles Glidden of Boston arrived in Calgary with a four-ton Napier automobile fitted with wheels to ride the rails. Glidden covered the ground between Calgary and Banff in just under two hours.

Five years later, Norman Lougheed made the car trip from Calgary to Banff on tires in eight hours. Lougheed took the south trail as far as the Cochrane Ferry, where he changed to the north side of the river and followed the Morley road through Exshaw and Dead Man's Flats to Banff. Here the vehicle was promptly impounded by the police. Apparently, Lougheed had violated a local ordinance forbidding motorized vehicles in the park.

Dream Chasing and Hang Gliding on Cochrane's Big Hill
Highway 1A, .5 miles (1 km) east of Cochrane

A physician and geologist, Sir James Hector of the Palliser Expedition—a group of men sent by the British government to determine western Canada's potential for settlement—was first to write of the Big Hill between Calgary and Cochrane, over which today's Highway 1A travels. Noting the magnificent view, Hector recommended calling the place Dream Hill.

Later, Matthew Cochrane, with a dream of his own when he looked down from the hill, started the first of the great free range cattle ranches here in 1881. In this century, according to an historical marker on the west side of the hill, just east of the present town of Cochrane, Willi Muller, the father of hang gliding, initiated the sport in Alberta on Cochrane's Big Hill. Today, hang gliders still soar through local skies every summer, chasing dreams or thrills in the tradition of Hector's Dream Hill.

First Big Ranch Comes to Alberta
At the Highway 1A and Highway 22 junction at Cochrane

Just west of the town of Cochrane, the Cochrane Ranch Provincial Historic Site is located at the original headquarters of the famous ranch. Today, Alberta grass feeds a quarter of the nation's beef cattle, and working ranches are found throughout the province. The excellent quality of the grass in Alberta's foothills is what first brought large-scale ranching operations to this area. Matthew Cochrane, the first of the big leasehold ranchers, is usually credited with starting commercial ranching in the province.

Cochrane established his ranch on land between today's Cochrane Ranch Provincial Historic Site and the Bow River. He leased 100,000 acres (40,470 hectares) of land from the Canadian government for just under one cent an acre (half a cent a hectare), then brought 3,000 head of range cattle in from Montana. With that one cattle drive, Cochrane had created the largest ranching operation in Alberta. He was not the first rancher, however. Cattle had been driven into Alberta since the 1830s from Red River country, following the North Saskatchewan River to Alberta fur posts and later to early Indian missions.

Despite being the first large-scale rancher in Alberta, Senator Cochrane didn't fare as well as most. The first year's cattle arrived late in the season. Having been pushed too hard up the trail from the Montana border, the animals were exhausted and hungry by the time they got to the Bow River. Before they had time to regain their strength, a snowstorm came out of the mountains and many of the cattle died. A hard winter followed, and the cattle never recovered from their long drive north.

In the spring, rotting carcasses littered the landscape. On the Cochrane roundup, cowboys were ordered to burn the Cochrane brand into every unbranded animal they came across. Neighboring settlers, friendly to the Cochrane outfit until this time, but fearing the loss of their mostly unbranded stock, began to collect and brand every cow, steer or calf they could put their hands on. On final tally, it was generally agreed that the Cochrane Ranch came up short.

In order to replenish his herd and further stock the ranch, Cochrane purchased 4,000 more head of cattle. These started out from Montana in August 1882. After a month and a half, near Fish Creek, another October snowstorm blew in. This time the cattle were in a fairly sheltered location. Word was sent to ranch manager, James Walker, an ex-Mountie, of the cattle's whereabouts. The Montana trail boss wanted to leave the herd where it was instead of continuing to the ranch as his contract stated. But Walker wanted the terms of the agreement carried out to the letter.

The cattle were pushed forward out of the cover of the creek and bound for the Bow River country through snow more than 12 inches (30 centimeters) deep. Walker was betting on a Chinook to clear the snow. One came, but it lasted only long enough to leave a coating of ice over the encrusted snow. The plight of the cattle grew worse. Throughout the winter, they died in distressing numbers. By the following spring, fewer than half the 7,000 cattle originally bought in Montana over the previous two summers were still alive.

With two bad winters under his belt, Cochrane decided to move his cattle operation south to the area around today's Waterton Park. Using the expedient of chartering a new company, Cochrane and his crew were able to obtain additional land from the government, so the combined ranches now totaled nearly 200,000 acres (81,000 hectares), for which Cochrane still paid under one cent an acre (half a cent a hectare).

Even with additional land, however, the Cochrane Ranch continued to be plagued by bad management and terrible luck. The ranch at Cochrane was left for sheep and horses. Here the winter of 1883–84 proved a generally good one with everything running smoothly until spring. Then a heavy snowfall in April created a bridge over the top of the corrals, and 300 sheep escaped and perished when they fell through rotting ice in a

nearby lake. Several hundred more succumbed to cold, hunger and timber wolves. In one final setback, the following spring saw a prairie fire kill still more of the Cochrane sheep.

Farther south, on the Cochrane's new ranch along the Waterton River, heavy snowfalls in the winter of 1883–84 made grazing poor. Cattle and profits suffered. Eventually, the Cochrane ranches did manage to recover. By the early part of the

Sheep on Senator Cochrane's Ranch west of Calgary, 1883.

new century, however, the days of open-range cattle ranching in southern Alberta were mostly over, and Cochrane's interests in the province, like many of the big ranches, were sold.

Although Cochrane's was the first of the huge leased cattle ranches in southern Alberta, Cochrane was not the region's first cattle rancher. The first cattle to graze the ranching area of southern Alberta were brought from Fort Edmonton in 1871 by the Morley missionary Reverend John McDougall, who used them to finance his mission work. The next year, McDougall brought 30 head more to Morley from Montana. In the next few years, other pioneer cattlemen also brought in small herds. For the most part, these herds were established near the Mounted Police post at Fort Macleod.

Sub-constable Robert Whitney of the North-West Mounted Police was, inadvertently, a leader in early ranching in the foothills. In a poker game in 1876, Whitney won 25 animals that had been driven up the trail from Montana to Fort Macleod. As a member of the Mounted Police, Whitney didn't have time to look after his new cattle, nor did he have any hay to carry them through the long winter. Whitney's answer to both problems was to turn the cattle out on the nearby prairie to rustle grub for themselves.

The general feeling at Fort Macleod that winter was that Whitney would never see his cattle again. People reasoned that even if the beasts weren't slaughtered by Indians, they couldn't live through a northern winter without hay. The following spring, however, when Whitney and a couple of helpers rode out on Alberta's first roundup, the merits of Alberta grass—grass that could cure like hay on the stem and be nearly as nutritious in winter as summer—were proven for the first time. Whitney's herd had survived the cold months without the loss of even a single animal.

Other would-be cattlemen soon followed Whitney's lead. A good many of them were ex-Mounties encouraged to take up ranching because of the land grants the government gave after three years of satisfactory service in the force. In 1877, about 30 ex-Mounties completing their terms of enlistment took up ranches in the Fort Macleod and Pincher Creek districts. In 1879, Tom Lynch and George Emerson brought 1,000 head of cattle from Miles City, Montana, to start a ranch near the old Spitzee Trading Post on the Highwood River.

First Canadian Hostel Established
Highway 22, 18.5 miles (30 km) south of Highway 1

At Bragg Creek an historical marker is dedicated to hosteling in Canada. The first hostel in the country was started by a group of outdoor enthusiasts from Calgary looking for ways to make the foothills and mountain country more accessible to visitors. They established their first hostel in Bragg Creek on July 1, 1933, when they erected a 12' x 14' rented tent in an unused campground. Within two years, other hostels were established in Jumping Pound, Morley, Canmore and Banff. This same group of Calgarians went on to establish hostels in eastern Canada.

Alberta's First Cheese Factory Established
Highway 1, .5 miles (1 km) west of Highway 22

On the south side of Highway 1, an historical marker commemorates the establishment of both the first cheese factory in Alberta and the commercial dairy industry of the province. Ebenezer Healy and his family started the factory in 1888. They made about three cheeses a day, which were soon marketed in Calgary. Not long after, Healy's cheeses were doing so well that several competitors launched their own businesses. By the turn of the century, the dairy industry was firmly established in Alberta.

McDougalls Establish Morley Indian Mission
Highway 1A, east side of Morley

George and John McDougall came to Edmonton from Ontario as Methodist missionaries in 1862. They built their first mission at Victoria, about 70 miles (113 kilometers) east of Edmonton, and worked there with their families until 1871. During that time, they won the trust of many Blackfoot and Cree, successfully ran their mission and then watched it decimated by smallpox in 1869. Lost in the tragedy, which took thousands of lives across the West, were John's wife and George's two daughters. John and George fought flare-ups of the disease for another year before abandoning the mission and returning to Edmonton.

Despite their grief, the McDougall families pressed on and soon built a church to continue their work. In 1875, they had established the Morley Mission, named after Reverend Morley Punshon, an well-known Methodist preacher. In the winter of 1876, tragedy struck once again when George McDougall died while returning home from a successful buffalo hunt. He was mourned by whites and Indians alike.

George McDougall Monument, Pakan, Alberta, 1956

John McDougall devoted himself to his and his father's missionary work for the next four decades. His activities included importing the first breeding cattle to southern Alberta to finance his work, railing against the whiskey trade and working with Indians and the government to ease the impact of white settlement in the West. He died in 1916 in Calgary, not far from where his father had died forty-one years earlier. Today, he is remembered as one of Alberta's most influential pioneers.

A cairn here is dedicated to the father-and-son missionaries. Just to the south of the cairn stands the first church constructed in southern Alberta. It was built in 1875.

Indians Burn Peigan Post
Highway 1, between Morley and Kananaskis

Near the mouth of Old Fort Creek on the Bow River in 1832 and 1833, J.E. Harriott built Peigan Post for the Hudson's Bay Company. This small fur trading post was meant to bring trade goods closer to Blackfoot territory and, it was hoped, to keep the tribes of the Blackfoot Confederacy from trading with the American Fur Company in Montana.

Peigan Post, as was true of other posts attempting to operate deep in Blackfoot territory until that time, was unsuccessful. The Bloods considered the land theirs and resented the whites' incursion. The Bloods also suspected that the Hudson's Bay Company might trade with their enemies the Stoneys and the Kootenay, and, indeed, that's exactly what the company intended to do. Finally, in 1834, Harriott decided Blackfoot tolerance had reached its limit, and he hurried back to Rocky Mountain House. Almost as soon as Harriott left, Bloods burned the small post to the ground. It would be more than 30 years before traders returned to the Bow.

Dead Man Found
Highway 1, approximately .6 miles (1 km) west of Exshaw at Dead Man's Flats

On the north side of Highway 1 at Dead Man's Flats, an historical marker offers two possible sources for the name *Dead Man's Flats*. One story says the name came about after a French immigrant named John Marret was murdered here in 1904. Marret established a small dairy farm in the area around the turn of the century. In 1901, his brother François joined him on the farm, but local people say that he often complained of pain and whining noises in his head. On May 10, 1904, François borrowed an ax from a neighbor, returned home and killed his brother. Arrested and tried for murder, François was found not guilty for reasons of insanity and committed to an asylum at Ponoka. According to this story, local residents have called the area Dead Man's Flats ever since.

Another explanation for the name comes from local Indians. Early in the century, when Banff National Park included most of the Bow River Valley, a small group of Stoney Indians were trapping beaver illegally on Pigeon Creek. When they saw a park warden, they knew they couldn't get away without being seen, so they rubbed themselves with beaver blood and played dead. The warden found the bodies and fell for the ploy. He returned to Canmore for help, but by the time he got back, the Stoneys had collected their pelts and returned to the reserve at Morley.

Chapter 4

David Thompson and Evergreen Country

Where Forest Meets Prairie

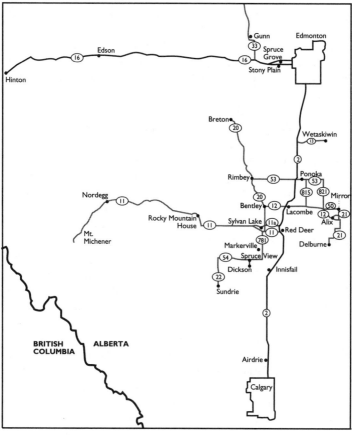

THE FORESTS of David Thompson and Evergreen Country spill from the mountains and foothills of western Alberta into the open prairies to the east. Bordering Jasper and Banff national parks, the gentle beauty of this region extends from the edge of the mountains to a jagged north–south line between Edmonton and Calgary. When Europeans first arrived in Alberta, David Thompson and Evergreen Country belonged to the Blackfoot, Stoney, Gros Ventre, Assiniboine and Cree.

Anthony Henday, an ex-smuggler employed by the Hudson's Bay Company, was the first European to come here. In the winter of 1854–55, Henday camped with a band of Cree traders southwest of present-day Red Deer. He had come to the prairies to entice local Indians to trade furs at York Factory on Hudson Bay. For the most part, prairie Indians ignored his proposals. In subsequent years, the Hudson's Bay Company, trying to lure trade from Montreal's North West Company, began to establish posts farther and farther west.

In 1792, both companies built their first fur posts on the North Saskatchewan River inside Alberta's present border. The North West Company's Fort George and the Hudson's Bay's Buckingham House were located near today's Highway 41 a few miles southeast of Elk Point.

In the fall of 1792, Peter Fidler, a Hudson's Bay Company surveyor, left Buckingham House with a band of Peigan Indians and spent the winter camping and traveling in the Alberta foothills. On an historic journey from November to March, he became the first to map Alberta's Rocky Mountains. He took compass readings on the Battle, Red Deer, Bow and Highwood rivers, and he accurately located Chief Mountain on today's Alberta–Montana border. Fidler traveled along the Oldman River between the Livingstone Range and the Porcupine Hills. He visited the site of Old Women's Buffalo Jump, and he discovered coal deposits on the Red Deer River. In addition to his charts and maps, Fidler also recorded intimate details of Blackfoot life and culture.

In the summer of 1795, the North West Company built Fort Augustus near present-day Fort Saskatchewan, and the Hudson's Bay Company built Edmonton House nearby in October. Although the Hudson's Bay Company changed the location of this post several times in the next two decades, Edmonton has been a name on Alberta maps ever since.

Fur Posts Come to David Thompson and Evergreen Country
Highway 11, Rocky Mountain House

About the time the first Edmonton House was built, two new fur companies, the XY and Olgilvie, made short-lived appearances in Alberta. The heightened competition encouraged the two major companies—the Hudson's Bay Company and the North West Company—to build Pembina House and Boggy Hall farther up the North Saskatchewan River, near present-day Lodgepole. Their plan was to get the two upstart companies to overextend themselves, and it worked.

In the meantime, the Hudson's Bay and North West companies pushed on to build Nelson House and Whitemud House even farther upriver. Finally, in 1799, Rocky Mountain House and Acton House were constructed near the present town of Rocky Mountain House. This completed a line of fur posts extending 808 miles (1,300 kilometers) on the North Saskatchewan River, from the river's mouth on Lake Winnipeg almost to the foot of the Rocky Mountains.

Although Acton House and Rocky Mountain House were virtually in the Peigan Indian's home territory, neither post was particularly successful. The Peigans and other members of the Blackfoot Confederacy were more likely to trade at Edmonton or with Americans on the Missouri River. The Kootenay Indians, already pushed into present-day British Columbia by the Blackfoot, rarely ventured over the mountains far enough to trade at the fort.

In the years after the amalgamation of the North West and Hudson's Bay companies in 1821, Rocky Mountain House was rarely used. Abandoned for a time, it played, at best, only a small role in the Hudson's Bay Company's larger operations. It was simply meant to capture some of the trade in Blackfoot territory that might otherwise have gone to the Americans.

Points of Interest Near Highway 11

The David Thompson Highway
Highway 11

David Thompson, Highway 11's namesake, began his apprenticeship with the Hudson's Bay Company at the young age of 14 fresh from a London orphanage. When he was 20, while recovering from a broken leg, he began to study surveying and map making. Afterward, he traveled to the Athabasca region as a company surveyor.

In 1797, dissatisfied with the Hudson's Bay Company's support for map making, Thompson joined the North West Company. Thompson was put in charge of surveying and mapping company posts and waterways. By 1799, when he had finished most of his work east of the mountains, Thompson became a company trader. Thereafter, his surveying and map making were limited by the time constraints imposed by his new responsibilities.

Nevertheless, Thompson completed his mapping east of the Rockies and in 1808 set out to open trade with Indians on the western side of the mountains. By the fall of 1810, he had completed two trips to the Columbia River country, using Rocky Mountain House as his eastern base and entering the mountains over a route followed by today's Highway 11.

In the summer of 1811, Thompson followed the Columbia River to its mouth, arriving there just a few weeks after American John Jacob Astor's Astoria Expedition. Thompson opened, or initiated the opening of, several trading posts on the western side of the mountains, but trading was always of secondary importance to him. His passion was to explore and map new areas of North America.

As a reluctant trader, Thompson also had misgivings about selling alcohol to Indians. When he began to trade on the western side of the mountains, Thompson asked that rum be omitted from his supply of trade goods. When company officials refused, Thompson loaded the kegs of liquor onto packhorses so they were sure to be broken. After reporting his rum lost en route on two trips, Thompson received the company's consent to travel without rum—making him the only fur trader in the West whose commerce did not include alcohol.

In 1812, Thompson retired to Upper Canada with his metis wife, Charlotte Small, and their family. He set himself up in business as a surveyor and map maker in Ontario. His most notable achievement during these years was to chart a boundary between the United States and Canada from the St. Lawrence to the Lake of the Woods. Business failures, however, left Thompson in poverty. In old age, he turned to writing narratives of his explorations in western Canada. These recollections, based on his extensive journals, are probably his greatest legacy. They describe much of the everyday life of the fur trade, Thompson's explorations in western Canada and much of what we know today of Indian life 200 years ago. In one fascinating account, for instance, Thompson describes how a band of Blackfoot left central Alberta in 1787 and rode 1,500 miles (2,400 kilometers) south into today's American southwest. Here they raided a Spanish pack train, stole about 30 horses and 12 mules, and then drove them back to Alberta. Despite his renown and achievements, David Thompson died blind and penniless at the age of 87.

Alberta's Only National Historic Park at Rocky Mountain House
Highway 11, Rocky Mountain House

Three forts were built at Rocky Mountain House during the fur trade. Today, just two chimneys from these fur posts remain. Parks Canada has established Alberta's only National Historic Park on this site. Summer interpretive programs cover different aspects of the fur trade, western exploration and aboriginal history.

Coal Mines Open in Nordegg
Highway 11, 49 miles (79 km) west of Rocky Mountain House at Nordegg

---

On the north side of Highway 11 just east of the Nordegg turnoff, an historical marker recounts the history of this coal-mining community. The town was established after Martin Nordegg came to Canada in 1906 to invest money for a German company called the Deutsches–Canada Syndicate. In the autumn of 1907, Nordegg developed an interest in the coal deposits of this area, and he spent the next seven years developing Brazeau Collieries. The company town was imaginatively planned, with a series of semi-circular streets for miners' houses radiating from a downtown core of stores and services. Over 250 small homes were built, along with churches, businesses, a dairy, police quarters, a hospital and a school.

Martin Nordegg's investment in Canada ended when this country went to war with Germany in World War I and wartime restrictions forced control of Brazeau Collieries from German hands. By 1923 the coal mine at Nordegg was the largest in Alberta. It continued to operate until 1955.

Mountain Named for Roland Michener
Highway 11, Abraham Lake

A road sign here points out a mountain named for Roland Michener, a former Governor General of Canada. Michener was born in Lacombe and raised in Alberta. After graduating from the University of Alberta, Michener received a Rhodes Scholarship to Oxford. While there, he met and became friends with another Canadian student, future Prime Minister Lester Pearson.

When Michener returned to Canada, he practiced law in Toronto, then became a Member of the Ontario Provincial Parliament in 1946 and a federal Member of Parliament in 1953. Michener served as Speaker of the House of Commons for five years until he failed to gain re-election in 1962. After spending a few years as high comissioner to India, he was, in 1967, appointed Governor General of Canada by his old friend Lester Pearson.

Traders Come to Kootenay Plains
Highway 11, 18 miles (29 km) east of Highway 93 or 5 miles (8 km) west of Cline River

On the south side of the highway, an historical marker looks out on Kootenay Plains. Rich in wildlife, the area was a favorite spot for intertribal trading in the eighteenth century. After Rocky Mountain House was built in 1799, whites, too, sometimes came to Kootenay Plains to trade with Indians—including the Kootenay Indians, who still occasionally ventured into the area from across the mountains, where they had more or less escaped permanently from their longtime enemies in the Blackfoot Confederacy. By 1820, fur-bearing animals throughout the region had been decimated by overtrapping, so white traders abandoned the area.

Points of Interest Near Highway 2
Between Calgary and Wetaskiwin

Trail Established Between Fort Edmonton and Calgary
Highway 2

The coming of the Canadian Pacific Railway to Calgary in 1883 turned the city into an important trading center.

After Rocky Mountain House was established in 1799, a trail developed from Fort Edmonton that ran due south to the forks of the Red Deer and Blindman rivers. The Indians called this trail the Wolf's Track. Near the forks of the rivers, the trail branched into three other trails. One trail turned west to Rocky Mountain House. Another went east to connect with other trails, including one through Blackfoot Crossing to Fort Macleod. The third trail continued south through a spot called Lone Pine, near today's town of Bowden. It then angled more southwesterly to the Ghost and Bow rivers. When the McDougall missionaries established Morley Mission in 1873, people began traveling this southern trail more frequently, sometimes as an alternate route to Fort Macleod.

Fort Calgary was established by the North-West Mounted Police in 1875, but nobody thought of the route between Edmonton, Morley, Calgary and Fort Macleod as the Calgary–Edmonton Trail. At the time, Calgary was only one of several minor stops along the way. As late as 1881, only approximately 30 people lived there. Morley, on the other hand, had more than twice as many people. Even the Cochrane Ranch, which had been established that year, had more people living on it than were at Fort Calgary.

After the Canadian Pacific Railway arrived in 1883, however, things quickly changed. Calgary became an important center for trade in Alberta. The section of the old trail leading through Morley was dispensed with as freighters pushed straight north through the Nose Creek Valley until they connected with the old trail. The new Calgary–Edmonton Trail, essentially today's Highway 2, had become a major Alberta trade route.

Ad MacPherson Makes First Run of the Calgary–Edmonton Stage
Highway 2, Airdrie

Addison MacPherson was an early buffalo hunter on the Alberta plains. For a time, he settled in what became known as MacPherson's Coulee at the head of Nose Creek near Airdrie. He used the coulee as a wintering spot for a number of years and, in the 1870s, established a trading post known as Fort Mac-Pherson. For a time, he evidently ran a few head of sheep on valley grass.

Later, MacPherson moved to the Red Deer area, where, among other things, he worked as a freighter. In July 1883, he teamed up with another freighter named Jim Coleman and established the Royal Mail Stage Lines. The name was more wishful thinking than descriptive—the impetus for the stage rested entirely on the hope of securing a mail contract. Once the Canadian Pacific Railway reached Calgary, MacPherson reasoned, people would need somebody to carry the mail to Edmonton.

The new stage scheduled departures from Edmonton every two weeks. On its first run, July 24, 1883, the stage left Edmonton behind a four-horse team with two passengers and an undisclosed amount of freight.

Soon after MacPherson's stage company got under way, another Calgary–Edmonton stage line started. It, too, hoped to carry the royal mail once the railroad reached Calgary. But when the railroad finally arrived on August 11, the government, dispensing with reason, decided to continue sending Edmonton's mail via the long, slow cart route through North Battleford. Even more baffling, they put the Calgary mail off the train at Medicine Hat and sent it by stage to Fort Macleod. Here the mail was put on a second stage bound for Calgary. It wasn't until the following year, after MacPherson and Coleman had gone out of business, that a contract for the Edmonton mail was given to a Calgary stage firm. Edmonton's mail service finally improved, but according to the local rumor mill, Calgary's mail still goes through Fort Macleod.

Dickson–Stevenson Stopping House Established
Highway 2, 5 miles (8 km) north of Airdrie at a rest stop

Several historical signs can be found at this highway stop. One tells of the Calgary–Edmonton Trail. Others outline the early settlement of MacPherson Coulee and area. A final sign telling of the Dickson–Stevenson Stopping House explains how this rest stop and former stopping house got its name.

The story begins in the mid-1880s when John Dickson came here from Calgary. He built several small buildings along this new leg of the Calgary–Edmonton Trail to serve as a stopping house and stables. In 1886, he filed for a homestead on the land where he had settled. Soon, though, Dickson decided to move on. Because he hadn't completed the requirements for a homestead, title reverted to the government. A settler on an adjoining homestead, Johnston Stevenson, took over the stopping house. Stevenson and Dickson squabbled for some time afterward over ownership, with Stevenson eventually paying Dickson for the buildings. Despite the rancor, people took to calling the place the Dickson–Stevenson Stopping House, and the name seems to have stuck.

Stage Holdup on Calgary–Edmonton Trail
Dickson–Stevenson Stopping House
Highway 2, 5 miles (8 km) north of Airdrie

A spot near the Dickson–Stevenson Stopping House was the scene of the only stage holdup on the Calgary–Edmonton Trail. In 1886, the same year John Dickson filed for homestead and began his stopping house and stables, two bandits stepped from the side of the road a few miles south of the stopping house and brought the royal mail to a halt. In Wild West fashion, they quickly relieved the passengers and driver of cash and valuables, ransacked the mail bags and then disappeared into the sunset— which in this particular case probably lay across the line in Montana. Nobody was ever charged with the crime.

Calgary–Edmonton Railroad Established
Highway 2

With regularly scheduled stage runs between Calgary and Edmonton, stopping houses like the Dickson–Stevenson were soon established all along the route. Most of the towns on the route we know today, however, were created after the Calgary–Edmonton Railway Company began operation in 1890.

The company planned to establish a town about every 20 miles (32 kilometers) regardless of where the old stopping houses were located. North of Airdrie, the new railroad, seeking better road grades, cut west of the old trail, passing through and creating the new stops of Crossfield, Carstairs, Didsbury, Olds and Bowden. Then the track angled close to the old trail again at Content's Stopping House and present-day Innisfail (then known as Poplar Grove).

Today, several museums are found along this route. They include the Roulston Museum at Carstairs, which is located in the community's Knox Presbyterian Church, the oldest surviving church in Carstairs. The museum features displays from early settlement days and a small library of local history books. An early Carstairs home is on display in the churchyard.

The Didsbury & District Museum and Cultural Centre features school, sports, military, aboriginal, household and agricultural exhibits. Olds Mountain View Museum features exhibits from the early years of settlement, and the Bowden Pioneer Museum features early memorabilia of the area, including an assortment of photography equipment. It also houses a good quantity of photographs of area subjects taken at the turn of the century.

The Innisfail Historical Village Museum is home to several pioneer buildings that house exhibits dating from aboriginal times to the 1930s. The buildings include The Spruces, a reconstituted stopping house from the days of the stagecoach. Also near Innisfail, look for the Dr. George House. Constructed in 1893 and now designated a Provincial Historic Site, the restored home of Dr. George, and later the Kemp family, houses a museum and tearoom. The natural history exhibits come from an original collection belonging to Dr. George.

Anthony Henday Becomes First European in Alberta
Highway 2, 3 miles (5 km) north of Innisfail

On the west side of the highway, an historical marker recounts Anthony Henday's visit to southern Alberta in 1754–55. Henday was the first European to set foot in what would become the province of Alberta. Although his journal contains no obvious reference to a mountain range, he was probably also the first white person to see the northern Rocky Mountains.

Fort Normandeau Established at Red Deer
Highway 2, .3 mile (.5 km) west on 32d Street exit at Red Deer, 3 miles (5 km) north at Fort Normandeau turnoff

---

During the Riel Rebellion in 1885, Alberta stayed relatively quiet and free from violence, except for the massacre at Frog Lake. Southern Alberta seemed far removed from the scenes of battle, but white settlers near Edmonton appeared to be in more peril. The first news of the rebellion came to Edmonton over the telegraph on March 27. "Metis attacked at Duck Lake yesterday," the message had said. "Ten police killed. Louis Riel and Gabriel Dumont victorious." Then the telegraph line went dead. Many residents from outlying communities fled to the protection of Fort Edmonton when they heard the news.

On April 8, still without a telegraph line and news from the outside world, James Mowatt volunteered to ride to Calgary for help. He left Fort Edmonton alone. Dropping in on four or five settlers along the trail to obtain fresh horses, he delivered his message to General T. Bland Strange in Calgary in just over 36 hours.

Strange, who had raised a volunteer militia called the Alberta Field Force—made up for the most part of southern Alberta ranchers and cowboys—had command of all government forces in Alberta. These included the Alberta Mounted Rifles, Steele's Scouts, under Sam Steele, and the 92nd Winnipeg Light Infantry, which had been deployed to Calgary after the rebellion began.

Strange and his troops, with the exception of part of the Winnipeg Light Infantry, which was sent south to help guard Fort Macleod, set off for Edmonton in separate contingents on April 15, 20 and 23. Two of the regiments took about 10 days to reach Fort Edmonton because of ruts and mud on the Calgary–Edmonton Trail. The other regiment took longer to arrive because it stopped to build three forts for the protection of settlers along the trail.

The first of these, Fort Normandeau, was built at Red Deer Crossing. The army used R. McLellon's abandoned hotel as the shell for the new fort. Rifle holes were cut in the building, and log walls were added 10 inches (25 centimeters) out from the original walls to reinforce them. The space between was filled with clay. The soldiers then built a 10-foot (3-meter) palisade, added three bastions, surrounded it all with a moat flooded from the river and named it after one of the unit's officers. Once built, the fort was never used. The following July, it was abandoned.

Points of Interest Near Highway 16

The Yellowhead Highway

Highway 16 extends from the Trans–Canada Highway in Manitoba across the western half of the country to Prince Rupert on the British Columbia coast. For all of that distance, the road is known as the Yellowhead, the name of the mountain pass it crosses west of the Jasper townsite in Jasper National Park.

The pass was named after Pierre Hatsination, a light-haired

Iroquois Indian who picked up the nickname Tête Jaune, or Yellow Head, from the voyageurs. Tête Jaune had moved to Alberta from the East to trap furs for the North West Company, and he kept a cache of them on the west side of what was known at the time as the Leather Pass. Later, it became known as the pass to Tête Jaune's cache, or Tête Jaune's Pass, which in translation is the name we know it by today.

In 1827, Tête Jaune, his brother Baptiste, their wives and children, were killed on the western side of the mountains by Beaver Indians.

Iroquois Indians Move to Alberta
Highway 16, .5 miles (1 km) west of Spruce Grove

On the south side of the highway, an historical marker commemorates the Iroquois Indians who came west to hunt and trap for the North West Company in the late eighteenth century. The Iroquois were particularly skilled hunters and trappers, but some also served the North West and Hudson's Bay companies as canoe men and laborers.

Many settled in northwestern Alberta. In 1878, Michel Callihoo, a descendant of Louis Harhiil, an early Iroquois leader, signed Treaty No. 6. This netted the Iroquois a little over 39 square miles (100 square kilometers) of reserve land.

Individually and collectively, the Iroquois were proud and self-reliant. They lived independently and hated dealing with the Indian Department. After years of wrangling with Ottawa officials, band members renounced their government status as Indians in 1958, took possession of their reserve and ceased to be "official" Indians. Many still live in this area today.

Saulteaux Refuse to Sign Treaty

A group of Alberta's Saulteaux, or Chippewa, Indians shared a history similar to the Iroquois. Like them, many of the Saulteaux originally came west to hunt and trap for the fur companies. In the early years of this century, the government tried to sign a treaty with them, but the Saulteaux ignored the requests. They preferred to live independently.

A fascinating legend surrounds one of these Saulteaux, a man named Jim O'Chiese. One night, when O'Chiese was a child, he became separated from other members of the band as they fled the area to avoid a party of enemy Indians. O'Chiese, who was only seven years old at the time, tried to follow the others but got lost and finally lay down to sleep under a clump of bushes. When he woke in the morning, he was being nosed about by a big bull buffalo.

It was spring, and O'Chiese stayed with the buffalo for the next few months, following the herd by day and snuggling up to their shaggy bodies to keep warm during the night. He ate whatever he found along the way. Late the next fall, O'Chiese's uncle, still searching for his missing nephew, discovered the boy crying in a dense coulee. The buffalo had abandoned the young O'Chiese only that morning.

O'Chiese grew up to be a chief of the Saulteaux and always refused to sign any treaty with the Canadian government, preferring instead to live in the traditional way, hunting and trapping in the foothills and mountains. So did his son, John, when he became chief after his father's death in 1932. In the 1940s, the government began pressuring the Saulteaux to sign a treaty and live on a reserve. In 1950, a group of about 15 families broke away from the traditional band and moved to a reserve near Rocky Mountain House. Other members of the band, under O'Chiese's grandson, Peter, refused. Some of these people continue to live in the area east of Jasper National Park.

Stony Plain: Town With the Painted Past
Highway 16, Stony Plain

Stony Plain is dubbed "The Town with the Painted Past" for fifteen larger-than-life murals that depict its important historical developments on the sides of buildings. The town's real name came from one of the area's first settlers, John McDonald, who registered the name when applying for postal services. Inspired by the plains of the Stoney Indians, McDonald decided to call the area Stoney Plain. He later dropped the *e* so potential settlers wouldn't think the fertile region was a rocky wasteland.

In 1891, the area began to attract German-speaking immigrants leaving eastern Europe for the New World. By the turn of the century, almost 600 had moved here from Germany, the United States and Ontario. In the first part of the twentieth century, Stony Plain's future seemed secure, so it was a considerable blow to McDonald and his fellow pioneers when the railroad they'd hoped for was laid five miles (eight kilometers) north of the settlement. Undaunted, the town picked up its belongings *and* buildings, and moved them to the present townsite around 1905.

As the town grew, so did its cast of spirited and important characters. Israel Umbach, Stony Plain's first sheriff, overseer and tax collector, proved his metal when the railway fell behind on its tax payments to the town. Umbach, who took his job seriously, chained one of the railway's locomotives to the tracks until the railway had paid the town in full. A replica of the chain, padlock and wheel now resides at the Stony Plain Multicultural Heritage Centre.

Another important figure in Stony Plain's development was Mrs. Cornelia Wood. At the age of 16, she secured a teaching contract stipulating she would not be paid if the job did not work out—and more than a few in town believed it would not. Wood not only persevered, but she succeeded and went on to become an outspoken and important Albertan. She sat as a minister in the Alberta legislature for more than thirty years and became a strong advocate for women's rights. During that time, she was known as "the lady with the hats" because she bought a new hat for each new session of the legislature. One hundred and four of those hats are now on display at the Multicultural Heritage Centre.

Trail Built from Edson to Peace River
Highway 16, Edson

In 1910, when the Grand Trunk Pacific Railway reached Edson, promoters billed it as the gateway to the Peace River country, which was just opening up to settlement. A trail was cut north through forests and muskeg for 199 miles (320 kilometers) to Sturgeon Lake. From there, it followed a comparatively easy trail to Grande Prairie, a mere 50 miles (80 kilometers) to the west.

By all accounts, however, the first leg of the trail was terrible. In spring and summer, it was often impassable. For the first year, there were no stopping houses or places to buy feed for horses. Mosquitoes and black flies tortured travelers and animals alike. In winter, the road was at its best, so long as one didn't mind all-day sleigh rides at –40°.

The trail was used until 1916, after which the Edmonton–Dunvegan and British Columbia Railway reached Grande Prairie.

Athabasca River Used as First Trans–Canada Highway
Highway 16, 14 miles (23 km) west of Hinton

On the north side of Highway 16, an historical marker recounts how, before the coming of railroads and automobiles, rivers and trails were the main arteries of travel. The Athabasca River was one such major route, and the Athabasca Pass near its headwaters became part of the fur traders' Trans–Canada Highway, the first link between eastern Canada and the Pacific Ocean.

Native people had been crossing back and forth over the mountains for centuries. In the early 1800s, Iroquois trappers working for the fur companies began crossing Alberta mountain passes. In 1810, an Iroquois known to history simply as Thomas led David Thompson over the Athabasca to the Columbia River. Thompson had first crossed the mountains west of Rocky Mountain House while working for the North West Company in 1808. In two successive years, he explored and established trading posts on the Kootenay and Columbia rivers. But Thompson's western trade with the Kootenays angered the Blackfoot. In the fall of 1810, while Thompson was back at Rocky Mountain House to gather supplies, the Blackfoot warned him to stop trading with their enemies across the mountains or suffer the consequences.

Ignoring their warning, Thompson left Rocky Mountain House and traveled back down the North Saskatchewan River toward Edmonton. At a point near modern Lodgepole, Thompson left the river and, following Thomas the Iroquois, traveled northwest to the Athabasca River at a point near today's Hinton on Highway 16.

From Hinton, Thompson traveled up the Athabasca and

over the pass into present-day British Columbia. It was early January. The following spring, he followed the Columbia to its mouth, where he discovered that John Jacob Astor's American company had arrived there only a few weeks earlier. Had the Blackfoot not prevented Thompson from following his original route over the mountains, the Canadian North West Company would have been the first to establish a fur post at the mouth of the Columbia in the Oregon country. Had that been the case, the history of the northwest, even the Canadian–American border, might have been dramatically different.

As it was, Thompson's route linking the Pacific with the East via Edmonton and the North Saskatchewan River became the main overland route for fur traders, travelers and gold prospectors until the Canadian Pacific Railway was completed in 1885.

ALTERNATE ROUTES THROUGH DAVID THOMPSON AND EVERGREEN COUNTRY

Points of Interest Near Highway 16

Alaska Highway Built
Highway 43, .5 miles (1 km) north of Highway 16

An historical marker on the east side of the road here commemorates the building of the Alaska Highway. As Americans' unofficial involvement in World War II intensified, so did fears of a Japanese attack on Alaska. Americans had been contemplating a route to their northern territory, but the Japanese bombing of Pearl Harbor in December 1941 officially brought the United States into the war and magnified the importance of a land connection to the far northwest. The old Klondike Trail from Edmonton was quickly chosen. A marvel of logistics and speedy construction even more than engineering, the 1514-mile (2,437-kilometer) road took less than nine months to build. Ten thousand troops and 17,000 civilians worked on the project. Today, this link with Alaska, which officially begins at Dawson Creek in Peace River country and terminates at Delta Junction, Alaska, brings many travelers through this part of Alberta.

Mission Established at Lac Ste. Anne
Highway 43, Gunn

Lac-La Biche Grey Nuns, 1895.

Lac Ste. Anne Mission was established in 1843 by Father Thibault, the first Roman Catholic missionary to come to Alberta. He arrived in Edmonton in 1842 and moved north the following year. Thibault located his mission at what was then known as Devil's Lake. He changed the name to Lac Ste. Anne in honor of the patron saint of voyageurs. In 1852, Father Albert Lacombe came west to replace Father Thibault. By 1859, the first group of Grey Nuns to come to Alberta arrived at Lac Ste. Anne.

Missionary activity focused on Lac Ste. Anne because of the large metis community that had grown up there. For years, the metis population of the West had grown far faster than the Hudson's Bay Company could supply jobs. The majority of metis built a livelihood around huge communal buffalo hunts that took to the open prairies each year, sometimes in armies with as many as 1,000 Red River carts. In the autumn and winter, the metis at Lac Ste. Anne also caught fish to sell to the Hudson's Bay Company. In 1856, an observer noted that 40,000 whitefish were taken from the lake in just five days.

Missionaries hoped to induce the metis at Lac Ste. Anne to

abandon the buffalo hunts and become farmers. These efforts met with almost total failure until the last of the prairie buffalo were exterminated in the late 1870s.

Georges Bugnet Immigrates to Alberta
Highway 33, .5 miles (1 km) north of Highway 43

On the east side of the highway, an historical marker commemorates the life of author, editor, horticulturist and activist Georges Bugnet (1879–1981). Bugnet emigrated from France in 1904 and later homesteaded in Rich Valley. A writer and homesteader, Bugnet experimented with trees and plants he obtained from around the world, developing hardy species that would survive northern Canadian winters.

Points of Interest West of Highway 2

University Studies Soil
Highway 20, .5 miles (1 km) south of Breton

On the east side of Highway 20, an historical marker recounts how agricultural research began at the University of Alberta's nearby experimental station. Soil scientists from the university began experimenting with crop rotation and fertilizers here in 1929 on plots of land leased from a local farmer. They hoped to develop better farming methods for Alberta's less productive Luvisolic soils. In 1946, the university bought the land. Breton Plots continues to be an important research facility today.

Mutual Telephone Companies Established
Highway 20, 11 miles (18 km) north of Bentley

On the east side of the highway, an historical marker commemorates the network of locally owned telephone cooperatives that once provided telephone service to rural Alberta beginning in the 1930s. Telephones in this area were provided by East View Mutual until 1980, when it was brought, along with nearly 1,000 other mutuals, into the Alberta Government Telephone system.

Finnish Settlers Come to Sylvan Lake
Highway 11A, 5 miles (8 km) west of Sylvan Lake

On the north side of Highway 11A west of Sylvan Lake an historical marker commemorates early Finnish settlers in Alberta. In 1902, Finns who'd migrated from Michigan settled near Sylvan Lake and Eckville. Other Finnish immigrants coming directly from the old country soon followed. Many of the new settlers had been miners in Michigan and Finland, and they found similar jobs in Alberta during the years they established their farms.

Icelandic Settlers Come to Markerville
Highway 54, 8 miles (13 km) east of Spruce View

At the Markerville turnoff on Highway 54, an historical marker commemorates the arrival of 50 Icelandic settlers from North Dakota on June 27, 1888. For many, coming to Alberta represented their third attempt to settle in North America. This time, though, most would succeed. A thriving Icelandic community soon developed in this area, and for several years, would-be homesteaders continued to arrive.

Main Street, Markerville, 1900.

In 1889, Stephan G. Stephansson came to the Markerville area with another group of Icelandic immigrants from the United States. Stephansson homesteaded and ran a dairy farm here. He also became famous for the poetry he wrote in his spare time. His poems often dealt with Canadian homesteading or ancient Icelandic sagas. Relatively unknown in this country, Stephansson is credited with helping to revive the Icelandic literary tradition in his homeland.

Today, the Stephansson House Historic Site is located on the old Stephansson homestead near Markerville. Visitors here can see the refurbished home and farmyard of the famous Icelandic poet and farmer. Programs are conducted by guides in period dress. A cairn has also been erected in Stephansson's honor next to Markerville's community park.

The Markerville Creamery recreates the workings of a small but productive creamery as it was in 1934. Established as a cooperative by local Icelandic farmers, the dairy operated from 1897 until 1972. Today, the creamery serves Markerville as a Provincial Historic Site and museum complete with a small restaurant offering Icelandic food. Special events are arranged during Dairy Month in June as well as on Cream Day, the third Sunday in August.

Danish Settlers Come to Dickson
Highway 54, Dickson

Dickson is the oldest Danish settlement in western Canada. An historical marker here recounts how the first Danish settlers in the region came from the American Midwest in the early 1900s. They were enticed north by a Canadian land agent sent to Nebraska in 1903. Danes settled in the Dickson area first, but later immigration led to the founding of Standard in 1910 and Dalum in 1917.

Today, the Dickson Store Museum in Dickson is operated by the Danish Heritage Society. The museum depicts a general store as it would have been around 1903, when the first Danes arrived in central Alberta.

Points of Interest East of Highway 2

Ernest Cashel Captured
Highway 53, 2.5 miles (4 km) east of Highway 2 at Ponoka

One of Alberta's most famous outlaw tales is set in turn-of-the-century Ponoka. It concerns a man named Ernest Cashel. An occasional barber and sometimes cowhand, Cashel was part of a Wyoming family with a mean reputation. He escaped prosecution in the United States by fleeing to Alberta in 1902, following his mother to Ponoka, where she had a job as a cook. Cashel had been in Alberta for only a short time before he was arrested in Ponoka for passing a bad check.

But Cashel never stood trial for the offense. On the train south for his court date in Calgary, he escaped from the guard and jumped through a train window. Somewhere near the tracks, he stole a pony and rode east toward the Mount Lake district. There he found a job working for a local homesteader named Isaac Belt. Within two weeks, Cashel murdered Belt and dumped his body in the Red Deer River. He also stole a horse, saddle, shotgun and a small amount of cash, including a $50 gold certificate.

Cashel evidently spent November and December in the vicinity of the Sarcee Indian Reserve near Calgary. By the first of the year, police had traced the fugitive to the Kananaskis district. Here, in separate incidents, Cashel stole a horse, a diamond ring and some clothing from a train near Canmore. On January 24, 1903, the stationmaster in Anthracite recognized Cashel and called the police. The fugitive was arrested again.

Although police were sure Cashel had murdered Belt, no body had been found, so murder charges weren't laid. But Cashel was convicted for stealing the horse, clothing and diamond ring, and he was sentenced to three years at Stony Mountain Penitentiary.

Later that summer, Belt's body was found floating in the Red Deer River. Cashel was charged immediately with the murder and later found guilty at a trial in Calgary. He was sentenced to hang on December 15, 1903. A month before the hanging, Cashel's older brother, John, arrived from Wyoming. Along with a Calgary clergyman, he began making weekly visits to his jailed brother.

Not long afterward, Cashel broke out of jail with the help of a pair of revolvers smuggled to him by his brother. The brother was arrested before he could flee across the American line, but Ernest Cashel disappeared. For over a month, he evaded what may have been the most intense manhunt in Alberta's frontier history.

Then on January 24, police discovered Cashel hiding under a bunkhouse at a ranch east of Calgary. They called for him to come out. When he refused, the bunkhouse was set on fire. As soon as the building got warm and smoke began to circulate, Cashel changed his mind and crawled out. He was hanged in Calgary nine days later.

Fort Ostell Built During Rebellion of 1885
Highway 53, 2.5 miles (4 km) east of Highway 2 at Ponoka

Fort Ostell, near modern Ponoka, was the second of three forts built on the Calgary–Edmonton Trail during the Riel Rebellion of 1885. Fearful that metis in Alberta would join Riel's rebellion, General T. Bland Strange of the Alberta Field Force dispatched a unit to build three forts along the trail. Fort Ostell was built around a Hudson's Bay post at the Battle River Crossing. Construction was similar to Fort Normandeau on the Red Deer River and included an 8-foot (2.5-meter) moat. Today, the memory of the old fort, but not the fort itself, is carried on at the Fort Ostell Museum in Ponoka. Exhibits are of area artifacts and memorabilia.

The last leg of the Calgary–Edmonton Trail travels north from Ponoka through the towns of Wetaskiwin and Leduc. This portion of the highway is included in Chapter 5, Battle River and Big Country.

Ex-Mountie Shoots It Out with Police
Highway 2A, Lacombe

Barnette's Stopping House near Lacombe was once the scene of a shoot-out between police and a pair of escaped prisoners from the jail at Fort Saskatchewan. One of the men, William "Crackerbox Bill" Johnson, had been imprisoned for drunkenness and vagrancy. His partner in crime was an ex-Mountie named Gallager.

The two men escaped on May 8, 1886, but were spotted on the Calgary–Edmonton Trail and arrested at Lone Pine, where they had stopped at a place known as the Hotel Rustle. The name developed because, it was said, the only way to get anything to eat at the place was to rustle it for yourself.

After capturing the two escaped prisoners, the police started north to return Gallager and Johnson to the hoosegow. They stopped for supper at Barnette's Stopping House, and as the meal ended, Gallager pulled a revolver from his boot and staged an impressive display of inaccurate shooting. Still, the fireworks allowed both Crackerbox and Gallager to make their getaway. They were never recaptured, and it is assumed they crossed the border into Montana a few days later.

Town of Lamerton Moves to Mirror
Highway 21, .5 miles (1 km) north of Mirror

On the east side of the highway, an historical marker describes how prairie settlement usually followed transportation patterns. Original settlements were most often along trails and rivers. These communities eventually gave way to new towns when railroads and highways came along.

In 1892, at a point where an early trail met Lamerton Creek half a mile (one kilometer) north of here, Fletcher Bredin capitalized on the crossroads traffic by opening the Buffalo Trading Post. Within a few years, the new town of Lamerton had a post office, general store, livery stable, hardware store, blacksmith shop, creamery, hotel, church, school and North-West Mounted Police detachment. Yet less than two decades after it began, Lamerton became a ghost town. As happened in so many other communities bypassed by the railroad, Lamerton's economy collapsed when the Grand Trunk Pacific Railway established a divisional point two miles (three kilometers) to the south at Mirror. Local businessmen quickly relocated, some taking their buildings with them, and the town of Lamerton became a memory.

Towns on Buffalo Lake Trail Disappear after Coming of Railroad
Highway 21, .5 miles (1 km) south of Delburne

On the west side of the highway, an historical marker re-counts the history of two former towns in the Buffalo Lake District. Between 1870 and 1880, the old metis settlement of Tail Creek was the largest settlement in western Canada. Its population stood at 2,000 at a time when Calgary had about 30 residents. Even Winnipeg, the metropolis of the Canadian West, had a population of less than 1,000 in 1880.

Tail Creek, by comparison, was a town with 400 cabins. It originally developed along with other communities near Indian and whiskey trails in the 1860s and 1870s. Several of these trails converged near Tail Creek, where a large metis buffalo hunt community developed, with the populations rising in winter and decreasing in summer. A North-West Mounted Police post was established here in 1875.

But Tail Creek's economy was built around the buffalo, and when the buffalo disappeared, the town's days were numbered. In 1898, a fire swept through the community, and all the cabins burned except one, which was later moved to Stettler. Nobody bothered to rebuild the town. Today, all that remains of the village of Tail Creek is the cemetery.

In the early twentieth century, the Buffalo Lake Trail linked the Rosebud and Blackfoot trails to the south with the Calgary–Edmonton Trail. By 1904, the village of Content had emerged as the local trading and marketing center for the Buffalo Lake District. Then in 1910, the Grand Trunk Pacific Railway bypassed Content, leaving the village to decline rapidly and eventually disappear.

Chapter 5

Battle River and Big Country

Land of Hills and Plains

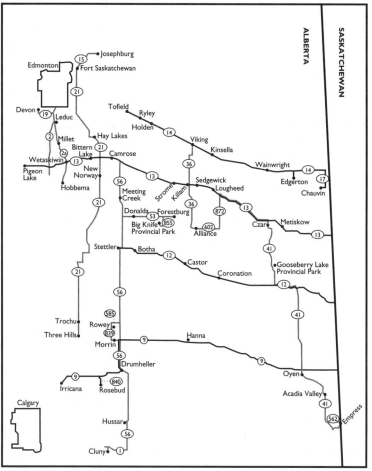

TRAVELERS CROSSING Battle River and Big Country today will find it a land of surprising contrasts. The level prairies of the region are regularly lined and dotted with high hills, fertile river valleys, badlands, parkland and arid plains. The watersheds of two rivers, the Battle and Red Deer, drain almost all of the region. History is here too: dinosaur bones, old trails and ancient buffalo jump sites. Somewhere near today's town of Chauvin, the first white man to come to today's Alberta arrived in 1754.

Although it's possible that French fur traders entered what we now call Alberta as early as 1751, the first documented visit to this part of the world by a European was made by the fur trader Anthony Henday. Henday had been a smuggler in England. Banished from his native country, he came to North America and went to work for the Hudson's Bay Company at York Factory on Hudson Bay.

While at the northern fur post, Henday volunteered to go to the prairies. By 1750, French traders already had inland posts on Lake Winnipeg and along the North Saskatchewan River. In the minds of Hudson's Bay traders, these French posts were intercepting furs that should have been going to them. Henday's mission was to get Indians on the prairies to trade with the Hudson's Bay Company instead.

Indians of the western prairies, however, had heard about Europeans long before any came here. Even before traders came to Hudson Bay in 1668, metal tools, coins and other articles of European origin began showing up regularly in prairie camps. By the end of the seventeenth century, the Cree had established a system of trade from Hudson Bay and Montreal with the tribes of the Blackfoot Confederacy. By 1730, Indians of southern Alberta had obtained guns. They were raising horses descended from those brought to North America by the Spanish, and they had already suffered their first experiences with European diseases. Still, it would be more than 20 years before any Blackfoot would actually see a European on the southern prairies.

During these years, horses and firearms changed the lives of the Indians profoundly. Horses made the buffalo hunts easier and more successful. Almost overnight, there was more time for recreational, artistic and spiritual pursuits. Guns gave the Blackfoot the means to both defend themselves from tribes that already had firearms and dominate others that lacked them. Additional trade in European goods with Indian merchants also contributed to making the Blackfoot one of the richest peoples on the North American plains.

Points of Interest Near Highway 14

Anthony Henday Comes to Alberta
Highway 14, at the Saskatchewan border

Following Cree guides, Anthony Henday left the Hudson Bay bound for the prairies in the summer of 1754. On September 11, somewhere along the Saskatchewan border near today's Highway 14, he became the first European to set foot in what would one day become the province of Alberta. "Level land, few woods, plenty of good water," he wrote in his journal. He then noted that his guides had killed several elk that day.

Although Henday's journey to Alberta was historic, his mission to bring Blackfoot trade to the Hudson Bay failed. Because of his journey, however, he discovered facts of the fur trade that no one else in the company understood.

Henday's route through central Alberta loosely followed the Battle River Valley. Somewhere near today's Stettler, he cut south and crossed the Red Deer River. Near today's town of Three Hills, he met with a small group of Indians who escorted him to a large camp of 2,000 or more Blackfoot.

The Blackfoot, not surprisingly, cared nothing for Henday's suggestion that they trade at York Factory. They already had everything they wanted from Europeans. It was unnecessary for them to travel even the relatively short distance to the French for trade goods. Why, they reasoned, would they want to travel all the way to the English at Hudson Bay.

"The distance is great and we don't know how to paddle," the Blackfoot chief told Henday, dismissing his suggestion with a wave of his hand. The Blackfoot already lived well off the buffalo and the land. What they needed from Europeans they could get easily enough trading pemmican and furs to the Cree merchants who went back and forth from the prairies to the Bay every year.

Henday spent the winter somewhere west of present-day Red Deer. During the cold months, he asked the Cree to trap furs to take north in the spring. The Indians ignored him or made good-humored excuses. It wasn't until the following May, when they started down the North Saskatchewan River on the way to York Factory, that Henday discovered why. The Cree he traveled with were traders not trappers.

After a few days on the river, Henday and his guides were met by the same band of Blackfoot he had tried to entice north the previous fall. Now, the Blackfoot traded pemmican and furs to the Cree for the European goods Henday wanted them to get at York Factory. Blackfoot pemmican was more important to the Cree traders than furs. Pemmican allowed the Cree and French, and later the English, metis, Scots and Canadians to travel the great distances covered in the fur trade without having to stop to hunt and gather food.

Several times during the early days of their journey to York Factory, Henday's Cree guides stopped to trade with bands of prairie and woodland Indians. It was a commerce beneficial to both parties. The Cree obtained furs to trade to Europeans, and the Blackfoot and other Indians obtained the European articles they wanted without having to travel long distances.

It was not an ideal system for increasing Hudson's Bay Company profits, however. And worst of all, from Henday's point of view, when his flotilla arrived at the first French fur post farther up the North Saskatchewan River, the Cree traded away the best of their furs. This left only the poorest pelts to be taken on to York Factory.

For years, men of the Hudson's Bay Company had been telling the Cree to bring other Indians with them when they returned to the Bay in the spring. Always the Cree had told them they would, but no new Indians ever came. Because of his trip to what we now call Alberta, Henday learned why. Not only were southern Indians unwilling to come to the English post, but the Cree didn't want them to come. Bringing other Indians to Hudson Bay would spoil their business.

Last of the Wild Buffalo Come to Wainwright
Highway 14, 2 miles (3 km) west of Wainwright at Camp Wainwright

---

On the south side of the highway, an historical marker recounts how the last wild herd of purebred plains buffalo came to what is today Camp Wainwright. The Canadian government bought the herd in Montana after the American government delayed an offer to purchase the animals from rancher Michel Pablo. American officials were somewhat chagrined at the oversight, especially after the U.S. National Bison Range was established in 1908 on land next to where the Pablo herd was located.

In a way, bringing the buffalo to Canada was just bringing them home. The Pablo herd started with four animals captured near the Montana–Alberta border. They were brought to Montana's Flathead Valley by a Pend d'Oreille Indian named Samuel Walking Coyote around 1872. Walking Coyote had skipped out on his wife that spring. He went to visit Peigan friends east of the mountains but soon decided to go home. As a peace offering, he drove four prairie buffalo back with him. Buffalo were not native to the Flathead Valley and, at least according to one story, Walking Coyote thought the novelty of seeing them might help patch things up with his wife.

No record tells if Walking Coyote's ploy was successful, but the buffalo he drove over the mountain trails did well in the Flathead Valley. He turned them loose on his reservation, and 11 years later, despite occasional feeds on buffalo meat, the herd had increased to 13 animals. That's when Michel Pablo and a partner bought them for $250 each. By this time, there were no wild buffalo left on the prairies, and Pablo guessed that some time in the future his small investment would pay off.

In 1893, Pablo also bought the remnants of a captive buffalo herd in Nebraska owned by C.R. "Buffalo" Jones. This herd, too, had at least partly originated in Canada. Jones had bought his foundation stock in Manitoba. Left to breed in Montana's Flathead Valley, the Pablo herd increased to about 700 animals. In 1906, they were sold to the Canadian government for $200,000. At the time of the sale, the buffalo ranged over such a large area that Pablo could only make a guess at how many animals he actually owned. A final count of more than 700 was reached only when the last animal had been shipped north.

Rounding up wild buffalo and loading them into cattle cars turned out to be harder than Pablo had anticipated. A 26-mile (42-kilometer) wing fence was built from the buffalo range to the shipping point at Ravalli, Montana. Log booms were placed in the Flathead River to prevent the beasts from swimming away. To bring them in, 75 cowboys were hired at five dollars a day plus beans. The cowboys were new to buffalo herding, though, and they were only able to load about 100 animals the first year. The next summer, they managed to ship about half the herd, but the wildest animals remained. It wasn't until 1912 that the last 68 buffalo were loaded and shipped to Wainwright.

Over 40,000 buffalo were born here. Their descendants were shipped all over North America and the world. During World War II, buffalo from what became Camp Wainwright were moved to Elk Island National Park near Edmonton, Wood Buffalo National Park in northern Alberta, and other points in Canada and the United States. Today, most of the buffalo alive in the world are descended from Pablo's original herd.

Ribstones Found Near Kinsella
Highway 14, 4 miles (7 km) west of Kinsella

On the south side of the highway, an historical marker describes two large stones carved to resemble the ribs of a buffalo. The stones are located three miles (five kilometers) south of the marker and probably once played a role in native Sun Dance ceremonies where, symbolically, the carvings would emphasize the importance of the buffalo in the lives of the prairie Indians. In Alberta, though rare, this type of carving is most often found on a high hill, most often within 100 miles (160 kilometers) of Sullivan Lake. Ribstone and similarly styled carvings of buffalo heads have also been found in Montana and the Dakotas.

Medicine wheels, once used in aboriginal spiritual ceremonies, are made of rocks placed in large circles, usually with spokes radiating from a central rock hub. They have been found at about 30 Alberta sites. The biggest is on the Suffield Military Range. Similar sites have been found in Saskatchewan and the northern United States.

When the first white settlers arrived in this area, Indians still regularly left gifts of beads, tobacco and food at the ribstone carving south of this spot. Today, a cairn erected by the Alberta government rests at the site, which has been designated a Provincial Historical Park. A small museum housed in a log building dating from the turn of the century is located in Kinsella.

Points of Interest On Highway 13

Plain Trail from Carlton Crosses Prairie
Highway 13, 6 miles (10 km) west of Metiskow

On the north side of the highway, an historical marker tells of the Plain Trail from Carlton. This was different from the more famous Carlton Trail between Winnipeg, Fort Carlton and Edmonton, which followed the north side of the Saskatchewan River.

The Plain Trail, too, terminated at Edmonton, but instead of cutting through the dense woodland that attracted freighters to the northern route, the Plain Trail passed through the more sparsely treed aspen parklands. It was originally used by native buffalo hunters until the destruction of the herds in the late 1870s.

After 1900, ranchers settled in the grazing land of the Neutral Hills and the Plain Trail to Edmonton experienced a brief revival. A stopping house on the trail was located 1 mile (1.5 kilometers) north of this marker. Then in 1910, when the Canadian Pacific Railway completed its line between Edmonton and Provost, the Plain Trail was abandoned.

Manitou Stone of Blackfoot and Cree Stolen
Iron Creek, north of Highway 13 near Killam (nothing to see today)

In 1865 or 1866, no one knows for sure, a band of Cree who had befriended the missionary John McDougall took him to a spot along Iron Creek near here to show him their Manitou Stone—a sacred rock for both Cree and Blackfoot. It played an important role in each tribe's mythology and ceremonies, as well as personal spiritual quests. Later that year, McDougall returned to Iron Creek and took the rock, which he recognized as a meteorite. In 1869, McDougall shipped the meteorite to Toronto. Eventually, it was put on display at the Royal Ontario Museum.

To the McDougall missionaries at Victoria, the Manitou Stone was a meteorite, nothing more, but to the Cree and Blackfoot, the theft of their stone was a sacrilege. Elders, whom the Reverend George McDougall called "the conjurers," declared that taking the Manitou Stone would bring sickness and war to Indian people. Because the stone was gone, they said, the buffalo would disappear.

McDougall made light of the accusations, but beginning in 1869, the same year that the Manitou Stone was shipped to Ontario, a smallpox epidemic wiped out half the Indians of Alberta. The following year, a last great battle between the Blackfoot and Cree was fought at today's city of Lethbridge. Within a few more years, the buffalo were gone.

It took more than 100 years, but the Manitou Stone has now been returned to Alberta. It has a new home at the Provincial Museum in Edmonton.

Norwegian Settlers Come to Alberta
Highway 13, 2.5 miles (4 km) west of Camrose

An historical marker on the south side of the highway commemorates the first Norwegian settlers to come to the Camrose district in 1893. Many were from Norwegian families who had immigrated to Minnesota and other American states earlier in·the century. Reports from the first settlers on the fertility of Alberta's soil soon brought an influx of more immigrants from the United States and Norway. What had been a trickle of settlers in the 1890s became a flood after the turn of the century.

Peter Fidler Crosses Battle River
Highway 13, Bittern Lake

In the autumn of 1792, Peter Fidler traveled through this area with a band of Peigan on their way to spend the winter in southwestern Alberta. Over the following five months, Fidler surveyed and mapped much of southern Alberta for the first time. He also accurately located many of Alberta's prominent mountain peaks, including Chief Mountain just across the line in Montana. Crossing the river south of here, Fidler wrote in his journal that the Peigan called it the Fighting or Battle River, and the name has been the Battle River ever since.

A few days after Fidler crossed the Battle, he noted that the Peigan called the next big river the Red Deer. On his way back to

Buckingham House the following spring, Fidler made the first discovery of coal in Alberta, noticing deposits near the mouth of Three Hills Creek on the Red Deer River near Drumheller.

Robert Rundle Comes to Alberta
Highway 13, approximately 12.5 miles (20 km) north, at Mission Beach on Pigeon Lake

Robert Terrill Rundle, representing the Wesleyan Society of London, was the first Methodist missionary to come to Alberta. He arrived at Fort Edmonton in the fall of 1840. Despite physical weaknesses, Rundle traveled extensively throughout the West, from modern-day Saskatoon to the foothills, and north into the Peace River country.

In 1847, Rundle founded Pigeon Lake Mission with fellow missionary James Sinclair. Soon afterward, however, Rundle broke a leg. When it didn't heal properly, he returned to England. The metis Sinclair continued to run the mission despite regular harassment by Blackfoot warriors. Then, in 1849, the Blackfoot killed several of Sinclair's Cree converts, and the mission at Pigeon Lake was abandoned. Today, a cairn at the north end of Pigeon Lake marks the site where Rundle and Sinclair built their mission.

Points of Interest Near Highway 12

Alberta Created as Part of North-West Territories
Highway 12, Coronation

On the north side of the highway, an historical marker recounts the creation of the District of Alberta in the North-West Territories on May 8, 1882. Alberta's name is the result of a visit to the Canadian West by the Governor General of Canada, the Marquess of Lorne, and Princess Louise Caroline Alberta in 1881. On his tour, the Governor General proposed creating a new Canadian province to be named after his wife, the Princess Louise. The government didn't care to have a new province at this time, however, so no action was taken.

The next year, however, the North-West Territories were

rearranged into four districts instead of the original three of Assiniboia, Athabasca and Saskatchewan. This created a new district for Princess Louise. Of course, North America already had a Louisiana. Carolina, both North and South, had also been taken. That left the princess's third name, and the new District of Alberta was born.

The District of Alberta was half the size of the eventual province. The District of Saskatchewan formed only the central portion of the current province, but it included the more important settlements of Prince Albert and Battleford. Assiniboia lay to the south and included much of the arid land of Palliser's triangle. Athabasca lay to the north.

Each district contained at least part of a major river valley, where lands, at least in the south, would be particularly attractive to early settlers. The Dominion government officially claimed that the districts had been created "for the convenience of settlers and for postal purposes." In fact, Canada was hoping to forestall the increasing agitation for self-government that was already rippling across the prairies. Eventually, the demands of the settlers won out, and the provinces of Alberta and Sask-atchewan were created in 1905. A cairn 8 miles (13 kilometers) south and 1 mile (1.5 kilometers) east of here marks the junction of the old boundaries of Assiniboia, Saskatchewan and Alberta.

Canada's First Manned Flight at Botha
Highway 12, Botha

On the north side of the highway, an historical marker tells of Canada's first manned airplane flight. It took place near here on August 10, 1907, when a craft piloted by John Underwood took off and remained airborne for almost 20 minutes. John and his brothers Elmer and George designed and built the flying machine on their farm three miles (five kilometers) east of Botha. Essentially, it was an elliptical, 26' x 42', wing-equipped vehicle with controls, a four-bladed propeller and a platform for engine and pilot.

Although the Underwood brothers had designed their flying wing to take off under its own power, they still had not found a suitable engine for their first test flight in 1907. On their initial voyage, they tethered their craft to the ground with a long rope, and the wind lifted it like a kite with John aboard.

In 1908, the brothers equipped their flying machine with a seven-horsepower motorcycle engine, but it didn't have enough power to lift the 450-pound (204-kilogram) wing. The cost of a more powerful engine was more than the homesteading brothers could afford, but for a short time they continued to fly their machine like a kite. The airstrip they laid out in a summer fallow field was probably the first airfield in Canada.

On the wall of the arena immediately to the north of Highway 12, a mural of the flying machine pays tribute to the inventiveness of the Underwoods.

Another Alberta aviation pioneer, Reginald Hunt, flew the first motorized plane in Alberta on September 7, 1909. Hunt flew his plane over today's west Edmonton for 35 minutes. It was the longest flight in Canada up to that time.

Hunt didn't stay with aviation. In 1910, his plane crashed during a demonstration flight. Later, he took a job in the north building boats for the Hudson's Bay Company. He never got around to rebuilding his airplane.

Alberta can also claim the first airmail service in Canada. In 1918, the barnstorming Texas pilot Katherine Stinson flew the Edmonton mail from Calgary in two hours and five minutes. Stinson's flight was not only the first airmail service in Canada, but it was also the first nonstop flight made between Calgary and Edmonton.

Stettler Starts at Blumenau
Highway 12, 1 mile (1.5 km) east of Stettler

On the north side of the highway, an historical marker recounts some of the history of the town of Blumenau and how that early prairie settlement led to the establishment of nearby Stettler. Carl Stettler (1861–1919) started the town of Blumenau when he opened a post office on his homestead in 1903. The name Blumenau comes from a German word that means "low-flowering meadow."

Stettler was a Swiss immigrant, and the community of Blumenau became a center for Swiss homesteaders in the surrounding countryside. It soon boasted two general stores, a lumberyard, hotel, blacksmith shop, bakery and feed store. When the railroad came through the area, however, it missed Blumenau. Undaunted, the townspeople moved the village 1 mile (1.5 kilometers) east and named the new town after the settlement's founder.

Today, in Stettler, you can get out of your automobile and climb on board an old-time railway car pulled by a 1920 steam locomotive. Alberta Prairie Railway Excursions operates every weekend (Friday, Saturday and Sunday afternoons). Trips last at least four hours, although the itinerary changes from week to week. Depending on the excursion, storytellers or musicians might be aboard, and the trip may be pleasantly interrupted by stops and visits to nearby museums. Special events include murder mystery programs, family trips and photographer excursions.

When you get off the train, you can visit the Stettler Town & Country Museum. Its displays are housed in a number of buildings, including some from the early days of the community. The eight-acre (three-hectare) site features an old Canadian Northern Railway station, a harness shop, log cabin, antique cars and more.

Points of Interest Near Highway 9

Palliser Expedition Comes to Alberta
Highway 9, 11 miles (18 km) west of Hanna

On the south side of the highway, an historical marker recounts the expedition led by Captain John Palliser in western Canada from 1857–59. The expedition was sponsored by the British government and came about because the charter for the Hudson's Bay Company was up for renewal in 1858. Although the charter was renewed, there was so much opposition to turning over such an extensive piece of property to a private company that Palliser was sent to examine the Canadian West and report on its suitability for agriculture and settlement.

Palliser's report was generally positive for the Cypress Hills and what he called the fertile belt in the parklands, but he had little good to say about the prairies themselves. The area in the south that has come to be called Palliser's Triangle he found totally unsuited for settlement, calling it too arid to support agriculture.

Eventually, most of Palliser's report would be ignored. The prairies would be settled, and for the most part, Palliser would be proved wrong. In the triangle itself, which runs approximately from the Canadian border in southwestern Manitoba to a pinnacle in east-central Alberta, then south to the American border again, Palliser was closer to right. In the heart of the triangle, homesteaders settled, but shortly afterward many abandoned the land, allowing it to be turned back into grasslands for livestock production. Even here, though, Palliser's estimate of the driest territory was too pessimistic—he didn't anticipate that some of the most arid land would later be irrigated.

First Settlers Come to Rosebud Valley
Secondary Road 840, 5.5 miles (9 km) south of Highway 9

On the west side of the road at the town of Rosebud, an historical marker recounts the history of the first settlers in the Rosebud Valley. In June 1885, James and Eliza Wishart and their family stopped to rest in the valley and decided to homestead on the site that would soon become the community of Redland. Before the end of the decade, other settlers would come to the valley. The area served by the communities of Redland, Rosebud and Beyon soon formed a center for ranching and grain production.

Interestingly, when whites began traveling through the area in the 1860s, it was the valley's profusion of saskatoon berries that gave the river running through the area its original name. Saskatoons are called service berries throughout much of the northern United States. Probably christened by an American trader, the river was called Service Berry Creek in the years before settlement. Today, a smaller stream flowing into the Rosebud nearby is called Service Berry Creek.

Pioneer Acres Demonstrates Historical Skills and Tools
Highway 9, Irricana

Pioneer Acres is operated by a provincewide, nonprofit society whose objectives are "to collect, restore, maintain and demonstrate artifacts which were used by the pioneers of Alberta." Programs using steam power equipment, vintage automobiles, trucks and tractors take place during summer. Early techniques in threshing grain, blacksmithing, baking and butter making are demonstrated. Old-time music is also part of the experience.

ALTERNATE ROUTES THROUGH BATTLE RIVER AND BIG COUNTRY

Points of Interest Near Highway 53

Anthony Henday Camps Near Forestburg
Highway 53, Forestburg

A plaque on a cairn at Devonian Park in Forestburg commemorates Anthony Henday's first trip to Alberta. Henday camped near Forestburg on October 4, 1754. Another plaque on the same cairn commemorates the incorporation of the village in 1919. A coal car on display at the park is typical of those used in nearby mines.

You can also visit the Forestburg and District Museum. It's housed in the old Masonic Temple, which is now a Provincial Historic Site. The Diplomat Mine Interpretive Site is five miles (eight kilometers) south of Forestburg on Secondary Road 855.

Fight at Big Knife Creek
Big Knife Provincial Park
Secondary Road 855, 4 miles (7 km) west of Forestburg and 6 miles (10 km) south

An historical marker here explains the overlapping territories of the Cree and Blackfoot in this area. According to one legend, Big Man (a Cree chief) and Knife (a Blackfoot chief) fought near this creek. Both warriors were killed in the battle. Afterward, the stream was known as Big Man/Knife Creek. Eventually, it was shortened to just Big Knife.

Points of Interest Near Highways 2 and 2A

Maskepatoon Murdered in Blackfoot Camp
Highway 2A, Hobbema

On the east side of the highway, an historical marker re-counts the life of Maskepatoon, a Cree chief noted for his efforts to arrange a permanent peace between his people and their tra-ditional enemy, the Blackfoot. Maskepatoon arranged at least two peace accords between the tribes during his life. The first was in 1850 but lasted only a short time.

For the next 20 years, Maskepatoon worked for peace at every opportunity. But no accord between the tribes ever held for more than a few months. In 1869, Maskepatoon was killed in a Blackfoot camp while attempting to negotiate a new truce. He was reportedly murdered by the fierce Blackfoot chief Big Swan, who then mutilated Maskepatoon's body.

Although the Methodist missionary George McDougall is sometimes credited with inspiring Maskepatoon's work, the Cree chief actually began counseling for peace with the Blackfoot a dozen years before McDougall arrived in Alberta. Much of what we know about Maskepatoon, however, comes to us from the writings of McDougall and his son, John. The missionaries undoubtedly made much of the Cree chief because of his interest in Christianity, but it is also clear that Maskepatoon was a remark-able man.

Riverside Cemetery Established
Secondary Road 822, 1.2 miles (2 km) north of Secondary Road 611

On the west side of the road, an historical marker com-memorates the first Scandinavian settlers in this region and the cemetery they established here. Many of these early Scandina-vians came to Canada from settlements in the United States. Before the turn of the century, the Canadian government gave the settlers, through the Congregational Church, land to estab-lish the Riverside Cemetery. At that time, a well-used trail passed by here from the Battle River. Soon after the cemetery was established, however, transportation patterns changed as more settlement developed. The local Congregational Church no longer drew parishioners from so wide an area, and Riverside Cemetery fell into disuse.

Wetaskiwin Gets Its Name
Highway 2, Wetaskiwin

The names of Wetaskiwin and the nearby Peace Hills commemorate several peace treaties arranged between the Blackfoot and Cree of this area. The word *Wetaskiwin* comes from the Cree phrase *Wetaskiwin Spatinow,* or "the place where peace was made." It was here that the famous Cree chief Maskepatoon tried for years to arrange lasting accords between the two tribes.

One legend says that the first truce between the Blackfoot and Cree occurred when a band from each tribe camped on opposite sides of the same hill without realizing the other was there. During the night, a chief from each camp walked to the top of the hill. When the chiefs discovered each other, they immediately started to fight. They battled for hours, and when morning came, they were still locked in combat.

Finally, in exhaustion, the two chiefs agreed to a time-out. The Cree chief caught his breath and then pulled out a pipe for a quick smoke. The Blackfoot chief did the same but discovered that his pipe had been broken in the scuffle. The Cree, too tired to think about the significance of his act, handed his own pipe to the Blackfoot, who took a few puffs. Then each realized that he had shared a pipe, an act that signified peace. The two Indians returned to their camps suggesting that if their chiefs could live in peace with each other, perhaps the tribes could do the same.

A good selection of aboriginal and local history exhibits are displayed at the Wetaskiwin and District Museum. It is located in the town's old Electric Light building. Separate rooms depict different aspects of the area's history, from a re-created hospital to early home life.

One of Alberta's finest museums, the Reynolds–Alberta, is located just west of Wetaskiwin on Highway 13. It features transportation, agricultural, industrial and aviation exhibits, including displays of vintage automobiles, aircraft and farm machinery. Several audio-video presentations are also available for viewing. The Canadian Aviation Hall of Fame, recognizing Canadians who have made significant contributions to aviation, is located in the museum's vintage aircraft hangar.

Leduc Oilfield Discovered
Highway 60, 12 miles (19 km) northwest of Leduc at Devon

On the east side of Highway 60, an historical marker commemorates the drilling of Imperial Oil's Leduc Number One, the oil well that opened the vast 200,000,000 barrel Leduc Oilfield. This discovery on February 13, 1947, was the first in a series of important oil and natural gas discoveries after World War II. Nearby towns grew with the oil industry. In some places, entirely new towns were built. Petroleum and petrochemical refining became a huge part of Alberta's economy. The oil industry brought thousands of new jobs, and then job seekers, to the province.

By 1947, Imperial Oil had already drilled 133 wells in the Leduc area without success. Company officials were so sure the new well would strike oil, however, that they invited over 500 businessmen, government officials and reporters to see the well blow in on that cold February day. The crowd watched in amazement as the company's prediction came true. The well erupted, spurting water, drilling mud and oil. The dawn of a new era for Alberta's economy had begun.

A replica of the original Leduc Oil Well Number One derrick has been constructed on the old site.

Points of Interest Near Highway 21

Galician Settlers Establish Josephburg
Highway 21, .5 miles (1 km) east of Fort Saskatchewan

On the south side of the highway, an historical marker commemorates Galician settlers in Alberta. In 1888, several families emigrated to Canada from Galicia in what was then the Austro–Hungarian Empire. They settled near Medicine Hat in a colony they named Josephburg after their village in the old country. Drought on the southern prairie forced them to move north in 1891. Most resettled near the present town of Josephburg.

Fort Saskatchewan Established
Highway 21, Fort Saskatchewan

An historical marker at the Fort Saskatchewan Museum tells how Fort Saskatchewan was founded by "A" Troop of the North-West Mounted Police in 1875. Under the command of Inspector W.D. Jarvis, Fort Saskatchewan was the first North-West Mounted Police fort in northern Alberta. In 1886, the fort became headquarters for "G" Division, which policed a vast area from Innisfail in the south to Peace River and Fort Simpson in the north. "G" Division moved to Edmonton in 1913, and in the next year, the Alberta government acquired the old fort to use as a provincial jail.

Today, on the site of the old police post overlooking the North Saskatchewan River, the Fort Saskatchewan Museum is

home to a variety of historical buildings. Exhibits at the Fort Saskatchewan Museum focus on the Royal Canadian Mounted Police, fur trade and pioneer history. Displays trace the community's history from its beginnings as a North-West Mounted Police post to the present. In addition to the main building, which was Fort Saskatchewan's first courthouse, the museum site includes a log farmhouse, one-room school, church, blacksmith shop and collection of antique cars, buggies and farm equipment.

A second historical marker on River Road in Fort Saskatchewan tells of the Canadian Northern spur line that ran past this point between 1913 and 1918. The line was used to haul gravel from the river to the main line of the Canadian Northern Railway and then on to Edmonton. Unfortunately, the operation never made money and was abandoned in 1918. When the Canadian Northern Railway lines through Fort Saskatchewan were removed in 1987, a small section of track was installed here to indicate where the old spur line and siding had been.

North-West Mounted Police in Fort Saskatchewan, 1884.

Telegraph Comes to Alberta
Highway 21, Hay Lakes

A provincial cairn 1 mile (1.5 kilometers) east of Hay Lakes marks the location of the old Hay Lakes telegraph office. This office, in the log home of the operator, was the western terminus for the first telegraph line in Alberta. Built in 1876–77, it followed the route of the proposed transcontinental railroad. In 1879, the telegraph was extended to Edmonton. Eventually, the Canadian Pacific Railway chose a southern route through Calgary, mostly in an attempt to lessen the influence of American railroads on the southern prairies.

Grand Trunk Railway Trestle Built
Highway 21, 5.5 miles (9 km) north of New Norway

On the east side of the highway, an historical marker tells of the old Grand Trunk Railway trestle that crossed the Battle River near here from 1910 until 1923. This bridge was the largest wooden trestle in the British Empire at that time. Rising 120 feet (37 meters) above the river flats, it was almost 4,000 feet (1,220 meters) long. Four million board feet of green British Columbia timber and 62 metric tons of bolts were used in the huge four-tier construction. Remnants of the pilings set 10 in a row and 14 feet (4 meters) apart can still be seen from the highway sign.

Laboucane Settlement Established
Highway 21, 5.5 miles (9 km) north of New Norway

Near the Grand Trunk Railway sign, another historical marker commemorates the Laboucane settlement. Metis buffalo hunters and freighters settled here on the south side of the Battle River Valley in the late 1870s. Prominent among them were the Laboucane brothers. In 1881, Father Bellevaire established the St. Thomas Duhamel Mission here and named it for the Archbishop of Ottawa. The church near today's road sign was built at the mission in 1883. In 1915, the log walls were covered with siding, and the steeple and sacristy were built. Today, the church is all that remains of the old settlement. It has been designated a Provincial Historic Site.

Armand Trochu Starts the St. Ann Ranch and Trading Company
Highway 21, Trochu

The St. Ann Ranch was established in 1903 by a French military officer named Armand Trochu. Soon a settlement, which would become the town of Trochu, developed around the ranch. During World War I, however, many of the original French settlers went back to Europe to help in the fight. Most never returned.

The St. Ann Ranch was bought by Martha and Ernest Frere in 1931. Members of the family still run a bed and breakfast in the 30-room main ranch house. Now a Provincial Historic Site, the St. Ann Ranch and Trading Company includes a pioneer log cabin, an old post office, museum displays and an interpretive center. Other buildings are in the process of being restored.

The Trochu and District Museum in Trochu focuses on the history of the village and area. Exhibits include an extensive photograph collection of the early years of the settlement, a dinosaur bone collection, and agricultural, mining and household displays.

Tail Creek Largest Settlement in the West
Highway 21, .5 miles (1 km) south of Highway 21A

On the east side of Highway 21, an historical marker tells of the old metis community of Tail Creek. During its heyday in the 1870s and 1880s, this community, with a population of as many as 2,000 people, was the largest town in the West—bigger than Calgary, Edmonton, Battleford or Winnipeg. In 1875, Sergeant Major Sam Steele established a North-West Mounted Police post here. But Tail Creek's economy depended on the buffalo, and when the last of the buffalo disappeared, people began to drift away. In 1898, a fire swept through the town. All of the buildings, with the exception of one cabin, were destroyed. Today, only the cemetery remains.

George Schech Builds Domed Dugout
Highway 21, 16 miles (26 km) west of Three Hills

Dugouts and sod houses were commonplace on the prairies in the early days of settlement. Usually, these were temporary places to live, but George Schech, an immigrant and stone mason from Wisconsin, built a dugout to last. In 1904, Schech homesteaded on land near Kneehills Creek. For many years, he lived in a dugout he constructed complete with stone steps, mortared walls and a domed roof. It was still a dugout, however, and was undoubtedly a damp, dark and cramped home.

Points of Interest Near Highway 56

Driedmeat Hill Named
Highway 56, 7 miles (11 km) north of Secondary Road 609

According to Joseph Burr Tyrrell, writing in 1866, the Cree called this hill *ka-ke-wuk* or "driedmeat." Later, white settlers retained the name in translation. An historical marker here explains the origin of the name, which is also applied to the nearby lake.

According to legend, the hill was called Driedmeat as a result of a love affair between a Cree woman and a Blackfoot man. Because their two tribes were bitter enemies, the couple decided to live apart from their families, hiding on their own to escape retribution. The couple hunted only when necessary and dried all of their meat rather than risk a fire. Unfortunately, they were discovered when a passing hunter noticed their meat drying on the hillside.

Meeting Creek Railway Station Refurbished
Highway 56, Meeting Creek

At the end of Main Street in Meeting Creek, the Canadian Northern Railway station, built in 1913, has been refurbished to appear as a typical branch-line depot of the 1940s. There's also a good collection of railway photographs, a grain elevator on display nearby and an adjacent park with a playground.

Swedish Settlements Established
Highway 56, 3 miles (5 km) south of Meeting Creek

An historical marker commemorates early Swedish settlers in central Alberta. Swedes from the United States and Sweden settled in the nearby communities of Thorsby, Calmar, Malmo, Falun and Edensville (Meeting Creek) from the 1890s to about 1920.

Estonian Settlements Established
Highway 56, 9 miles (15 km) south of Stettler

On the west side of the highway, an historical marker commemorates early Estonian immigrants. The Kingsep brothers were the first Estonians to come to Alberta. They homesteaded north of Red Deer in 1898. Afterward, several Estonian settlements sprang up around the province. The largest were at Eckville and in the Linda Hall district south of Stettler.

Epiphany Mission Built at Hartshorn
Secondary Road 589, 16 miles (26 km) east of Highway 56

On the south side of the road, an historical marker recounts the history of the community of Hartshorn and the Anglican Epiphany Mission that was once here. The Hartshorn Post Office was established in 1908. From 1911 until 1925, Hartshorn flourished as a community and recreational center. When the Canadian Northern Railway completed a branch line to nearby Byemoor in 1925, the community quickly dissolved. The general store and Farmers' Cooperative Creamery were moved to a location near the railroad. Soon the Anglican mission was all that remained of the old village.

The Reverend H.E. Scallon had directed construction of Epiphany Mission in 1914. The church served as the community center of Hartshorn. Over the years, it sometimes served as post office, courthouse, polling station, Red Cross branch and flu epidemic relief center. When a fire destroyed the building in 1920, it was quickly rebuilt.

Reverend Scallon stayed in Hartshorn for three years after the railroad bypassed the town. The mission continued to serve the community until 1934. Then the main building was moved to Byemoor, where it was rededicated as St. Paul's Anglican Church.

Drumheller Gets Name
Highway 56, Drumheller

Drumheller, shown here in 1915, was named after Jerome Drumheller, an early coal mining entrepreneur in the area.

Jerome Drumheller was from an entrepreneurial family who owned coal mines in the United States. He came to the Red Deer Valley looking for farmland. Near present-day Drumheller, he stopped at the cabin of a man named Greentree. No one was home when Drumheller arrived, but following the frontier custom, he went in to make himself at home. He noticed a bucket of coal near the stove. Realizing the coal would have been dug locally, Drumheller went back outside and followed a well-worn path in the snow to a coal seam near the river. Drumheller dropped the idea of farming and started acquiring land to develop the first of the area's rich coal mines. When the railroad came, today's town was given the name *Drumheller* in honor of the local mine owner.

Dinosaur Bones Found Near Drumheller
Highway 56, Drumheller

The arid Red Deer Valley with its hoodoos and rugged terrain looks the part of the Old West. While visiting Drumheller and other nearby valley communities, you can, among other things, stop to take pictures at Horseshoe Canyon, cross the Red Deer River on the Rosedale suspension bridge (for foot traffic only), take pictures of the valley's slowly disappearing hoodoos or stop for a cold drink at the Last Chance Saloon in Wayne. Museums in the area include the Atlas Coal Mine Museum, the Homestead Antique Museum and the East Coulee School Museum. The Drumheller Dinosaur and Fossil Museum is located in Drumheller near the Tourist Information Centre.

For a dose of really ancient history, visit the Royal Tyrrell Museum of Palaeontology, which has been ranked one of the five best museums in the world. Dinosaurs disappeared from this valley 65,000,000 years ago, but they left one of the richest sources of fossils in North America in this area.

The Royal Tyrrell Museum is named after Joseph B. Tyrrell. In 1884, while working for the Geological Survey of Canada, Tyrrell discovered dinosaur bones a short distance from today's museum. His discovery was called an Albertosaurus. Thirty-five different species of dinosaurs have since been found in the Red Deer Valley.

The Royal Tyrrell's field station at Dinosaur Provincial Park is worth going out of your way to visit. After you leave the Royal Tyrrell, one route to the park takes you across the Red Deer River on the Finnegan Ferry southeast of Dorthy. This is one of the few remaining operating ferries in Alberta.

Points of Interest Near Highways 36 and 41

Battleford–Edmonton Trail Abandoned
Highway 36, 6 miles (10 km) north of Highway 14

On the east side of the highway, an historical marker recounts the history of the Battleford–Edmonton Trail. This trail was surveyed in 1876 in anticipation of a transcontinental railroad. A trail was cleared, and a telegraph line strung from Battleford to Hay Lakes south of Edmonton the following year. Afterward, the trail was used by freighters and the North-West Mounted Police during years when Battleford was capital of the North-West Territories. In 1883, the anticipated railroad took the southern route across the prairies to Calgary instead. The capital of the territories was moved to Regina, and the telegraph trail fell into disuse. In 1887, even the telegraph was rerouted. After that, except for short sections used for local traffic, the trail was abandoned.

Neutral Hills Cairn
Highway 41, 17 miles (27 km) north of Consort

A cairn on the east side of the highway here tells of the history and beauty of the surrounding Neutral Hills. There's a legend about how the hills got their name. At one time, before the hills were created, Cree and Blackfoot warriors fought regularly in this area. Each side claimed the land as its own. The great spirit tired of this fighting and put the hills between the two tribes. The Cree got the land north of the hills, the Blackfoot the land south of them. The hills themselves were a neutral zone.

Chesterfield House Built in Indian Country
Off Secondary Road 562, at the confluence of the Red Deer and South Saskatchewan rivers, approximately 6 miles (10 km) east of Highway 41 in Saskatchewan

In 1800, the intense competition between the North West and Hudson's Bay companies spurred traders to look to the South Saskatchewan River for more opportunities. The South Saskatchewan was Indian country—home of the Blackfoot, Assiniboine and Gros Ventre. Traders had never been welcome here, but near where the Red Deer River joins the South Saskatchewan River, traders from each company built a new trading post. To protect themselves from the Indians, traders built a common stockade around the two posts and called them both Chesterfield House.

At first, the Blackfoot tolerated the traders' presence, mostly because they liked being able to obtain guns and ammunition there. But the traders for each company sold firearms to the Gros Ventre and Assiniboine as well, so each tribe despised the fur men for dealing with its enemies. Blackfoot and Gros Ventre animosity ran particularly high.

Peter Fidler was in charge of the Hudson's Bay Company post at Chesterfield House. As always, he brought along his surveying equipment to map the area. He also continued to keep a journal of his activities and observations. That winter he wrote the first European report of the presence of the Cypress Hills along today's Saskatchewan and Alberta border.

Chesterfield House, though, continued to arouse Indian hostility. In 1802, after two winters, Fidler abandoned the area when a band of Gros Ventre killed 14 traders nearby. It would take 20 years before traders once more tried to open a post at the junction of the Red Deer and South Saskatchewan rivers. A final attempt was made when Hudson's Bay Company men, members of the Bow River Expedition, came here in 1822. But the Blackfoot and Gros Ventre were no more welcoming. After a short time, these traders, too, made a swift and, this time, permanent retreat from the ill-fated Chesterfield House.

Chapter 6

Lakeland

The Great
North Woods

THE LAKELAND TOURIST ZONE stretches north from the Battle River to the border of the Northwest Territories. In this vast region, the grain fields and poplar stands of Alberta's south soon give way to the lakes and forests of the north. It was to this still sparsely populated wilderness that Alberta's first white residents came in the late 1700s. It was here, where traders sought the pelts of beaver, lynx, muskrat and mink, that the exploration of Alberta began.

The Treaty of Paris ended the French fur trade in western Canada in 1763. Within a short time, however, an equally aggressive competitor of the Hudson's Bay Company sprang to life. Independent, mostly Scottish traders from Montreal established an empire from the network of men and waterways the French left behind. As a result, furs that might otherwise have gone to the Hudson's Bay Company continued to be diverted to Quebec as they had been for nearly 100 years.

By the late 1770s, Montreal fur traders had combined forces to form the North West Company. About the same time, Hudson's Bay traders began establishing their own inland posts. For the following 40 years, the two great fur companies engaged in a fierce, sometimes bloody, rivalry. In the process, they exploited the Indians and decimated the fur-bearing animals of the northwest.

From the beginning, the North West Company was the more enterprising. Each year, it reached deeper into the heart of the Canadian wilderness. Montreal traders had already established a post on the Churchill River by 1775. In 1778, Peter Pond, a North West Company employee and surveyor, followed the Churchill to its headwaters and crossed over the Methy Portage into what is today Alberta. He followed the Clearwater River to the Athabasca. Once on that great river, Pond continued to Lake Athabasca. He then backtracked 40 miles (64 kilometers) and built the first trading post in the future province of Alberta.

As the province's first white resident, Pond raised Alberta's first agricultural crop by growing potatoes in his garden. He traded so many furs his first year in the Athabasca that he didn't have men or canoes enough to take everything back to Montreal. Half the pelts had to be left behind. With a prejudice characteristic of his time, Pond assumed the local Indians would steal the pelts he left and then try to trade them back to him when he returned. The following year, however, he found that none of the furs had been touched by the Indians.

Career in Fur Trade Ends in Murder
Athabasca River

Peter Pond established successful trade in the Athabasca country. His reputation, though, was marred by his tendency to shoot people. At 16, Pond had joined the British Colonial Army during the French and Indian War. After the war, instead of returning to his home in Connecticut, Pond entered the fur trade. While working at Detroit, he killed a trader in a pistol dual. As Pond wrote in his journal, "the pore fellow was unfortenat."

After this first killing, Pond moved north to trade along the Saskatchewan River. Backed by Simon McTavish, the man who engineered the formation of the North West Company, Pond had a successful first season and returned to the northwest the following spring. By the end of 1777, traders from the Hudson's Bay Company had built a post close to his, so Pond decided to move farther west and north. Typical of North West Company traders, Pond outflanked the rival trading company with this move.

Despite his Athabasca successes, the expense of taking furs all the way back to Montreal was formidable. Pond dreamed of finding an easier and cheaper route to world markets. The answer, he believed, lay farther west, on the Pacific. After hearing stories from Indians of a river flowing west out of Great Slave Lake, Pond concluded from the scant knowledge of the northwest then available that the river might be his hoped-for waterway to the ocean. He developed an impressive, though flawed, map of North America, with a river from Great Slave Lake leading west toward the Pacific. Before Pond could explore this river and discover if it did in fact lead to the Pacific, his troublesome tendency to shoot people terminated his career in the Canadian fur trade.

In 1881, Pond shot and killed trader Jean-Etienne Waden at Lac La Ronge. The two had been rivals within the North West Company. After the shooting, Pond, fearing retribution, left the north for a short time. When he returned, another rivalry, this time with a North West Company trader named John Ross, ended predictably with Ross's untimely death. This time, Pond left the northwest for good.

In all likelihood, if Pond hadn't been so easily provoked to murder, he would have followed in succeeding years the trails he outlined on his map. He would have traveled to the Mackenzie River and mapped its course, and he probably would have led the first white men across the mountains to the Pacific. Instead, those honors went to Pond's second-in-command in Alberta's Athabasca country, Alexander Mackenzie.

Fort Chipewyan Oldest Continuously Occupied White Settlement in Alberta
Lake Athabasca

Fort Chipewyan on Lake Athabasca, 1901. Today, it is Alberta's oldest continuously occupied white settlement.

In 1789, Alexander Mackenzie ordered the construction of Fort Chipewyan on the northwestern shore of Lake Athabasca. Here he established the headquarters of the North West Company for the region. Unlike other early fur posts in Alberta, Fort

Chipewyan was destined to last. Today, it is the oldest continuously occupied white settlement in the province.

Soon after the post was built, Mackenzie used it as the starting point for his first attempt to reach the Pacific. From Fort Chipewyan, Mackenzie traveled up the Slave River to Great Slave Lake. He was looking for the elusive westerly flowing river on a map drawn by Peter Pond. Like Pond, Mackenzie hoped the river would lead him to the Pacific and to easier access to world markets. To Mackenzie's disappointment, however, the stream he followed west from the lake turned north. Eventually, it took him to the shores of the Arctic Ocean. Mackenzie called it the "River of Disappointment." We now know it as the Mackenzie River.

Points of Interest Near Highway 63

Road Building to Fort McMurray Bogs Down
Highway 63, Fort McMurray

Today, Highway 63 carries travelers north on smooth pavement, but the first attempts at overland roads to Fort McMurray were failures. As Henry Moberly explains in his book *When Fur Was King*, Roman Catholic missionaries attempted to build a road from Lac La Biche in 1871. After spending $1,100 on what grew to seem an impossible task through bogs and muskeg, they gave up. The Hudson's Bay Company was next to attempt building a road. In 1872, after horses for the crew that was cutting a walking trail from Lac La Biche died in the mosquito-infested bush, they, too, gave up. Moberly later reported that when he was asked to build a road the following year, he told his employer it was impossible. Traffic bound for Fort McMurray would continue to use the Athabasca River until the Alberta Great Waterways Railway reached the community in 1921.

Oil Sands Developed at Fort McMurray
Highway 63, Fort McMurray

Eight years after Peter Pond of the North West Company first came to what would become Alberta, a second North West Company fur post was established at present-day Fort McMurray. But this post at the forks of the Clearwater and Athabasca rivers was used intermittently. It wasn't until 1870, after Chief Factor William McMurray sent Henry John Moberly to build a post at the mouth of the Clearwater that a permanent settlement came to Fort McMurray.

Until nearly the turn of the century, Fort McMurray was a minor trading post on the Athabasca River. After the Hudson's Bay Company moved its post downriver to Fort McKay (at the end of today's Highway 63), most communities like Fort Mc-Murray would have disappeared. Fort McMurray, though, had two things going for it. The town was the northern terminus for steam traffic on the Athabasca, and it had some potentially profitable oil deposits.

Whites had known of Fort McMurray's oil sands for nearly 200 years. The first report of them came around 1715, long before any white man had arrived on the Athabasca. At that time, a Cree trader named Swan traveled through the area on a mission to promote peace between the Cree and Beaver Indians. When Swan returned to York Factory, he told traders of the Athabasca's oil sands. He even brought samples of the tars he had found seeping from the riverbanks. Nearly 200 years later, not long after the Hudson's Bay store moved downriver, the first drilling rigs arrived in the Fort McMurray area.

Today, Fort McMurray's economy is closely tied to the development of the oil sands. You can learn something of the history and geology of the sands at the Fort McMurray Oil Sands Interpretive Centre. Information about some of the technical innovations that advanced oil sands development is also displayed here. Nearby Heritage Park has a collection of some of Fort McMurray's early buildings. It includes a museum housed in an old drugstore, as well as an old log mission building, a replica schoolhouse and a North-West Mounted Police building.

Points of Interest Near Highway 41

Fur Trade Moves into Alberta
Highway 41, 5 miles (8 km) south of Elk Point

On the west side of the highway, an historical marker tells about Fort George and Buckingham House, the first fur posts on the North Saskatchewan River inside Alberta's present border. The posts, built side by side by the North West and Hudson's Bay companies, were located a few miles east of here on the riverbank. By about 1800, trappers had depleted the furs in this region, so both companies moved on. Within two years, Fort George and Buckingham House had been burned to the ground.

Angus Shaw and William Tomison Start Posts
Highway 41, Elk Point

An historical marker about Fort George and Buckingham House can be found at the Elk Point campground. It recounts some of the history of the two forts not mentioned on the marker located five miles (eight kilometers) south of Elk Point on Highway 41. Angus Shaw, one of the North West Company's Scottish wintering partners who worked in the fur country instead of Montreal, was responsible for the construction of Fort George. Earlier the same summer, William Tomison of the rival Hudson's Bay Company supervised the construction of Buckingham House. Despite being rivals in the fur trade, the two companies, with trading posts within calling distance of each other along the North Saskatchewan River, shared a common well.

Fort George/Buckingham House Established
Secondary Road 646, 7 miles (11 km) southeast of Elk Point

Today, the Fort George/Buckingham House Provincial Historic Site has been established at the original location of the two fur posts built by the North West and Hudson's Bay companies. A small interpretive center offers displays and presentations of the early years of the Alberta fur trade. Neither of the old forts has been rebuilt, although their locations have been marked. Because of the limited development at the site and its surrounding area, Fort George/Buckingham House Provincial Historic Site looks much the way it must have in 1792 before the first fort was built.

A short trail runs from the interpretive center to the old fort sites, and some beautiful views of the river can be found along the way. Saskatoon and choke cherry bushes grow among the poplar trees near the trail. To my mind, the natural setting and limited development make this one of the most pleasant historical stops in the province. You can also visit the Fort George Museum at nearby Elk Point. A mural depicting the local history of the area is on display at the town's park.

Fur Trade Comes to Southern Alberta
North Saskatchewan River

Fort George and Buckingham House were the first fur posts on the North Saskatchewan River inside Alberta's present border, but at the time of their construction nothing about them was extraordinary. They were simply two more trading posts in the fiercely competitive Canadian fur trade. By the time they were built, that trade was already 250 years old.

The fur trade had begun as an offshoot of an early explorer's attempts to find a northwest passage across the continent. In 1535, when Jacques Cartier discovered the St. Lawrence River, he thought he'd found the mythical waterway to the East. But the river proved unnavigable past the rapids above present-day Montreal.

Disappointed, Cartier stopped long enough on the St. Lawrence to trade for furs and other articles with local Indians. He then returned to France, where his furs (especially beaver pelts) found a quick market. Other French traders soon returned to the St. Lawrence to take up the fur trade in an organized fashion.

Business was so good that by the 1600s fur-bearing animals began to disappear from the areas closest to the river. In the quest for additional furs, French and Indian voyageurs took to the waterways that had served for centuries as travel and trade routes for native people.

By the 1650s, the French fur trade had reached the Great Lakes. By 1670, the French were competing with the newly formed Hudson's Bay Company on waters that emptied into the Bay, and by the time the Hudson's Bay man Anthony Henday became the first European to come to what would one day be Alberta, French fur forts had penetrated the Saskatchewan River country almost to the present Alberta–Saskatchewan border.

This put pressure on the Hudson's Bay Company to establish posts inland or lose the bulk of the continent's furs to the French. After Henday completed his first journey to Alberta in 1755, several more Hudson's Bay employees were sent up the Saskatchewan River. In 1759, Henday made a trip back to the prairies with another trader, Joseph Smith. The following spring, the pair returned to York Factory with 61 canoes loaded with furs.

In 1763, a treaty between Britain and France ended French claims in North America and left the men of the Hudson's Bay Company as the only traders in the northwest. If Hudson's Bay traders thought they would be able to retreat to their post at York Factory, however, they were wrong. Soon new traders from Montreal were plying the waters of the Saskatchewan led by the same voyageurs who had labored for French traders before the treaty. Competition became even more vigorous than before. Eventually, a loose association of these Montreal traders led to the formation of the North West Company.

While a lively trade in furs developed on the prairies, pelts were never as plentiful here as in the north. But buffalo and the pemmican made from their meat were sought by fur traders almost as eagerly as furs. Pemmican allowed the men of the fur brigades to travel swiftly without having to stop to hunt. This was crucial in freighting goods between Saskatchewan River country and either the Hudson Bay or Montreal.

Just as the Saskatchewan River system was the gateway to the North, the watershed also took traders to the southern half of Alberta. Traders bound for Athabasca country and the far North crossed over to the Churchill River from the Saskatchewan at Cumberland House. Central and southern traders simply followed the river into present-day Alberta.

Competition between the Hudson's Bay and North West companies was such that as soon as one company, usually the Nor'Westers, would open a new post on the Saskatchewan, the other company would build a fort nearby. By 1785, both companies had fur posts nearly as far up the river as today's Alberta–Saskatchewan border. In addition, employees of each company regularly spent the winter with southern Alberta Indians. These traders learned the native languages, developed influential friendships and, when they were successful, returned in the spring with large quantities of furs.

In 1792, the two companies built Fort George and Buckingham House. Within only three years, however, pelts in this region were depleted to such an extent that the fur companies moved upriver, building Fort Augustus and the first Edmonton House in 1795. In 1799, the two companies each built a post at Rocky Mountain House, effectively penetrating Saskatchewan River country as far as it was practical to navigate.

Points of Interest Near Highway 16

Barr Colonists Come to Alberta
Highway 16, 1 mile (1.5 km) west of Lloydminster

Barr colonists and a sod house near present-day Lloydminster (c. 1900). Although most of the Barr colonists were inexperienced farmers, the colony eventually prospered.

On the south side of the highway, an historical marker tells of the Barr colonists. In 1903, Reverend Isaac Barr led 2,000 settlers from Britain to the Alberta–Saskatchewan border area. Many British settlers followed in 1904 and 1905.

Before the first of them arrived at their new home near what would become Lloydminster, Barr was accused of mismanagement and fraud. The charges of outright fraud were probably unfair, but it was true that the Barr colonist settlement seemed beyond Barr's meager managerial skills. Instead of staying to defend himself, Barr departed his troubled colony and Reverend G.E. Lloyd took over as guide and leader.

Only a few of the Barr colonists knew anything about farming, and many stories were told about the hardships and follies of those particularly lacking in rural knowledge. One man afraid of cutting himself with an ax was seen chopping a tree while standing in a large barrel. Another used a flat rock for a chopping block because, he said, he kept splitting the wooden blocks.

On the trail to the colony from Saskatoon, Saskatchewan, one Barr settler—under the impression that hobbles were designed to slow the downhill progress of horses and oxen—hobbled his bovine team at the crest of a large hill. This precipitated a rather incredible combination of momentum and recalcitrance that destroyed his wagon as it tried to pass over the top of his hobbled oxen.

Another man drove a team of horses to a river for a drink. He was unaware that the horses' heads were held by a check-rein, so he didn't understand why the animals wouldn't bend their heads to drink. After studying the problem for a few moments, he tried to lift the rear of the wagon and thereby tilt the horses' heads down to the water.

Another colonist asked a seasoned westerner how to dig a well. When it was suggested that he start at the top, the colonist gravely thanked his advisor and went to work with his shovel.

Many of the stories about the early settlers' inept homesteading skills were undoubtedly exaggerated. Despite early setbacks, most of the Barr colonists survived and eventually prospered in their new community. In fact, many became excellent farmers. In 1911, a crop of oats from the colony was judged in Chicago as the best one grown in North America that year.

Border Divides City and Colony
Highway 16, Lloydminster

When the Alberta and Saskatchewan provincial borders were determined in 1905, the Barr colonists, who'd come from Britain with Reverend Isaac Barr, suddenly found themselves divided. The new boundary split the colony into two parts, one in Saskatchewan and the other in Alberta. It also divided the colony's new village of Lloydminster, named for the Reverend G.E. Lloyd, through its center. This confusing state of affairs was ameliorated in 1930, when an act in both the Alberta and Saskatchewan provincial legislatures united each province's part of Lloydminster into a single governmental body.

Highway 17 (which at Lloydminster runs north and south through the heart of the town's business district) marks the Alberta–Saskatchewan border for most of its 99-mile (160-kilometer) length. In places, the road angles slightly west into Alberta, while in other places it moves back into Saskatchewan. Mostly, the center of the road is the dividing line. Both provinces share the highway's maintenance costs.

No Rats Allowed in Alberta
Highway 16, 1 mile (1.5 km) west of Lloydminster

On the north side of the highway, an historical marker tells of Alberta's remarkable rat extermination program. The Norway rat came to North America on sailing vessels as early as 1775. In the years that followed, it steadily spread across the continent. The first rats reached the southeastern part of Alberta in 1950. By the fall of 1951, many more rat infestations were reported. In 1954, the Alberta Department of Agriculture initiated a comprehensive rat control program, concentrating on a 18-mile- (29-kilomete-) wide rat control zone along the Saskatchewan border. Public education and effective rat eradication measures since then have made this province one of the few areas in the world that can claim to be rat free.

Cree Indians Massacre Civilians at Frog Lake
Highway 16, Kitscoty

On the north side of the highway here, an historical marker gives an account of the Frog Lake Massacre. It took place 34 miles (55 kilometers) north of the marker in the community of Frog Lake. During the North-West Rebellion of 1885, Big Bear and his band of Plains Cree killed nine white men and took three other whites who lived in the mostly Indian community hostage.

The scene of the Frog Lake Massacre, 1885. A group of Big Bear's Cree, led by the war chief Wandering Spirit, killed nine white men and took two women and a young Hudson's Bay employee prisoner.

Frog Lake Cairn
Secondary Road 897, 25 miles (40 km) north of Marwayne and 1.2 miles (2 km) east of Frog Lake

Two miles (three kilometers) east of Frog Lake Store on Secondary Road 867, a cairn and seven grave markers commemorate what has become known as the Frog Lake Massacre. On April 2, 1885, anticipating a widespread rebellion after Louis Riel's initial victory at Duck Lake, members of Big Bear's Cree band executed nine men, including two priests. The Indians then took Frog Lake's other white residents, two women and a young Hudson's Bay Company employee, hostage.

Big Bear's Plains Cree were not permanent residents at Frog Lake. The reserve surrounding the community belonged to the Woods Cree. Big Bear's band had only spent the previous winter there. On the day of the massacre, all of the community's white residents, except an employee of the Hudson's Bay Company, were in the Catholic church. While they were there, Wandering Spirit and a group of his followers arrived and ordered the whites to come with them to their nearby camp. Thomas Quinn, a tall man who was part Sioux and had acted as the community's Indian agent, left the church but refused to go farther. Wandering Spirit shot him through the heart for his insubordination.

As Quinn fell, Father Fafard rushed toward him. Wandering Spirit shot the priest through the neck. Then someone shot the other priest. Within moments, the dead also included John Delaney, the farming instructor; Gowenlock, the millwright; Dill, the trader; Gilchrist, the clerk; Williscraft, the mechanic; and Gouin, a metis.

Monument to the Frog Lake Massacre, 1949.

Big Bear had not taken part in the killing. He had, in fact, counseled against it. Afterward, though, he led his people to Fort Pitt, where they drove the police away and then burned and looted much of the fort. Although General Strange of the Alberta Field Force gathered his troops and pursued Big Bear and his men, he was never able to catch them. Only after the rebellion ended two months later did Big Bear allow his Plains Cree to surrender.

District of Alberta Created
Highway 16, Innisfree

A plaque mounted on a cairn at this location tells how, in 1882, the North-West Territories was divided into the districts of Alberta, Assiniboia, Athabasca and Saskatchewan.

Alberta received its name after a visit to western Canada in

1881 by the Governor General, the Marquess of Lorne, and Princess Louise Caroline Alberta. At that time, the Governor General proposed creating a new Canadian province named after his wife, the Princess Louise.

The government didn't care to have a new province, however, so no action was taken on the Governor General's request. But the following year, the North-West Territories were rearranged into four districts instead of the original three (Assiniboia, Athabasca and Saskatchewan). This created a new district to be named after Princess Louise Caroline Alberta. Of course, North America already had a Louisiana. Carolina, both North and South, had likewise been taken. Fortunately, the princess had a third name. The new district became Alberta.

French Canadians Establish Ukrainian Town
Highway 16A, Vegreville

An historical marker at this spot commemorates the founding of Vegreville. Today, Vegreville is a renowned center for Ukrainian culture on the prairies. But the town was originally settled when French Canadians who had immigrated to Kansas returned to Canada to homestead in this area in the 1890s. Most of these early settlers came to escape drought-stricken Kansas homesteads. They named their community after a Roman Catholic priest, Father Valentin Vegreville.

English and Ukrainian settlers came to the area after the turn of the century. When the Canadian Northern Railway bypassed the town in 1905, determined residents used steam tractors to tow the town's buildings to a new place along the tracks.

Galician Pioneers Settle in Alberta
Secondary Road 855, 8.5 miles (14 km) south of Highway 16 and Mundare

On the east side of the road, an historical marker chronicles the early settlement of this area by people from the district of Galicia, now Halychyna, in the Ukraine. The region's Ukrainian heritage is reflected in its St. John the Baptist Ukrainian Catholic Church, Hall and Cemetery; the St. Anthony Polish Roman

Catholic Church and Cemetery; and the M. Drahomanov Literary Society Hall.

First Ukrainians Come to Alberta
Highway 16, 2 miles (3 km) east of Secondary Road 834

An historical marker at this site recounts how the first Ukrainian settlers in Alberta, Ivan Pylypiw and Wasyl Elyniak, came to Canada in 1891. Within a year, an initial group of Ukrainian immigrants also began homesteading in the vicinity of Edna-Star, two miles (three kilometers) north of the present town of Lamont. In the following years, thousands of others followed their lead and came to settle on lands across the prairies.

Ukrainian Cultural Heritage Village
Highway 16, 18.5 miles (30 km) west of Mundare

The Ukrainian Cultural Heritage Village is one of the best historical interest stops in the province. It offers displays and re-enactments of village and farm life in early Alberta. Buildings, machinery and tools of all kinds are on display. Guides dress in period costumes and play the roles of men and women from the past, explaining life during the early years of settlement in Alberta.

Points of Interest Near Highway 36

Notre Dame des Victoires Mission Established
Highway 36, .5 miles (1 km) south of Lac La Biche

On the east side of the highway, an historical marker commemorates the founding of the Notre Dame des Victoires Mission. After eight years of occasional visits from itinerant Oblate missionaries, the mission properly began when Father Remi Remas built a log cabin near the Hudson's Bay Company post at Lac La Biche in 1853.

In 1855, the Oblates moved the mission 8 miles (13 kilometers) west to its present location. The Notre Dame des Victoires Mission served as a headquarters for other Oblate missions in the Peace, Athabasca and Mackenzie River districts. Warehouses, boat construction facilities, a multilingual printing press, a school, a convent and a sawmill were all once part of life at the mission.

In its heyday, the mission became the site of many "firsts." The first farm in Alberta to grow wheat in commercial quantities was located here. The first grist mill in the province, built in 1863, was here, and the first book ever printed in Alberta, *Histoire Sainte,* came off mission presses in 1878.

Today, Notre Dame Des Victoires Mission is a Provincial Historic Site, and many of the mission buildings have been restored.

Steinhauer Establishes Mission Near Whitefish Lake
Off Highway 36, 12.5 miles (20 km) southeast of Kikino

West of Highway 36 near Whitefish and Goodfish lakes, Henry Bird Steinhauer, an Ojibwa missionary from the East, established a mission in 1855. Later, Steinhauer translated part of the Bible into Cree. Steinhauer's great-grandson, Ralph S. Steinhauer, served as Lieutenant Governor of Alberta from 1974–79.

Edmond Brosseau Comes to the North Saskatchewan River
Highway 36, Brosseau

Brosseau is named after Edmond Brosseau, a frontiersman and prospector born in Quebec but raised in St. Paul, Minnesota. Brosseau fought in the American Civil War, prospected for gold in California, British Columbia and Alberta, and then spent some time as a trader in the Peace River area. He also ran a store in Edmonton during the 1890s.

Around the turn of the century, Brosseau sold his store on Jasper Avenue, loaded a scow with trade goods and floated down the North Saskatchewan River. Near the site of Father Lacombe's abandoned St. Paul des Cris Mission, Brosseau opened a new store and started a horse ranch.

In time, a prosperous town known as Brosseau grew up around his store. Within a few years, however, after the area's railroads had bypassed the town, local businesses left for the new railroad towns, and Brosseau withered. But Edmond Brosseau stayed on. He continued to farm and run his store until just before his death in 1918.

Father Lacombe Establishes St. Paul des Cris Mission
Highway 36, Duvernay

Reverend Father Lacombe; Jean L'Heureux, Three Bulls (half-brother of Crowfoot); Crowfoot, Blackfoot Chief; Red Crow, Blood Chief; North Ace, Peigan Chief; One Spot, Blood SubChief (1886).

On the east side of the highway, an historical marker commemorates the mission of St. Paul des Cris, which was founded by Father Lacombe in 1865. Priests here attempted to teach farming to the Plains Cree of the area, but the Indians preferred to follow their traditional culture based on hunting and trapping. Cree men considered planting crops and working in the fields beneath their dignity. Cree women agreed to plant the crops, but every summer they left the fields untended to follow the buffalo. After several years, Father Lacombe gave up. The mission was abandoned in 1873. In the following years, many Catholic priests took a lesson from Father Lacombe's experience and instead traveled regularly with the Indians as they followed their traditional life on the plains.

Points of Interest Near Highway 55

Portage La Biche Used from 1798 to 1825
Highway 55, Lac La Biche

On the south side of the highway, an historical marker commemorates the once busy fur trade route of Portage La Biche. It connected the North Saskatchewan and Churchill rivers with the Athabasca River. In 1798, David Thompson traveled over Portage La Biche en route to establish Red Deer's Lake House for the North West Company at today's Lac La Biche. In 1799, Peter Fidler also crossed this height of land to build Greenwich House, the first Hudson's Bay Company post outside Rupert's Land, the huge area of today's western Canada that had been granted to the company by Royal Charter in 1669.

When David Thompson opened the Columbia River country in 1811, Portage La Biche became part of the first practical transportation route across the continent. Fur traders used the Beaver River, paralleling the edge of the forest, to avoid confrontations with hostile Indians on the North Saskatchewan River. From Lac La Biche, they crossed to the Athabasca, and then over its pass in the Rockies to the Columbia River.

The Beaver River–Portage La Biche route, however, was long and difficult, with dozens of hard portages. After the amalgamation of the Hudson's Bay and North West companies, Governor George Simpson replaced the Portage La Biche route with the

Fort Assiniboine Trail between Edmonton and the Athabasca River.

Trading Posts Established at Lac La Biche
Highway 55, Lac La Biche

On the south side of the highway, an historical marker tells of two original trading posts at Lac La Biche. David Thompson established Red Deer's Lake House for the North West Company in 1798. Peter Fidler built Greenwich House nearby for the Hudson's Bay Company in 1799. Both posts were on the Portage La Biche, between Beaver Lake and Red Deer's Lake (today's Lac La Biche).

Lac La Biche is famous throughout Canada today not so much because of the mission here or its days in the fur trade, but because of Robert Service's famous poem about Athabasca Dick. The poem begins,

> *When the boys come out from Lac La Biche in the lure of the early spring*
> *To take the pay of the Hudson's Bay as their father's did before*
> *They're all a-glee for the jamboree, and they make the landing ring*
> *With a whoop and a whirl, and a 'Grab your girl,'*
> *and a rip and a skip and a roar.*

Points of Interest Near Highway 28

Duclos Mission Established
Highway 28, .5 miles (1 km) west of Bonnyville

On the south side of the highway, an historical marker commemorates the Duclos Mission. It was established near this spot by Reverend John Duclos in 1916. Duclos came to the area from Edmonton when several French–Canadian families in the Bonnyville area converted to Protestantism. Using the mission here as a base, Duclos worked for nearly a quarter of a century to establish hospitals, schools and churches in the Bonnyville, St. Paul and Cold Lake regions.

Shaw House Established
Highway 28, 3 miles (5 km) south of Bonnyville

On the east side of the highway, an historical marker tells of Shaw House, an old North West Company trading post that once stood near here. In 1789, Angus Shaw opened the fur post on the northwest corner of Moose Lake. For a time, Shaw House was the farthest south of Alberta's fur posts, but in 1792, the Hudson's Bay Company built Buckingham House on the North Saskatchewan River south of here. To counter the influence of this new fort, Shaw closed his post on Moose Lake and built Fort George close to the Hudson's Bay Company's post.

St. Paul des Metis Colony Founded by Father Lacombe
Highway 28, St. Paul

The town of St. Paul is named for St. Paul des Metis Colony, founded by the Roman Catholic missionary Father Albert Lacombe in 1895. Father Lacombe obtained a grant of 144 square miles (373 square kilometers) of land here from the Canadian government to encourage metis families to go into farming. In the late 1800s, though, most of the metis, who had been as dependent on prairie buffalo as their Indian cousins, had little interest in agriculture. The colony languished, particularly after a fire destroyed the mission and school in 1905. In 1909, the project was abandoned.

Victoria Settlement Established
Highway 28, Smoky Lake

On the south side of the highway, an historical marker recounts some of the history of the Victoria settlement. This largely metis community was located on the North Saskatchewan River 7 miles (11 kilometers) south of here. The village grew up around a mission for Cree Indians established in 1863 by the Methodist clergymen George and John McDougall. In 1864, the Hudson's Bay Company built a trading post next to the Victoria Mission. The following year, metis families were establishing farms and settling along the river on each side of the new fur post.

The Victoria Mission continued to operate until the late 1880s, when local Indians moved to reserves. Even when the mission closed, the settlement lived on. When a post office opened in 1887, the settlement was named Pakan, after the Woods Cree chief, Pakannuk. When the railroad came to nearby Smoky Lake in 1918, however, Pakan's economy began to decline. By the end of World War II, it was a ghost town.

In 1971, Victoria Settlement became an Provincial Historic Site. To visit the old village, take Secondary Road 855 south from Smoky Lake. Site interpreters offer guided tours. The clerk's quarters built in 1864 represent Alberta's oldest building still on its original foundation. An interpretive center is housed in a community church built in 1906. Additional exhibits pertaining to the area can be seen at the Smoky Lake Museum in Smoky Lake.

Points of Interest Near Highway 45

Fort Vermilion Cairn
Secondary Road 897, 6 miles (10 km) north of Highway 45

A cairn on the north bank of the North Saskatchewan River marks the location of two fur trade posts built at the mouth of the Vermilion River around 1802. Both posts, one built by the Hudson's Bay Company, the other by the North West Company, were called Fort Vermilion, and both were housed inside a single palisade. Sometimes called Paint Creek House, the posts closed in 1816.

Ferry on North Saskatchewan River at Desjarlais Crossing
10.5 miles (17 km) north of Hairy Hill

On the south bank of the North Saskatchewan River, north of Hairy Hill, an historical marker gives an account of the history of the Desjarlais Ferry. It was operated by the North-West Territories government beginning in 1901. The ferry was named for the Desjarlais family, who ran a general store and post office near the ferry dock during the ferry's initial years of operation. Later, the Desjarlaises moved their store to a small community

1 mile (1.5 kilometers) west. The ferry operated for another 60 years.

Early Settlement Comes to Soda Lake District
Secondary Road 637, 3.5 miles (6 km) west of Hairy Hill

On the north side of the road, an historical marker commemorates the settling of the Soda Lake district. The name Soda Lake was first applied to the nearby lake but came into official use for the district in 1904, when the Soda Lake (later renamed Hairy Hill) School was established. A post office of the same name opened in 1907. The Soda Lake Holy Trinity Anglican Church was built in 1915.

Soda Lake was an important district service center during the early part of the century. Its economic decline began with the construction of the Canadian Pacific Railway branch line through nearby Hairy Hill in 1927.

First Romanian Settlers Arrive in Alberta
Highway 45, 4 miles (7 km) west of Hairy Hill

On the north side of the highway, an historical marker recounts the first settlement of Romanian immigrants in Alberta. In 1899, Ikim Yurko and Elie Raviliuk led a small group of settlers on the long journey from a village in Romania to establish the new community of Boian near today's Willingdon. They named their new settlement after their old one. Many local residents are descended from this original community of Romanian settlers.

Trail Town of Andrew Moves to Railroad
Highway 45, .5 miles (1 km) west of Andrew

Just west of Andrew on the south side of the highway, an historical marker tells of the founding of the nearby town in 1898. The town began when a land guide in this region, John Borwick, built a roadhouse at the junction of the Winnipeg and Calgary–Pakan trails. He called the place the Andrew Hotel after his friend Andrew Whitford, who had lived on the property since 1893, when it had been given to him in recognition of his service as a guide during the Riel Rebellion. The town of Andrew grew up around Borwick's hotel, but when the Canadian Pacific Railway built a branch line near here in 1928, Andrew moved buildings and people to an adjacent quarter section of land to be closer to the tracks. The new Andrew was incorporated as a village in 1930.

Polish Settlers Build Churches
Highway 45, 23 miles (37 km) west of Andrew

On the south side of Highway 45, an historical marker commemorates the first major settlement of Polish immigrants in Alberta and gives an account of some of the many churches they built. The first Polish settlers came to the Beaver Hill Creek district in 1897. During the first 20 years of this century, the Polish immigrant community built 19 Roman Catholic churches in central Alberta alone. The first, Our Lady of Good Counsel Chapel, was built at Skaro in 1901.

Points of Interest Near Highway 15

First Moravian Settlement Comes to Alberta
Highway 15, .5 miles (1 km) west of Highway 45 near Bruderheim

On the north side of Highway 15, an historical marker tells of Alberta's first Moravian settlement. The Moravians were a German-speaking people, religious followers of John Huss, an early Protestant leader burned at the stake in 1415. For centuries, Moravians migrated from country to country in Europe to escape persecution. In 1894, a number of families from Volhynia in Russia came here to homestead on a tract of land set aside for them by the Canadian government. The following spring, under the leadership of Andreas Lilge, they organized the first congregation of the Moravian Church in western Canada and named it Bruderheim, "Home of the Brethren." In the following years, several other Moravian settlements developed in Alberta.

Chapter 7

Edmonton and the Land of the Midnight Twilight

The Northern Heartland

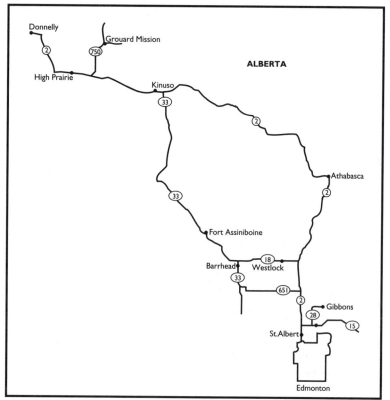

EDMONTON LIES AT THE TOP of North America's Great Plains. Cattle pastures and grain farms crowd the city's borders, molding the Alberta capital into a prairie metropolis. But Edmonton is partly of the North as well. In reach and spirit, the North has always been close. A relatively short drive can take you from an urban shopping mall well into the northern forest.

Almost from its birth in the fur trade, Edmonton has been located where the road to the North begins. Early in the nineteenth century, Edmonton House became an administrative center and distribution point for the Hudson's Bay Company's vast northern empire. As a young city, Edmonton billed itself as the gateway to the Klondike. Later, it became the starting point for the road to Peace River country. All through this century, it has been a supply point for much of the oil and mineral development that has taken place in northern Alberta and the Northwest Territories. Edmonton even claims to be the starting point for travel to the Alaska and Mackenzie highways.

The first Edmonton House was built in 1795. The North West Company had gained a trade advantage that year by building a new post, Fort Augustus, farther upriver than any previous fort. To nullify this advantage, William Tomison of the Hudson's Bay Company ordered Edmonton House built next door to Fort Augustus. He named the new post after an English estate owned by James Winter Lake, the Deputy Governor of the company.

Ever since then, Edmonton has had a place on the maps of western Canada. Edmonton's location changed three times, though, before it was permanently established at its present site. In 1802, traders abandoned the original site near Fort Saskatchewan and moved to a place on the river near where Edmonton's 105th Street bridge would one day be built. Indians burned the buildings at the original location almost immediately, a common fate for empty fur posts at the time.

In 1810, Edmonton House and its rival Fort Augustus moved again. This time the companies chose a site on the North Saskatchewan River near today's Smoky Lake, but after three years, they returned to a site at today's Edmonton. Once again, the old buildings had been burned, so Edmonton House and Fort Augustus were rebuilt. The companies cooperated long enough to surround both posts with a common stockade. Since that time, Edmonton's present site has been continuously occupied.

There would, however, be two more Fort Edmontons. John Rowand took charge of Hudson's Bay Company operations at the post after the Hudson's Bay amalgamated with the North West Company in 1821. In 1830, when a flood drove traders to higher ground, Rowand decided to build a new and better post. He selected a site above the earlier fort, below today's Legislature buildings. It took two years to complete, but in 1832, Rowand opened the grandest fur post ever built in the northwest.

The new Fort Edmonton was much larger than earlier ones. It was decorated inside and out with paintings and ornaments calculated to please its native customers. Trade was carried out here until well into the twentieth century. Then in 1914, although Fort Edmonton's buildings were still sound, politicians of the day decided to demolish the old fur post. It was felt the fort detracted from the grandeur of the newly constructed Legislature. As for historical significance, the Edmonton Board of Trade

Fort Edmonton (c. 1850). Sixty years later, the fort, still structurally sound, would be torn down in an attempt to improve the appearance of the legislature grounds. According to the Edmonton Board of Trade at the time, the city had no historic buildings worth preserving.

declared that the city was "too young to have any buildings of historical interest."

Today, there's a new Fort Edmonton, a replica of the earlier one, on display at Fort Edmonton Park on the southwest side of the city. In addition to seeing the old fur post, visitors to the park can ride a steam-powered train or travel on a streetcar down "1905 Street." They can also visit "1885 Street" and see a replica of a homesteader's farm, watch a blacksmith at work or stop in a local store. Special presentations are held throughout the year. Of special note is the Fort Edmonton Storytelling Festival held every Labour Day weekend.

An historical marker on the Legislature grounds also tells some of the history of Fort Edmonton.

John Rowand, the Hudson's Bay Company's factor at Edmonton from 1825–54, first came west from Montreal in 1803.

Points of Interest In and About Edmonton

Rowand Puts Edmonton on Trans–Canada Highway
Old Fort Edmonton

Born in Montreal, John Rowand went to work for the North West Company as a young man in 1803. A few years later, while hunting alone, he fell from his horse and broke a leg. Unable to move, Rowand lay where he fell until a young Indian woman found him and saved his life. Rowand was plagued with a serious limp from then on, but the woman who saved him became his wife. They lived together until her death at Fort Edmonton in 1848.

When the Hudson's Bay Company took over the North West Company in 1821, John Rowand was one of the North West men looked on with favor by the company's officers, particularly Hudson's Bay Governor George Simpson. In 1823, Rowand was appointed chief factor at Edmonton House. A few years later, he was put in charge of the entire Saskatchewan district, which included most of today's Alberta outside the far north and Peace River areas.

Along with the massive reorganization going on throughout the Hudson's Bay Company after its amalgamation with the North West Company, Rowand began to institute changes. For the next 30 years, during what was in many respects the heyday of the monopolistic Hudson's Bay Company, Rowand oversaw the fur trade of the area. He also played a powerful role in much of the day-to-day life of the region.

One of Rowand's first chores after taking over Edmonton House was to upgrade the Trans–Canada route to the Oregon territory, which then included the region of present-day Oregon and Washington. Rowand realized that Edmonton was destined to become the most important fur post west of York Factory. He also saw that it could be a major stopping place on the Trans–Canada route.

With this in mind, he ordered Fort Assiniboine built on the Athabasca River, 80 miles (129 kilometers) northwest of Edmonton just off today's Highway 33. Rowand planned Fort Assiniboine to serve as a stopover between Edmonton and the upper Athabasca, as well as the Lesser Slave Lake and Peace River regions. A trail from Fort Edmonton to Fort Assiniboine, Rowand reasoned, could replace the difficult portages to the Athabasca River through Lac La Biche.

To cover the distance between Edmonton and the Athabasca River faster and easier, Rowand had a pack trail cut. This was the first deliberately cut pack trail in Alberta. Some of the old trail follows, roughly, today's Highway 33 between Barrhead and modern Fort Assiniboine. With his network of fur posts throughout Alberta and his strategic spot on the road to Oregon, Rowand was then able to keep in close contact with people and happenings spread over almost a quarter of the continent.

Rowand Becomes First Albertan to Vacation in Honolulu

In addition to the fur brigades that traveled to and from Edmonton, and the Hudson's Bay Company employees passing through on their way to and from the Pacific, other visitors began to arrive in Edmonton. The first missionaries, Fathers François Blanchet and Modeste Demers, came to Alberta in 1838. The Wesleyan missionary John Rundle arrived two years later. Beginning in 1841, settlers bound for the Oregon territory also started to pass through John Rowand's fort.

One of the best accounts of Fort Edmonton recorded during the period can be found in the memoirs of the artist Paul Kane, who visited Edmonton in 1845 on his way to the Oregon country and Vancouver Island. During the winter of 1846–47, he was there again, on his way home to Ontario. Kane later recounted these visits in his book *Wanderings of an Artist among the Indians of North America* . . .

"Edmonton is a large establishment," Kane wrote, where "a large supply is always kept on hand, consisting of dried meat, tongues and pemmican. There are usually here a chief factor and a clerk, with 40 or 50 men with their wives and children, amounting altogether to about 130 who all live within the pickets of the fort. Their employment consists chiefly in building boats for the [fur] trade, sawing timber—most of which they raft down the river from 90 miles [145 kilometers] higher up—[and] cutting up the small poplar which abounds on the margin of the river for firewood, 800 cords of which are consumed every winter to supply the numerous fires in the establishment. The employment of the women, who are all, without a single exception . . . [Indians] or half-breeds, consists of making moccasins and clothing for the men, and converting the dried meat into pemmican."

In the fall of 1841, John Rowand traveled the transcontinental route himself. Along with George Simpson, Rowand went first to Fort Vancouver on the Columbia River in the Oregon territory. From there, the two men shipped off to Honolulu, in what was then known as the Sandwich Islands. Simpson continued on to London via Asia, but Rowand spent the winter in Honolulu. In the spring, he returned to Edmonton, thus becoming the first Albertan to take a winter holiday in Hawaii.

Fur Trade Declines
Old Fort Edmonton

Although visitors from outside the fur trade might have created pleasant diversions for the residents of Fort Edmonton, their increasing numbers reflected changing times. Civilization was coming to Alberta, albeit slowly. By 1854, the fur trade was already beginning to decline. John Rowand, the Hudson's Bay employee who had led much of Alberta through its fur-trading heyday, had just died. Years of overtrapping had diminished the number of fur-bearing animals. Free traders also were becoming troublesome. American traders who were moving farther north would soon encroach on Hudson's Bay Company territory.

Within a few years, gold prospectors would scour the Saskatchewan River. Others would travel through Edmonton bound for the gold fields of British Columbia. In 1874, the first contingent of North-West Mounted Police reached Alberta, and the new country of Canada began to assert control over the vast region that had once belonged to the Hudson's Bay Company.

Fort Edmonton Prepares for Battle During Rebellion of 1885
Old Fort Edmonton

The first report of the Riel Rebellion in 1885 reached Edmonton over the telegraph. "Metis attacked at Duck Lake yesterday," the message said. "Ten police killed. Louis Riel and Gabriel Dumont victorious." Then the telegraph line went dead. No more messages were sent or received until after the rebellion.

Louis Riel returned to Canada to lead the North-West Rebellion of 1885, an event that sparked the creation of militia units throughout Alberta, although no actual fighting occurred here.

Rumors began to fly. Settlers fled the surrounding area for the protection of the fort. On April 8, James Mowatt volunteered to ride for help to Calgary, which was connected to the outside world by rail and telegraph. Alone, but dropping in on four or five settlers along the trail to obtain fresh horses, Mowatt arrived to deliver his message to General Strange in just over 36 hours.

Back at Fort Edmonton, all the arms and ammunition that could be gathered in the district were brought to the fort. An old Hudson's Bay Company cannon that had overlooked the river outside the fort for nearly 50 years was hauled inside and prepared for battle.

The only trouble was that nobody remembered how to load the heavy brass artillery piece. An old whaler named Malcolm Groat was the only man there who had actually fired a cannon of similar size. Groat said he couldn't recall if the load was one pound of powder and one pound of shot or five pounds of powder and one pound of shot, or even five pounds of powder and five pounds of shot. It was finally decided that, just to be safe, the higher quantity of shot and powder should be used.

Of course, the Riel Rebellion ended without a gun being fired in battle anywhere near Fort Edmonton, and the cannon was forgotten for some time. When somebody finally remembered it, all concern about the quantities of powder and shot had been forgotten. It also seemed easier to shoot the cannon than unload it. A minor celebration was planned. A crowd gathered. Somebody lit the cannon's fuse.

People said the resulting explosion sounded as if the world had blown up. Numerous Indians, convinced whites were trying to slaughter them, took flight. The cannon sailed backward, flattening everything on the ground in its path and finally lodged in the palisade wall. None of the shot was ever recovered, and people present at the time claimed it would soon circle the globe or, perhaps, shoot down the moon.

Halfway House Built
18 Street and 195 Avenue

At this intersection, an historical marker tells about an Edmonton landmark that survived until the late 1920s, the Halfway Hotel. The original hotel had been called a halfway house at the junction of the old Fort and Athabasca trails, halfway between Edmonton and Fort Saskatchewan. This building, constructed originally in 1883, burned to the ground on April 3, 1896. A new building, the Halfway Hotel, was built later that year. By the 1920s, the old system of cart trails had been replaced by railroads and automobile traffic. Within the decade, the Halfway Hotel fell into disuse and was closed.

Railroad Almost Comes to Edmonton
Old Strathcona, Whyte Avenue in south Edmonton

Strathcona's Whyte Avenue in 1901 vied with Jasper Avenue across the river in Edmonton as the commercial center of what would one day be the amalgamated City of Edmonton.

When talk of a transcontinental railroad first began, everyone assumed the Canadian Pacific Railway (CPR) would run through Edmonton. But in 1882, the CPR decided to follow a southern route across the prairies through the little fort town of Calgary. This left Edmonton, a community that had come to think of itself as the major settlement in the region, more than 200 miles (322 kilometers) from a railroad.

It wasn't until August 1891 that a branch line was built north from Calgary. Then, to the anger of almost everyone in Edmonton, the CPR stopped on the south side of the North Saskatchewan River. No bridge was built to take the railroad across to the existing community. A new town that the CPR christened South Edmonton was born. Later, the name would be changed to Strathcona.

Railroad Finally Crosses North Saskatchewan River

The first railroad to actually cross the river and link Edmonton to the rest of the world by rail came on November 8, 1902. Originally conceived as a railroad to connect Edmonton with the Klondike gold fields, the new line settled for something more modest. Instead of 1,500 miles (2,414 kilometers) of track leading to Whitehorse, it started business with a 4,000-yard (3,658-meter) railway. The important thing about the new railroad was that it crossed the Low Level Bridge to connect with the Canadian Pacific Railway (CPR) Calgary-to-Edmonton line, which had stopped on the south side of the North Saskatchewan River and left Edmonton residents still with no direct rail link to the CPR.

Before the connection was made, the CPR upset Edmonton residents once more, though only briefly. Anxious to keep the end of the rails on the south side of the river, the CPR sent a crew to keep an engine driving back and forth over the track where the new railroad wanted to connect. This kept workers from tapping into the CPR line. Toward the end of the day, though, the CPR engine was removed to allow the regular train from Calgary to pass.

As soon as the tracks were clear, workers from the new railroad dashed from their hiding places in some nearby trees and completed the connection. Finally, Edmonton was linked to the rest of the country by rail. Three years later, the Canadian Northern Railway reached Edmonton, giving the city its own transcontinental line.

Rivalry Between Edmonton, Calgary and Strathcona

From the time the Canadian Pacific Railway chose to put Calgary on the first cross-Canada rail route, a rivalry developed between Edmonton and the southern city. Both towns wanted to be the capital when Alberta became a province in 1905. Both wanted to be chosen as the home for the University of Alberta. Today, both cities want their respective hockey teams to win the Stanley Cup, particularly if they can do it by defeating their rival at the opposite end of the Calgary-to-Edmonton highway.

People have almost forgotten now, but there was once an equally intense rivalry between Edmonton and Strathcona. When the Canadian Pacific Railway (CPR) stopped on the south side of the North Saskatchewan River, only 700 people lived north of the river in Edmonton. Many of them moved to the south side almost immediately to set up shop near the railroad. Some thought Edmonton would gradually disappear in favor of the new town.

In 1892, merchants on the south side of the river, thriving on the business of early immigrants, thought the local land titles office should reside in their community instead of across the river in Edmonton. With an appropriate amount of conniving in Ottawa, merchants arranged to do this. When the moving wagon was sent to fetch the office's furniture and records, however, an angry crowd of 200 Edmonton residents descended on the movers, pulling off the wagon's wheels and unhitching the horses.

Telegrams were sent to Ottawa by supporters of both land office sites. The North-West Mounted Police were called in, but all they dared do was keep a watchful eye on the office records. Officials in Ottawa had to decide which community would be favored. Edmontonians, expecting to be betrayed, organized a defense force. Almost every available man turned out, fully armed, to prevent the theft of the land titles office.

When this information reached Ottawa, it was decided that the government land office would remain in Edmonton. In typically Canadian fashion, a branch office was opened across the river. A new land titles office, which survives to this day, was built in Edmonton in 1893.

A few years later, the Klondike Gold Rush of 1897–98 helped ensure that Edmonton would remain a prominent place on the map. The Calgary and Edmonton Railroad happened to be the closest rail link with the Yukon at that time and hundreds of misguided gold seekers decided to head north overland from the end of rails. When they got to Strathcona, most of them, anxious to get on to the gold fields, crossed the river before spending their money on gear and supplies. As a consequence, just at a time when many thought Edmonton was about to disappear, it experienced a commercial boom.

A few years later, in 1905, Alberta became a province and Edmonton was chosen as the permanent seat of government. The Canadian Northern Railway put Edmonton on a transcontinental route the same year. Then, in 1912, Edmonton and Strathcona buried the hatchet and amalgamated.

Route to the Klondike Starts at Edmonton

For thousands of gold seekers, the end of the rail line at Edmonton seemed like the logical place to embark for the Yukon gold fields. This was a plan especially espoused by the merchants of Edmonton, who stood to gain the most from travelers on the "all Canadian route" through their town. Unfortunately for those inexperienced in northern travel, the route from Edmonton through the Peace River country and northern British Columbia to the Yukon Territory was virtually impassable. Only one in every five who started from Edmonton actually made it to Dawson City. The lucky ones were those who gave up early and turned back. Despite the drawbacks of the overland route to the Klondike, Edmonton benefited from the commercial boom that accompanied the Klondike stampede, sparking the community's population growth from several hundred to several thousand by the early years of the century. It also provided local people with a fair amount of entertainment as they watched one inexperienced group of gold seekers after another set off for the Klondike.

One of the most ingenuous devices for travel to the Klondike was a contraption built by a man known as Texas Smith. Smith's invention was essentially three huge barrels fixed on shafts and hitched to a horse tricycle fashion. He presumed the barrels would roll over the muskeg and swamps all the way to Dawson. Inside the barrels, he carried his prospecting supplies. Unfortunately, the hoops came off the barrels 7 miles (11 kilometers) out of Edmonton, and Texas Smith followed a trail of beans and flour all the way back to the North Saskatchewan River.

Another group of gold seekers built an ice boat. They figured they could sail to the Yukon on a bed of northern ice. Unfortunately, even if there had been clear sailing all the way to Dawson, the weight of the boat was too much for any wind short of a hurricane to budge.

The route overland from Edmonton was undoubtedly the hardest way to reach the Yukon in 1897. Only a few of the hundreds of Klondikers who started from Edmonton, like this group from Chicago, actually reached the gold fields.

Perhaps the greatest boondoggle was the great steam sleigh constructed by a group from Chicago. Powered with a boiler and a marine engine, the sleigh got its traction from studding the engine wheels with spikelike teeth. These wheels, it was reasoned, would then be able to pull a train of four railroad cars riding on sleigh runners behind. On the day of its departure, the steam sleigh's engine was started, and the studded wheels began to spin. Instead of moving down the road, however, they dug the sleigh into the ground as if it were digging a mine instead of heading for the Yukon. The steam sleigh was abandoned, but years later a local entrepreneur bought the machinery to use for a sawmill.

Mrs. Garner was the first woman to reach the Klondike over the Edmonton route.

A.C. Rutherford Becomes First Alberta Premier
11153 Saskatchewan Drive

Alberta became a province of Canada in 1905, and Alexander Cameron Rutherford became its first premier. In the first election, his Liberal party took 23 of the 25 seats available, though there appears to have been some gerrymandering of constituency boundaries to help the cause.

Despite Rutherford's huge majority, he was sharply criticized for having a personal interest in the government's agreement to insure bonds of the Alberta Great Waterways Railway. He resigned in 1910. Rutherford's major accomplishment while premier was probably his work to establish the University of Alberta in 1907.

When the matter came up in the legislature, Calgary representatives felt their city should be the home of the provincial university. After all, Calgary had been passed over when Edmonton became the capital. Rutherford lived in Strathcona, however, and with Edmonton votes to support him, he saw to it that the university came to his city. In later years, Rutherford became a chancellor at the university. Today, you can visit the home of Alberta's first premier, restored to circa 1915, on Saskatchewan Drive on the University of Alberta campus.

Edmonton Has First Dial Telephones in North America
10437 – 83 Avenue

The first telephones in Alberta were in Edmonton. They were a pair of phones installed between the telegraph office and a local store. Before long, other telephones were connected to the line, and a city telephone system gradually developed. By 1908, over 500 homes and businesses in Edmonton had telephones. Another 600 had applied to get them, but the company contracted to manufacture the phones kept postponing the delivery date.

In exasperation, the city arranged to buy 1,200 new dial telephones from the new Strowger Automatic Telephone Company in Chicago. By the end of April, more than 1,100 dial telephones had been installed. This made Edmonton the first city in North America where, if you had phone service, you could let your fingers do the walking.

Today, you can visit the largest telephone museum in North America in Old Strathcona. The Edmonton Telephone Historical Museum is the only accredited telecommunications museum in Canada. Alberta Government Telephones (AGT) also houses an historical collection in the AGT Tower in downtown Edmonton.

Hudson's Bay Company Makes Jasper Avenue 100 Feet Wide
Jasper Avenue

In 1880, the Hudson's Bay Company hired a surveyor to subdivide the southern portion of its 1,000-acre (405-hectare) land reserve around Fort Edmonton. Before work began, the company called a public meeting to ask residents which street they thought should be the main thoroughfare of the growing village. Local people suggested it run from George McDougall's Methodist Church on the east to Dr. Newton's Anglican Church on the west. Coincidentally, the 14th Base Line lay almost perfectly along this route, so the surveyor staked the street 100 feet (30 meters) wide along that line. Because the road pointed due west toward the old fur post in the mountains, the Hudson's Bay Company named the proposed thoroughfare Jasper Avenue.

John Brown Refuses to Move Store
Jasper Avenue

Jasper Avenue hasn't always been 100 feet (30 meters) wide despite an early survey that mapped out the road for local people. Early residents of Edmonton didn't pay much attention to property lines. Land wasn't worth much at the time, and space was abundant. People built where it was convenient, which sometimes happened to be in the middle of surveyed streets. Once talk of railroads and imminent development began, though, building lots and roads became more important. For a time, a vigilante committee was even formed to keep squatters off previously claimed land.

By 1892, Edmonton was incorporated as a town and officials started to demand that people build houses and stores on their own property. A number of stores on 95, 97 and 99 streets were moved back to straighten the roads. A merchant on Jasper Avenue, John Brown, was also asked to move his store, which sat approximately in what should have been the middle of the street.

John Brown, however, didn't care to move. He told town officials that people could darn well go around his store. After all, they'd been doing that for 10 years. The town offered Brown $3,000 to cover his expenses, but Brown still refused. A year of court action followed. Brown lost the first case but appealed. The appeal court sided with the town of Edmonton. It ordered Brown to pay all court costs, all legal expenses for the town and then to move his building out of the middle of Jasper Avenue. After doing that and paying his lawyer, Brown, no doubt, wished he had taken the town up on its original offer of $3,000.

Nellie McClung Elected to Alberta Legislature

Nellie McClung moved to Edmonton in 1914, after gaining national prominence as a leader in the Manitoba Political Equality League. In Alberta, she joined women activists such as Emily Murphy and others in the Edmonton Equal Franchise League. The year before, when a delegation from the league had gone to the Legislature to lobby Premier Sifton for equal rights, the premier had told the women to go back home and wash up their luncheon dishes.

About this time, however, through the efforts of women in several organizations across the province, things began to change in Alberta. The political franchise was extended to women in 1916, the same year that Emily Murphy was appointed the first female police magistrate in Canada. In 1917, Louise McKinney of Claresholm and nursing Sister Roberta McAdams were elected to the Alberta Legislature. McAdams was one of two armed services representatives, and she and McKinney were the first women in Alberta, Canada and Great Britain to be elected to any legislative assembly. In 1918, the federal franchise was extended to women.

In 1921, McClung was elected as a Liberal to the provincial legislature from her riding in Edmonton. She also confessed to being too independent to be a good party member. The same year that McClung was elected, Mary Parlby also became a member of the Alberta Legislature. Parlby was appointed as a minister without portfolio in the new United Farmers of Alberta government. She assigned herself the role of responsibility for women's rights.

In 1928, McClung, Parlby, Murphy, McKinney and Henrietta Edwards went to court to seek a judgment about whether women were legally "persons" under the Canadian constitution and, as such, entitled to full rights of citizenship, particularly appointment to the Senate. After first losing the case in the Supreme Court of Canada, which declared that while women were human beings, they (along with lunatics, criminals and children) were not "fit and qualified" to be members of the Senate.

The five Alberta women appealed the case to the Privy Council, which overruled the Supreme Court decision in 1929. The Privy Council stated that women were, indeed, persons under the act and could, therefore, be appointed to the Senate. In 1930, Cairine Wilson of Ontario became the first woman to serve in the Canadian Senate. Emily Murphy hoped to be the first from Alberta, but it would take more than 50 years before any Alberta woman would be appointed. Martha Bielish became Alberta's first woman Senator in 1979. Today, the house where Emily Murphy lived from 1919 until her death in 1933 has been preserved as a Provincial Historic Site.

Points of Interest Near Highway 2
Between Edmonton and Donnelly

Father Lacombe Comes to Alberta
Father Lacombe Chapel
7 Rue St. Vital, just off Highway 2 in St. Albert

The Father Lacombe Chapel, built in 1861, is Alberta's oldest surviving building. It was used as a church until 1870, then put to use in various other ways until it was made into a museum in 1929.

Father Albert Lacombe came to Alberta in 1852 and, except for a 10-year stay in Manitoba, remained in the province for over 70 years. He worked with Cree and Blackfoot all over the West and started several missions and churches in addition to the chapel at St. Albert. In 1865, he was severely wounded while trying to stop a battle between Blackfoot and Cree warriors. Both sides withdrew when they discovered what had happened to the white priest who had tried to stand between them.

In 1883, when Crowfoot, chief of the Blackfoot, attempted to halt construction of the Canadian Pacific Railway, Lacombe went to the chief and negotiated a settlement between the Blackfoot and government officials. Lacombe also wrote a Cree grammar and dictionary. He died near Calgary in 1916.

Father Albert Lacombe arrived in Edmonton in 1852 and worked throughout the West until his death in 1916.

Athabasca River Part of First Trans–Canada Highway
Highway 16, 14 miles (23 km) west of Hinton

At the town of Athabasca, an historical marker recounts the importance of the Athabasca River and the overland route from Edmonton in the days before the railroad. From this point, known as Athabasca Landing, fur traders went up the river and over Athabasca Pass on the transcontinental route to the Pacific. The lower reaches of the river carried canoes, York boats and eventually steamboats to and from Canada's vast northland.

Also in Athabasca, look for the Athabasca Landing Cairn and the Ukrainian Memorial Cairn. Both commemorative markers are along the river near the campground.

Treaty No. 8 Signed by Moostoos and Keenooshayo
Highway 2, .5 miles (1 km) east of the Grouard turnoff

On the north side of the highway, an historical marker recounts the 1899 signing of Treaty No. 8 with the Indians of northern Alberta and adjacent areas in British Columbia, Saskatchewan and the North-West Territories. The first negotiations between the government commission headed by David Laird and the principal Indian spokesmen, Moostoos and Keenooshayo, were held near Lesser Slave Lake about 10 miles (16 kilometers) north of this point. As a result of the treaty signed at this location on June 21, and at other points in succeeding weeks, an immense tract of land was transferred to the government of Canada.

The Northern Woods and Water Route Cairn
Highway 2, McLennan

This cairn can be found near Lake Kimiwam at the edge of town. The Northern Woods and Water Route runs across western Canada from Hudson's Hope, British Columbia, to Winnipeg, Manitoba. For most of that distance, it stays, as its name implies, in the northern parts of all four western provinces. A plaque on the cairn explains that this route came about largely through the efforts of one of McLennan's former residents, George Stephanson.

You can also do some bird watching at the lake, which is at the intersection of three North American fly routes, or check out the exhibits in the nearby migratory bird center. There's also a museum room with local history displays at the Town Centre in McLennan and a Northern Alberta Railway coach with displays of railroad artifacts in Centennial Park.

Points of Interest Near Highway 33

Klondike Trail Through Alberta a Hazardous Route
Highway 18, .5 miles (1 km) east of Highway 33

On the north side of the highway, an historical marker commemorates the Klondike gold discovery of 1896 and the overland route to the gold fields that began at Edmonton. The Yukon gold strike drew thousands of fortune seekers to Alaska and the Yukon Territory. Most went up the Inside Passage along the West Coast, then over the Chilcoot Trail to the gold fields of the Yukon.

Thousands of others, though, chose the overland route through Edmonton and northern Alberta. Parts of this route had been used for years by fur traders. For inexperienced travelers, however, crossing the northern bush country was plagued with misery and misfortune. The lucky ones turned back early. Many died along the route. Only a few of those who attempted it actually completed the trail to the Yukon.

Lac La Nonne Supplies Hudson's Bay Posts
Highway 33, .3 miles (.5 km) north of Secondary Road 651

On the east side of the highway, an historical marker recounts the development of the Lac La Nonne area as a supply post for the Hudson's Bay Company in the nineteenth century. Fish from the lake were used to supply Fort Assiniboine, 31 miles (50 kilometers) north of this point on the Athabasca River, while the meadows around the lake served to pasture horses used on the Fort Assiniboine Trail. As Fort Assiniboine declined in importance after 1860, when the new overland trail to the Athabasca Pass became widely used, the fishery and pasturage at Lac La Nonne were abandoned. In 1870, Lac La Nonne House, a Hudson's Bay Company trading post, was established to cater to the Indian and the metis people who had migrated into the region. This post closed in 1894.

Fort Assiniboine Link on First Trans–Canada Highway
Highway 33, 2.5 miles (4 km) southeast of Fort Assiniboine turnoff

On the north side of the highway, an historical marker tells of the original Fort Assiniboine. The fur post was established in 1823, but its strategic location made it an important stop in the transcontinental fur trade the following year, when a trail was completed from Fort Edmonton. After 1860, when alternate routes to the Athabasca region began to be used, Fort Assiniboine reverted to a local trading post. There was little business in the area, however, and in 1877 the post was abandoned. In 1898, the post was revived after a large number of people moved into the area during the Klondike Gold Rush. A replica of the original post is located in the present town of Fort Assiniboine.

Wolf King of Alberta Builds Cabin in Swan Hills
Highway 33, 17 miles (27 km) north of Fort Assiniboine

At Trapper Leas Cabin Campground, an historical marker recounts the life of George W. Leas, a native of Michigan who moved north to trap furs in the late 1930s. In 1938, he built the smaller of the two log cabins located on this site today. Five years later, he expanded his living quarters to include the larger "Home" cabin. In 1943, Leas was named Wolf King of Alberta after trapping more wolves than anyone else in the province. Leas lived and trapped in the Swan Hills area until the early 1960s, when he returned to Michigan. Between 1977 and 1981, the Swan Hills Chamber of Commerce restored both of Trapper Leas' cabins as a local community project.

This marker is, according to another highway sign nearby, slightly north of the geographical center of Alberta.

Points of Interest Near Highway 55

Black Settlers Come to Amber Valley
Highway 55, 14 miles (23 km) east of Athabasca

On the north side of the highway, an historical marker recounts the immigration of Black settlers to Alberta in the early years of this century. More than 160 of them came from Oklahoma to settle near here in the spring of 1910. Originally cotton, tobacco and corn farmers, they quickly adapted to new conditions and began raising wheat and other grain crops. In 1932, the community included a school, church and post office and was known as Pine Creek. It was later renamed Amber Valley. In the years since then, the Amber Valley area has declined in population, but the heritage of many black Albertans can be traced to this and other early black communities across the province.

Points of Interest Near Highway 18

Edison Settlement Established
Highway 18, 2 miles (3 km) west of Highway 2

On the north side of the road, an historical marker describes the early settlement of this area. In 1902, the four Edgson brothers built a stopping place in a clearing near here known as the Little Grande Prairie. The stopping house soon formed the center of a community of new settlers from eastern Canada, the United States, Great Britain and Europe. Because of the common misspelling of the brothers' last name, the little village became known as the Edison settlement.

Located about two and a half miles (four kilometers) west of the present sign, the settlement grew quickly. By 1908, a church and a school had been built. Within the next five years, though, the Canadian Northern Railway and the Edmonton–Dunvegan and British Columbia Railway both bypassed Edison, and the community declined as new towns developed elsewhere along the rail lines.

Families from Netherlands Settle in Alberta
Highway 18, 2 miles (3 km) east of Highway 33

On the north side of the road, an historical marker here commemorates the settlement of Neerlandia, established by immigrants from the Netherlands in 1912. Many Dutch–Canadians still farm and work in this area.

Points of Interest Near Highway 28

Lamoureux Brothers Come from Quebec
East of Highway 28, near the junction of highways 15 and 28

On the north side of Highway 15 at Highway 37, an historical marker tells of the Lamoureux brothers, Joseph and François, who settled on the north bank of the river near here in 1872. Four years later, Joseph brought his family to the area from Quebec. The Lamoureuxs farmed and cut timber, rafting lumber on a steamboat. Both brothers remained prominent in the community during the years of settlement, and both became Justices of the Peace in the district.

Other early settlers in this community included Jean-Baptiste Beaupré, James Reid, John Bourque and Henri Lambert, all of whom had moved here from Quebec by 1876. As in many early settlements, optimism ran high. The town was subdivided and called the City of Saskatchewan, a name also given to the 1885 School District of Saskatchewan, the first Roman Catholic school district in Alberta. For a time, the settlement had two general stores, a blacksmith shop, hotel, church, school, sawmill, flour mill and post office. However, the main development in the area took place across the river at Fort Saskatchewan. After a time, the Lamoureux settlement dwindled in favor of the larger community.

Athabasca Landing Gateway to the North
Highway 28, 3.5 miles (6 km) north of Gibbons

On the east side of the highway, an historical marker recounts the days when the Athabasca Landing Trail passed through this valley, running from southeast to northwest. The trail became important in the 1870s, when it linked the Athabasca River with the North Saskatchewan River at Edmonton. Trade goods were hauled by cart and wagon to Athabasca Landing and then shipped on the river to the fur trade posts of the North. Wagons returning to Edmonton were piled high with furs.

The trail became outmoded in 1912, when the Canadian Northern Railway, forerunner of the modern Canadian National Railway, completed a line to Athabasca.

Chapter 8

Game Country and the Mighty Peace

Oasis in the Northern Forest

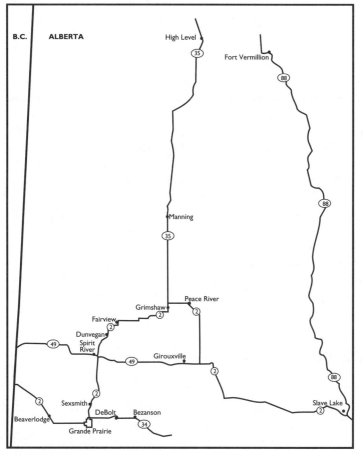

GAME COUNTRY AND THE MIGHTY PEACE tourist zones, plus an area around High Prairie west of Lesser Slave Lake, make up Alberta's remarkable Peace River country. This region is the most northerly major agricultural district on the continent. It's both farther north and farther west than any other farming area in Alberta.

A drive through the region at the beginning of harvest reveals the duality of the Peace country. All around, fields of ripened grain look as they do in southern farming districts. But the land still feels northerly. The vast northern forest looms all around. Summer sunsets come late. Fields of wheat, barley, baled hay and bright yellow canola in full blossom testify to the region's agricultural bounty, and through the heart of this agricultural oasis flows the mighty Peace River.

In the 1700s, the Peace River became an unspoken dividing line between the Indian lands of the Cree and the Beaver. Armed with guns from English traders, the Cree had expanded their territory at the expense of the Beaver and most other neighboring tribes. At the same time, many of the Cree became fur traders. These Indian middlemen exchanged European goods obtained from the Hudson's Bay Company for the furs of Indians from other tribes. For these native traders, war was counterproductive. They wished for peace among the Indians as much as the European traders did and for the same reasons.

Most Indians, however, continued to make war on their traditional enemies. Eventually, the Cree pushed the gunless Beaver north and west of today's Peace River. But after a time, the Beaver, too, obtained rifles. Ironically, most of the Beaver's guns came from Cree traders. Soon, the strength of the two tribes became more equal, particularly after a wave of smallpox weakened the Cree in 1781. Sometime afterward, a peace accord was reached at a point about 50 miles (80 kilometers) above the mouth of the river we still call the Peace.

First White Traders Come to the Peace
Highway 88, Fort Vermilion

By rights, Peter Pond should have been the first white trader to come to the Peace country. And he might have been. No one knows with any certainty. Pond established a post on the

Athabasca River within 100 miles of the Peace River in 1778. Pond's journals from this time have been lost, however, so it can't be said with certainty that he or anyone working with him in the Athabasca country traveled to the Peace.

But Pond was interested in the Peace River area, both as a trader and because of his desire to find an easy route to the Pacific. Pond even devised a map of the northwest based on stories he'd heard from Indians and from his own conjecture. This map included the Peace, as well as a river flowing west, perhaps to the Pacific, from Great Slave Lake. Later, Pond's interest in a direct route to the ocean was passed to his successor on the Athabasca, Alexander Mackenzie. Mackenzie took over Pond House in 1787, when Pond fled the northwest after killing a trader.

Almost immediately after taking charge at Lake Athabasca, Mackenzie sent two traders, Alexander McLeod and Charles Boyer, to trade with Beaver Indians to the west. A record was not made of how far Boyer and McLeod traveled, so we don't know if they actually reached the Peace River. The Beaver the traders encountered were anxious to trade, however, so in the fall of 1788, Boyer was sent to build a trading post on the Peace. He chose a spot near present-day Fort Vermilion. With the construction of this post, the first European entry into the Peace River country can be confirmed.

Points of Interest Near Highway 2

Mackenzie Travels to the Pacific
Fort Fork, south of Peace River townsite

Alexander Mackenzie embraced Peter Pond's dream of finding an easy route to the Pacific. In 1788, he ordered Fort Chipewyan built on the southwestern shore of Lake Athabasca. Here he promptly set up regional headquarters for the North West Company. Then, in the spring of 1789, he set out for Great Slave Lake, where he followed the westerly flowing river on a map drawn by North West Company trader Peter Pond.

After a few days, the waterway turned north instead of continuing toward the Pacific as the map indicated. Mackenzie followed the river all the way to its mouth on the Arctic Ocean before giving up on Pond's dream. Then, bitterly, he returned to Fort Chipewyan. In his journal, Mackenzie called the waterway he followed the "River of Disappointment." Today, we know it as the Mackenzie River.

Alexander Mackenzie copy negative of a photo taken from Alexander Mackenzie's Voyage to the Pacific Ocean in 1793.

Although his first venture failed to discover an outlet to the Pacific, Mackenzie refused to abandon his quest. He went back to England in the spring of 1791 and studied astronomy and surveying. In the fall of 1792, he returned to Fort Chipewyan. Soon afterward, he moved the North West Company into the heart of the Peace River area by establishing Fort Fork, southwest of the present town of Peace River.

Mackenzie spent the winter near the forks of the Peace and Smoky rivers. Then, in an amazing journey that took him up the Peace River, over the divide, partway down the Fraser River and finally over the coastal mountains, he reached the Pacific Ocean on July 22, 1793. In doing so, he and his men became the first to cross the North American continent north of Mexico. Mackenzie's achievement came more than a decade before the Lewis and Clark Expedition completed the continent's second crossing.

In later years, the Peace was used as an avenue to much of the fur trading areas of northern British Columbia. David Thompson, the great Canadian geographer, mapped the Peace between 1802 and 1803.

Twelve-Foot Davis Comes to the Peace
Highway 2, Peace River

The Peace River country remained a land for fur traders and Indians until the 1850s, when gold prospectors began to come into the area. The great Caribou Gold Rush in the 1850s and 1860s sparked much of this activity. Many of these gold seekers from the British Columbia diggings gradually worked their way north. In the upper reaches of the Peace, it became a logical step to follow the river into today's Alberta.

One such prospector was Twelve-Foot Davis. Contrary to his name (and the size of his statue in Peace River), Davis was a small man, but he was smart and strong. It was said he often packed 200 pounds (91 kilograms) when he brought supplies into the Peace country. Born in Vermont in 1820, Davis went west to California in the gold rush of 1849. Like so many other California miners, Davis ended up in British Columbia a few years later during the Caribou Gold Rush. In the Caribou, while his peers searched the mountains and valleys for gold after the big strikes had been made, Davis decided there might be other ways to find his bonanza. Working in the evening, after miners along the creeks had stopped for the day, Davis set about measuring each of the 100-foot (30-meter) claims in the richest areas of the diggings.

Several times, Davis found claims slightly larger than the

allotted 100 feet. He kept quiet about what he had found until he discovered two claims, side by side, that added up to 212 feet (65 meters). The next day, Davis staked a claim on the extra 12 feet (3.5 meters). His new claim didn't make him a millionaire. But he took between $12,000 and $20,000 worth of gold from it before moving on with his new nickname. The money he took from his 12-foot claim was enough to set himself up as a trader near the headwaters of the Peace River.

The Hudson's Bay Company discouraged competition in its territory, driving most out of business by fair means or foul. Unlike other independent traders, however, Davis had enough of a stake to make a proper start. The large company couldn't do much about him. Davis also had a sharp business sense. Gradually, he moved east along the Peace, establishing first one, then another post near the river. As Indian families moved north, following the fur-bearing animals downstream, Davis periodically moved his posts with them. All along the way, Davis was remembered for his kindness, honesty, good humor and the fine pumpkin pies he baked. Davis said that what people needed most in life was food and a few laughs, and they could get both from him.

Davis's success in the Peace country is all the more remarkable because he never learned to read or write. In Fort Vermilion, where Davis established his last post, Reverend Garrioch, a local missionary, observed that it was probably better that Davis never learned to read. "Thereby," said the minister, "his kindness got the better of his smartness."

At the turn of the century, Davis, then 80, was still trading in the Peace River country. On a return trip from Edmonton in 1900, he stopped at Bishop Grouard's Mission on Lesser Slave Lake. Before he could resume his journey, he collapsed and died. Davis was buried at Grouard, but 12 years later, his body was reburied at the top of the hill overlooking today's town of Peace River. Davis had often climbed the hill to take in the spectacular view. Several times he told friends that he wanted to be buried there.

Today, a monument and plaque telling of Davis's life are located near the crest of the hill at the grave site. On the way up, the road passes a park and then a cairn dedicated to Dr. Greene, an early Peace River doctor who founded the Greene Valley Nature Trail. From Davis's monument at the top, there is, perhaps, the grandest sight in the Peace River country. The view overlooks the town, the forks of the Peace and Smoky rivers, the Peace River Bridge and Highway 2 trailing west toward the sunset.

The Twelve-Foot Davis statue in Peace River honors one of the Peace River area's most prominent pioneers.

Mackenzie Winters at Fort Fork
Secondary Road 684, 2.5 miles (4 km) south of Peace River

South of Peace River on Shaftsbury Road (Secondary Road 684), a cairn marks a spot directly across the river from Fort Fork, where Alexander Mackenzie spent the winter of 1792–93. The following spring, Mackenzie followed the Peace River into today's British Columbia, where he became the first to cross the North American continent north of Mexico.

Also on Shaftsbury, watch for the McLeod's Fort Cairn and the nearby "Fur Trade Posts on the Peace" sign. The sign tells of some of the history of fur trading along this stretch of the Peace River. From the time the North West Company first came to the Peace in 1781, the Peace River became an important transportation route and a rich source of furs.

In 1790, Alexander McLeod of the North West Company established McLeod's Fort near the mouth of Whitemud River about 34 miles (55 kilometers) downstream from the historical marker on Shaftsbury Road. In 1792, the post was moved to Fort Fork on the south bank of the Peace just above the mouth of the Smoky River. It was here that Alexander Mackenzie wintered in 1792–93 before traveling to the Pacific Ocean.

In 1818, the Hudson's Bay Company built St. Mary's House on the south bank of the Peace River, near the Smoky River. In 1819, the post was moved across the river to the location of the present sign. In 1820, St. Mary's House was moved again, this time to a spot near today's town of Peace River. Finally, in 1821, the Hudson's Bay and North West companies merged. St. Mary's House closed and Fort Dunvegan, the old North West Company headquarters, became the main post in this area of the Peace.

If you're looking for an alternate route south from Peace River, continue down Shaftsbury Road to Blakley Landing. Here you and your car can cross the Peace on one of the few river ferries remaining in Alberta. While you wait to board, you can read the plaque telling of the ferry's history as a private ferry operated by a local farmer. On the south shore of the Peace, the ferry docks on Secondary Road 740.

Mackenzie Highway Built to Northwest Territories
Highway 2, Grimshaw

At the Mile Zero Mackenzie Highway Monument, an historical marker recounts the origins of the highway. The first road north from this point was the old Battle River Trail, which dates back to 1914. Gold and other mineral discoveries in the Northwest Territories in the 1930s led to the building of a winter road from Grimshaw to Yellowknife in 1938–39. The first cat train over the road arrived in Yellowknife, April 12, 1939.

On November 3, 1945, the federal and Alberta governments signed an agreement to build an all-weather highway from Grimshaw to Hay River. Completed by 1950, the government of the Northwest Territories named the new road the Mackenzie Highway in honor of the North West Company explorer Alexander Mackenzie.

Homesteaders Follow the Old Fort St. John Trail
Highway 2, Fairview

An historical marker at the Fairview and District Lion Heart Scout Camp recounts the development of today's highway system through this area. In the early days, travel between the towns of Peace River, Alberta, and Fort St. John, British Columbia, was over a network of ill-defined Indian and fur-trade trails. By 1870, long use had produced two well-marked trails that led from the Smoky–Peace River forks to Fort St. John by way of Fort Dunvegan. The route north of the Peace River from Dunvegan to Fort St. John was longer but easier to travel. Much of the route south of the river was forested. Dunvegan could also be bypassed on the northern route.

The Canadian government sent two North-West Mounted Police trail expeditions through this area after the start of the Klondike Gold Rush in 1897–98. At the time of the first expedition, many gold seekers were attempting to reach the Yukon over the Fort St. John Trail. Inspector J.D. Moodie was under orders to compile information on the best route overland to the Klondike. It took him over a year. This was somewhat longer than the 90 days claimed by the boosters of the overland trails in Edmonton but quite fast compared to the length of time it took many Klondikers who started out from Edmonton in 1897. Some of these spent nearly two years, and two full winters, wandering through the northern wilderness. Of all the routes that could be used to get to the Yukon, the overland trail from Edmonton was undoubtedly the worst. The second North-West Mounted Police expedition, led by Superintendent Charles Constantine, wasn't attempted until 1905. Large numbers of settlers began arriving in this region after 1910.

Waterhole on Dunvegan–Peace River Trail
Highway 2, 3 miles (5 km) south of Fairview

On the east side of the highway, an historical marker commemorates what was once the village of Waterhole. This somewhat unimaginatively named town was established in the early days of settlement three miles (five kilometers) south of today's Fairview. It was located at a watering place on the overland trail between Dunvegan and the town of Peace River. At that time, there were few places on this trail with easy access to good water.

By 1911, pioneer homesteaders had taken up the land surrounding Waterhole. Soon the community grew to 150 people. By 1928, Waterhole had a hospital, churches, banks, hotels, restaurants, garages, livery stables, a telephone and telegraph office, and a variety of retail businesses. But that year, the Central Canada Railway, now called the Northern Alberta Railway, was extended to a point four miles (six kilometers) north of the town. Here the village of Fairview was born. Waterhole, without a railroad, declined and soon passed into history.

Fort Dunvegan: Heart of Peace River Fur Trade
Highway 2, Fort Dunvegan Historic Site

Dunvegan is one of the earliest fur trading posts in Alberta and one of the most important fur posts on the Peace River. Archibald N. McLeod built the post in the summer of 1805, probably on the recommendation of David Thompson. Thompson mentioned the site in his journal when he passed here in 1804. The name comes from the ancestral castle of the McLeod family on the island of Skye in Scotland.

Dunvegan played a major part in the area's fur trade almost continuously from its founding until the Peace River country was settled in the early years of the twentieth century. For much of that time, it was the most important post in the Peace River area. It was assumed that, like Edmonton, Winnipeg and other important fur posts, Dunvegan would grow into a major city. At the very least, people were confident it would be the major settlement in the Peace River district.

When the area began to be settled, surveyors descended on Dunvegan, laying out a town 5 miles square (13 kilometers square). The proposed town lay on both sides of the river, with many of the surveyed lots on the steep hillside and riverbanks. Property went for between $100 and $200 per lot, with business lots in the heart of the planned town going even higher. Investors from as far away as Europe bought property, confident the place would be a boomtown once the railroad arrived.

When a railroad was proposed for the region, it was named the Edmonton–Dunvegan and British Columbia. This served to heighten speculation in Dunvegan real estate. But when the new railroad finally came, it bypassed the old fur post. Like so many other towns missed by the railroads, the hoped-for city never materialized and the existing community declined.

One of the stories told about Dunvegan at the height of the real estate boom was of an Edmonton investor who came north to see his new property. The parcel turned out to be one of the steep riverbank lots that would have been useless even if the railroad had come to Dunvegan. When this unfortunate investor returned to Edmonton, he was asked by a friend if he had stayed on his land. "I can't say as I stayed on it," the investor said, "but I got to lean against it."

When the old fur post closed in 1918, it looked as if Dunvegan would slip into obscurity. Instead, history saved it. Dunvegan has been made a Provincial Historic Site. Visitors can learn about Dunvegan's past at the interpretive center, then walk the grounds and look at the St. Charles Mission Church and the old factor's cabin, built in 1877, among other sights. On the day I was there, guides had samples of freshly roasted bannock for visitors.

The nearby Dunvegan Bridge is the largest suspension bridge for automobiles in Alberta. It's also the only suspension bridge for automobiles in Alberta.

Before the bridge was built, the area was served by a ferry. In the early years, the ferry operator, Joe Bizzette, was said to be somewhat cantankerous. But passengers had to get along with him or find another way to cross the river. He wouldn't operate the ferry for anyone he didn't like. "Go around," Bizzette would tell them when they asked to go across. "Go around."

Grande Prairie of the Peace River Country
Highway 2, Grande Prairie

The town of Grande Prairie got its name for obvious reasons. The area was, indeed, a grand prairie when Europeans first came here. Unlike the prairie regions farther south, however, the prairies of the Peace River country were created by forest fires. With a rich subsoil, grasslands thrived in the wake of the fires. These same fertile soils encouraged the development of agriculture once homesteaders arrived early in this century.

The grasslands of the region also meant buffalo were abundant when the first Europeans came to the Peace country. Unlike buffalo in southern Alberta, which were killed off over several decades, the Peace River herds were virtually destroyed in one winter. Deep snows made killing buffalo easy in the winter of 1829–30. Hard winters, of course, had killed huge numbers of buffalo many times before. Always, though, enough animals remained to replenish the herds.

Once Europeans arrived, however, fur traders found it profitable for Indians to kill buffalo even after their domestic needs had been met. By the spring of 1830, when the traders finally said they wouldn't buy any more buffalo meat, it was already too late. Even then, the slaughter continued until the buffalo of the area were virtually wiped out. For a few years afterward, one or two animals would be sighted in some sheltered place. But never again would herds of wild buffalo roam the Peace River country.

Points of Interest Near Highway 35
and Fort Vermilion

The Mackenzie Highway
Highway 35, .5 miles (1 km) north of Highway 2

An historical marker on the east side of the highway gives a brief account of Alexander Mackenzie's journey to the Pacific Ocean in 1792 and the building of the Mackenzie Highway in 1950. (See "Mackenzie Highway Cairn" under "Points of Interest on Highway 2" in this section.)

Battle on Banks of Notikewin River
Battle River Pioneer Museum
Highway 35, south of Manning near the agricultural grounds

The Battle River Pioneer Museum features displays ranging from an albino moose to old farm machinery. The name of the museum comes from the translated name of the nearby Notikewin River. The name *Battle River* was also used by early homesteaders to refer to this area and in the early days was sometimes used for the river itself.

An Indian battle fought along the Notikewin's shores more than 200 years ago gave rise to the river's name. At that time, the Cree used guns obtained from European traders to push the Beaver Indians, their traditional enemies, farther and farther west. One autumn, close to the mouth of the river, a large band of Cree came to drive the Beaver even farther west. Many of the Cree were from as far away as the North Saskatchewan River.

The wind blew briskly from the west that day. The Cree warriors slipped quietly along the riverbank to a horseshoe bend, where they hid in the high, frost-killed grass. They planned to ambush the Beaver as they came down the river. Unknown to the Cree, however, a small band of Beaver were already hiding in the grass on the opposite shore.

The Beaver, many with their own guns now, saw their chance. They circled back to the west, then crossed the river and set fire to the paper-dry grass where the Cree were hiding. In a flash, the wind whipped the flames through the grass, driving the Cree lucky enough to escape into the river and away.

Many Cree were consumed by the fire or caught and killed. The Beaver were exalted in their victory. Finally, just west of the Peace, they had been able to defeat the gun-toting Cree. The Cree remembered the river, too. They called it the Notikewin, or "river of the fight."

Fort Vermilion an Old Establishment
Highway 35, 2.5 miles (4 km) south of High Level

Hudson's Bay Company buildings at Fort Vermilion about 1900.

On the east side of the highway, an historical marker tells of some of the early fur posts on the northern arc of the Peace River and the eventual settlement of Fort Vermilion. Today's town of Fort Vermilion, 50 miles (80 kilometers) southeast of the historical marker on Highway 88, began as the North West Company fur trading post Old Establishment. It was built by Charles Boyer in 1788. This fort was replaced upstream by Aspen House in 1792 and La Fleur's Post in 1798–99.

Trade with Beaver, Cree and Déné Indians created keen competition between the North West and Hudson's Bay companies in this area. In 1802, the Hudson's Bay Company built Mansfield House across the river from today's Fort Vermilion. The North West Company built Fort Liard nearby. In 1831, after the two companies had merged, the Hudson's Bay post was moved across the river to the site of today's town of Fort Vermilion.

North West Company Controls Trade on the Peace
Highway 88, 4 miles (7 km) north of Fort Vermilion

On the west side of Highway 88, an historical marker tells some of the history of the fur trade in the Fort Vermilion area. The first fur post, built by the North West Company, was located a few miles downstream from this sign. The North West Company continued to control most of the trade on the Peace, ruthlessly forcing the closure of rival establishments until its union with the Hudson's Bay Company in 1821.

Nor'Westers Starve Bay Men
Highway 88, Fort Vermilion

In the winter of 1815–16, one of the most gruesome chapters in the long war between the North West and Hudson's Bay companies took place up and down the Peace River from Fort Vermilion. Until 1815, trade in the Peace River country had been controlled by the Nor'Westers, the men of the North West Company. That autumn, John Clarke of the Hudson's Bay Company led nearly 100 men to Lake Athabasca in an another attempt by the Hudson's Bay Company to gain some of this trade. Clarke built a post on Potato Island directly across from the North West's Fort Chipewyan.

Clarke's plan was to use the new post as an entry point to the Peace River country. But Clarke failed to measure the extent of the Nor'Westers' opposition to sharing the trade. It was about this time that the fierce competition between the two companies came to a peak (the Battle at Seven Oaks on the Red River was only a few months away), and John MacGillivray, visiting Fort Chipewyan from his post at Dunvegan, decided to starve the Bay men out.

Clarke, who was short of food but had planned to trade with Indians for provisions once he entered the Peace country, recognized his predicament too late. He divided his force, hoping smaller groups would be able to find food easier than a single, large one. He and 50 of his men went up the Peace, where they hoped to make contact with Indians willing to trade. MacGillivray and his men had left earlier for Dunvegan, however. All along the way, MacGillivray had encouraged Indians to scatter the game away from the river. He also gave the Indians strict orders not to give the Bay men food.

The tragedy played itself out over the early part of the winter. Clarke left the bulk of his men and continued upriver. The Indians continued to ignore the plight of the Hudson's Bay men. Clarke went as far up the Peace as Horseshoe House, at a point east of today's Notikewin, but MacGillivray had spread the word to Indians there, too.

By February, Clarke gave up and exchanged what goods he had with the Nor'Westers for food enough to return to Fort Chipewyan. Some of his men had already surrendered to the North West Company at Fort Vermilion. Here they were fed but kept under guard. Later, they were taken to Fort Dunvegan and then back to Edmonton. Over the course of the tragedy, 16 Hudson's Bay employees had starved to death.

Sheridan Lawrence Ranch Historic Site
On the Peace River a few miles north of Fort Vermilion

The Sheridan Lawrence family came to the Peace River country in 1879 to work at the Anglican mission at Fort Vermilion. They also established a farm and trading operation. At its peak, the ranch encompassed 1,000 acres (405 hectares) of land, 35 buildings and 2 steamboat landings.

Points of Interest Near Highway 34

Bezanson Dreams of City
Highway 34, Bezanson

A.M. Bezanson, one of the early Peace River district's biggest promoters, first came to this area in 1906. That first summer, he traveled the country taking photographs. The following winter, Bezanson spent in Edmonton writing a short book called *The Peace River Trail*, which extolled the virtues of the new Peace River country. The book was published by the *Edmonton Journal*, and the federal government bought several thousand copies to distribute to potential homesteaders.

The next spring, Bezanson headed north again, intent on

establishing a new town, perhaps even a city. Bezanson felt sure a railroad would come to the Peace River district, and he knew major towns would be located along the railroad. After reading George M. Dawson's 1879 report recommending a railroad through the Peace River country, Bezanson found surveyors' stakes he assumed Dawson had driven to mark the line of his proposed railroad. The stakes were near the forks of the Smoky and Simonette rivers, and Bezanson speculated that a future railroad through the Peace River past this point would create the logical place for a town or even a small city.

Bezanson filed for a homestead on this land, and over the next few years established a small farm. Once he had free title to the property, he began trying to promote it as a new townsite. The railroad, of course, had not yet come, but Bezanson went ahead and wrote a pamphlet describing his planned community. He recruited a sales agent in Vancouver. Officials of the Canadian Northern Railway even helped out by assuring all who would listen that they were nearly ready to begin building a railroad along the route Bezanson described. (They didn't add that what they were waiting for was government financing.)

In 1913, Bezanson drove the first automobile into the Peace country over the Edson Trail from Edmonton. He took A.J. Davidson, a well-known land promoter, on a 2,000-mile (3,218-kilometer) tour of the Peace River district. One story claims that during this trip, the two men crossed Lesser Slave Lake at 65 miles (105 kilometers) an hour, trying to stay ahead of the collapsing ice behind them. Bezanson and Davidson made it safely back to Edmonton, however, and Davidson, too, went to work selling lots in Bezanson's proposed town.

It was 1916 before a railroad finally came to the Peace River. When it did, it crossed the Smoky many miles downstream from Bezanson's site, at the mouth of the Simonette. Bezanson's dream of a town vanished, or almost vanished, since the present village a few miles northwest of the original Bezanson was named in his honor. Rumor has it that several people in Edmonton inherited deeds to town lots at the original Bezanson site and have been paying taxes on them ever since.

Prehistoric River Delta Forms Kleskun Hills
Highway 34, 11 miles (18 km) east of Grande Prairie

On the north side of the highway, an historical marker describes the Kleskun Hills located north and west of this point. The hills were created from the eroded remnants of a prehistoric river delta formed more than 70,000,000 years ago. Badlands developed here in rich beds of decayed volcanic dust. These and the famous Cretaceous dinosaur badlands of the Drumheller area are outcroppings of the same underground strata. The Grande Prairie plains, the remains of a glacial lake, lie southwest of the hills.

Blacksmith One of First in Sexsmith
Highway 34, 10.5 miles (17 km) east of Grande Prairie

On the north side of the highway, an historical marker tells of the Sexsmith Blacksmith Shop. The town of Sexsmith sprang to life in 1916 with the construction of the Grande Prairie branch of the Edmonton–Dunvegan and British Columbia Railway. Dave Bozarth's blacksmith shop was one of the first commercial establishments in the new town. By 1920, Bozarth also operated a livery barn and implement dealership. Nels Johnson, who joined the business in 1920, had come to Canada from Jantland, Sweden, in 1909. He bought the shop from Bozarth in 1928 and operated it until 1974.

Today, Bozarth's log blacksmith shop has become a museum. It still contains most of the original equipment and tools.

Chapter 9

Mountain Country

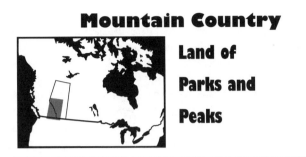

Land of

Parks and

Peaks

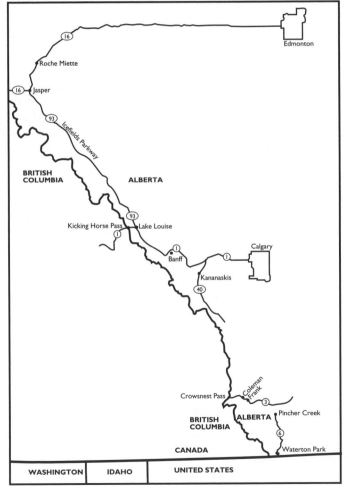

Edmonton

16

Roche Miette

16 Jasper

93 Icefields Parkway

BRITISH COLUMBIA   **ALBERTA**

93

Kicking Horse Pass ● ● Lake Louise

1

● Banff

Calgary

1

Kananaskis

40

Crowsnest Pass   Coleman Frank

3

Pincher Creek

BRITISH COLUMBIA   **ALBERTA**

6

Waterton Park

CANADA

WASHINGTON	IDAHO	UNITED STATES

FEW PLACES CAN BOAST of scenery as breathtaking as Alberta's Mountain Country. Jagged, snow-capped peaks, deep turquoise glacial lakes, forested mountainsides, boulder-strewn river rapids. Spectacular views crowd one after another in Mountain Country. In addition to panoramic scenes, sights close to the highway might include mountain goats, herds of elk or deer and maybe even a bear.

For the purposes of this book, Mountain Country encompasses the eastern side of the Rocky Mountains along the southern half of Alberta's western border. The region stretches 435 miles (700 kilometers) from north to south. Yet only four highways through four mountain passes cross over the divide into British Columbia.

Travel in Mountain Country has always been limited because of its often treacherous mountain passes. Europeans first discovered Indian trails over the Continental Divide about 1800. These passes opened the first regularly traveled routes across North America. Later came the search for suitable mountain passes for the transcontinental railroad. The building of the railroad in turn led to mining, forestry and the establishment of national parks. All have played significant roles in the history of Mountain Country.

Today, Alberta's three mountain national parks—Waterton, Banff and Jasper—cover more than two-thirds of Mountain Country. Peter Lougheed Provincial Park, Willmore Wilderness Park and the Rocky Mountains Forest Reserve account for most of the rest.

Waterton Lakes National Park

"Kootenai" Brown First Superintendent at Waterton
Waterton National Park
Highway 6, 31 miles (50 km) south of Pincher Creek

The history of Waterton Lakes National Park is linked to one of the most colorful characters in Alberta's history, John George "Kootenai" Brown, one of the earliest white men to settle near what was then known as Kootenay Lakes, in today's park. He moved to the region in the early 1870s, but he first came to the Kootenay (Waterton) Lakes area in 1865.

At that time, Brown was traveling with a small party of men who had been prospecting in southeastern British Columbia. They'd crossed the mountains at Kootenay Pass, and Brown had traded with Indians for a horse somewhere along the way. Some say Brown stole the horse, although he denied the accusation. According to legend, however, Brown and his companions rode swiftly from the Waterton area with a band of Kootenay Indians close on their heels.

Coming out of the mountains, Brown followed the Waterton River north, heading for Fort Edmonton, where he planned to prospect for gold along the North Saskatchewan River. Unfortunately, Brown and his companions had only a sketchy knowledge of Fort Edmonton's location. Within a few days, they were 200 miles (322 kilometers) off course.

Near the Cypress Hills, Brown and his friends ran into more Indians. On the banks of Seven Persons Creek, they were attacked by a small band of Blackfoot. The prospectors eventually fought their way out of this skirmish but not before Brown had been shot in the back with an arrow. Sometimes when telling the story, Brown would claim the wound had been somewhat lower.

No matter where the puncture was located, it turned out to be enough to persuade Brown to leave Alberta. He headed south to Montana and the Dakotas. In the following years, he became an army dispatch rider and scout, a buffalo hunter, a storekeeper and a whiskey trader.

While working in this last occupation, Brown stabbed and killed a man in a fight. He spent a short stint in the hoosegow before a Montana jury decided it had been a fair fight. Free again, Brown moved back to the Waterton Lakes area and opened a trading post. After 1874, he made his living hunting and fishing, supplying the Mounties at Fort Macleod with meat. Later, Brown became a guide. Eventually, he added his voice to those advocating the creation of Waterton Lakes National Park.

In 1911, the government finally consented. They named the park Waterton after Charles Waterton, a midnineteenth century naturalist. Kootenai Brown was appointed the park's first superintendent. In 1932, Waterton Lakes National Park and Montana's Glacier National Park were united to form Waterton–Glacier International Peace Park. This created more than 1,700 square miles (4,403 square kilometers) of contiguous parkland.

Kootenai Brown's grave, Waterton Lakes, August 1957.

Kootenai Brown's metis wife died not long after the couple moved to the Waterton area. Some time later, Brown met a young Saskatchewan Cree woman who was visiting relatives on the Blackfoot reservation in nearby Babb, Montana. Brown was so taken with Chee-Nee-Pay-Tha-Quo-Ka-Soon, whose name meant "Flash of Blue Lightning," that he traded five horses for her soon after they met. The couple stayed together until his death in 1916. Today, she is buried next to Brown and his first wife, just beyond the park gate. Markers are located near the side of the highway.

First Oil Well in Alberta Found at Waterton
Akamina Parkway, 4 miles (7 km) from Waterton townsite

A plaque marking the site of western Canada's first producing oil well can be found on Akamina Parkway in Waterton Park. John George "Kootenai" Brown, Waterton Lakes National Park's first superintendent, had a hand in this oil discovery as he did in much of Waterton's early history. According to Brown, in 1876 George Dawson of the Geological Survey of Canada asked him if he'd watch for crude oil in the nearby mountains. Brown told Dawson that he wouldn't know what to look for. In response, Dawson gave him a jar containing a mixture of kerosene and grease. This, said Dawson, resembled what he might find.

Some years later, Brown showed the mixture to some visiting Stoney Indians. One Indian told him of a place on Cameron Creek where something much like the mixture could be found. Again, Brown didn't do anything about the oil for several years. Then one summer, Bill Aldredge, whom Brown had hired to cut hay, needed some oil for the mowing machine. Brown told him about the oil on Cameron Creek. Aldredge, who had worked in oil fields in Texas, immediately quit his job. Within the week, he had set himself up for business near the oil pool. Aldredge strained the oil through a gunny sack, then sold it to local farmers for lubricating oil, antiseptic gargle and sore throat cure. In 1901, Aldredge's pool was taken over by an oil company.

The Crowsnest Pass
Points of Interest Near Highway 3

Coal Discovered in Crowsnest Pass
Highway 3, 5.5 miles (9 km) west of Highway 22 and Highway 3 junction

On the north side of the highway, an historical marker tells of the discovery of lead, copper and zinc during the 1890s in southeastern British Columbia. These discoveries stimulated American investment in this area. In an attempt to keep financial control of the area's resources in Canada, the Liberal government backed the construction of a Canadian Pacific Railway line over the Crowsnest Pass. About the same time, coal deposits were discovered on the eastern side of the mountains in Alberta. Prairie settlement during this era, along with the new railroad's steam-powered engines, created a steady market for coal. Mines were opened, and within a few years, the Crowsnest Pass area became Alberta's largest coal-mining district.

Rock Slide Buries Town of Frank
Highway 3, Frank Slide

The day after the Frank Slide in 1903 at Frank, Alberta.

On Highway 3 at Frank Slide, an historical marker tells of the early morning of April 29, 1903, when a gigantic wedge of limestone—459 feet (140 meters) deep, 2,625 feet (800 meters) across and 1,805 feet (550 meters) high—dislodged from Turtle Mountain and thundered down onto the sleeping town of Frank, Alberta. At 4:10 A.M., 82,000,000 tonnes of rock swept 1 mile (1.5 kilometers) across the Crowsnest valley in less than two minutes. The rock slide took at least 68 lives, destroyed a large part of the town, covered the rail line and buried the mine.

Miners working the night shift deep inside Turtle Mountain managed to dig their way to the mine's entrance only to find devastation outside. Although the mine reopened for a while, the original town of Frank never recovered. The townsite was moved to its new location east of the slide. Remnants of the old town are still visible at the western edge of the slide.

The Frank Slide Interpretive Centre is located 1 mile (1.5 kilometers) off Highway 3 in the Municipality of the Crowsnest Pass. In addition to offering information about the Frank Slide, the center details much of the history and geology of the region. It's open year-round and features a variety of interpretive programs, presentations and special events. The audio-visual program "In the Mountain's Shadow" is shown daily.

Explosion at Hillcrest Mine
Highway 3, Hillcrest Mine

At the Hillcrest Cemetery in the Crowsnest Pass, an historical marker tells of the difficulties early coal miners encountered. Methane gas and the highly combustible coal dust found in mines continually endangered their lives. Two explosions rocked the Bellevue Mine near Hillcrest in 1910 and another followed in 1912. A total of 30 miners were killed in the three accidents. However, the worst was yet to come.

At 9:30 on the morning of June 19, 1914, a violent explosion ripped through the tunnels and slopes of the Hillcrest Mine, killing 189 men and boys. A small explosion of the seeping methane gas known as firedamp had triggered the ignition of coal dust. The extent of the devastation became evident when rescue teams were able to locate only 48 survivors of the 237 miners working that morning.

Although the Hillcrest Mine reopened soon after, the mass graves located in this cemetery lie as a silent testimony to the largest coal-mining tragedy in Canadian history.

Visit the Crowsnest Museum in Coleman and the Crowsnest Pass Ecomuseum in Blairmore for additional history of coal mining in this area.

Volcanic Rock in Crowsnest Pass Older than Rocky Mountains
Highway 3, 1.5 mile (2 km) west of Coleman

On the north side of Highway 3, an historical marker tells about the outcroppings of volcanic rock in this vicinity. These are the only major occurrences of volcanic rock in Alberta. Up to 1,600 feet (488 meters) thick, the rocks consist of ash and cinders with some large blocks similar to the pumice stone bombs thrown out by many modern volcanoes. There is little actual lava, which suggests violent explosive eruptions of the type produced by volcanoes like Mount Vesuvius in Italy. These rocks, approximately 100,000,000 years old, are older than the Rocky Mountains.

South Kananaskis Country to the Crowsnest Pass
Points of Interest Near Highway 40

Kananaskis Named
Highway 40, Kananaskis River

Two stories explain how the Kananaskis River got its name. A Stoney Indian legend tells of a warrior struck in the head with a tomahawk near the river. According to some people, Kananaskis is a white corruption of the Stoney words for "man with tomahawk in the head."

Others say the name comes from a similarly corrupted pronunciation of the words for "place where two waters meet." Since the Bow and Kananaskis rivers come together at a point on the old Bow River Trail near the present town of Kananaskis, this also seems a logical name for the river. Members of the Palliser Expedition in 1858 were the first whites to use the name.

Search for Lemon Gold Mine Continues
Highway 40, Highwood River

Tales of the lost Lemon Mine have circulated in Alberta for over 100 years. They revolve around a Montana prospector named Frank Lemon and a trader named Lafayette French. Lemon had prospected on the North Saskatchewan River before coming to southern Alberta in the fall of 1870. Either in the upper Highwood River area, or perhaps farther south near the Crowsnest Pass, Lemon and a partner named Blackjack discovered a rich gold deposit.

As is often the case when business partnerships start to make money, an argument soon developed over what to do about their good fortune. Blackjack wanted to spend the winter working the claim. Lemon wanted to stake the find and return to the Tobacco Plains area of Montana to wait for spring. Tempers flared. Loud words were exchanged. Sometime after nightfall, Lemon seized an ax and struck Blackjack in the head.

Lemon would have escaped immediately, but it was too late and too dark to abandon camp that night. While waiting for morning, Lemon heard eerie wails coming from the darkness. Unknown to either Blackjack or Lemon, two Stoney Indians had watched the prospectors that day as they panned the creek for gold. They'd watched when the two prospectors dug a 5-foot (1.5-meter) hole through rocks and soil littered with gold. They'd watched the argument develop, and they'd watched when Lemon struck Blackjack with the ax. Then the Indians amused themselves by tormenting Lemon with their screams and wails all through the long night. Lemon ran from the camp at first light.

The two Indians took the news of the white men, the gold and the murder back to their band. Chief Bearpaw made them swear to keep quiet about what they had seen, so white men wouldn't flock to the area. Lemon, meanwhile, returned to Tobacco Plains, where he confessed his evil deed to a priest. The priest sent a metis by the name of John McDougall to bury Blackjack. Bearpaw's Indians soon found the grave, and the crude marker and all evidence of the camp were scattered. After that, the Indians stopped hunting in the area so the trails would grow over.

The next spring, Lemon started north with a number of

prospectors. After they camped at Crow's Nest Lake, however, Lemon became irrational. Soon he appeared to be raving mad. The whole party returned to Montana. The following year, the priest advised Lemon to lead another party to the gold. Once more, soon after they passed the Crows Nest Lake, Lemon went insane.

Others took up the quest for the gold, notably Lafayette French. Year after year, French went into the mountains looking for the mine. Always, though, something would happen to drive him out. French even had a piece of a map he said had been given to him by Lemon. It showed the headwaters and three forks of the same river. At the head of one of the streams was an *X* that French said marked the spot where the gold would be found.

Finally, in the winter of 1912, French made one more attempt to find the Lemon Mine. On his return from this expedition, he stopped at an old cabin at a place known as Emerson Crossing. That night, the cabin caught fire, and though French managed to escape, he was badly burned. Men from a nearby ranch took him to the hospital in High River. Here, close to death, French requested that Senator Dan Riley be summoned. When Riley—who had financed many of French's expeditions into the mountains— arrived, French told him in a faint whisper that he'd learned the secret of the Lemon Mine. Then the old prospector lapsed into a coma. He never regained consciousness.

Since then, dozens of others have looked for the Lemon Mine. Many say there never was a mine, but they offer no proof. Other stories tell of men going in search of the gold but never returning. It's said the Indians have put a curse on the mine, and anyone who touches the gold will die. One story tells of a skeleton found at the headwaters of the Oldman River. Supposedly, the skeleton had been bleached white in the sun, and one bony hand still clutched a bag of gold.

Banff National Park

Along the upper reaches of the Bow River, on the eastern slopes of the Rocky Mountains, Banff National Park preserves 2,317 square miles (6,600 square kilometers) of mountain forests, lakes and meadows. Banff became Canada's first national park in 1887, two years after the area around the Cave and Basin hot springs had been set aside as a federal reserve.

*In 1883, the year the CPR arrived, Banff was known as "Siding 29."
Later that year, the name was changed in honor of Banffshire,
Scotland, the birth place of two important CPR officials.*

The name *Banff* is shortened from Banffshire, a county in Scotland where Canadian Pacific Railway magnates Donald Smith and George Stephen were born. When the railroad first came through in 1883, the townsite was named Siding 29. It was renamed Banff later that year. The name *Banff* wasn't applied to the park until 1949, when the original name, Rocky Mountain Park, was officially changed to Banff National Park.

Sanitarium Comes to Banff
Park Administration Building
Highway 1, Banff

In 1886, Dr. R.G. Brett, a medical supervisor for the Canadian Pacific Railway, built a hospital and spa at Banff. He called it the Brett Sanitarium. Even now, hot springs are considered therapeutic by many people, but in the 1880s, when modern medicine was only beginning, the benefits of hot mineral water fresh from the ground were even more widely extolled. Many visitors to Dr. Brett's sanitarium testified to the healing powers of the water. In the early years, so many crutches were being left behind in Banff by people who said they didn't need them anymore that skeptics accused Dr. Brett of issuing crutches to his guests as they got off the train. In 1933, the Brett Sanitarium, by then known as the Bretton Hall Hotel, burned to the ground. In 1936, today's Park Administration Building on Banff Avenue was built on the old sanitarium site.

Banff Springs Hotel Built
Highway 1, Banff

Construction of the Canadian Pacific Railway's (CPR) first and most famous Chateau-style hotel began in 1886. The following summer, CPR General Manager William Van Horne visited the site and discovered that the hotel kitchen had a view overlooking the Bow River while guests' rooms looked out on a wall of forest. Alterations were quickly made, and the hotel opened on the first of June in 1888. After the turn of the century, the hotel was expanded several times. Today, it can accommodate more than 1,000 guests in nearly 600 rooms.

Prime Minister's Wife Given Sack of Flour
Banff Railroad Station
Highway 1, Banff

Isabella Macdonald, the wife of Canada's first Prime Minister, was one of Banff's early visitors. When her train left Calgary, Canadian Pacific Railway officials wired the Banff station master with orders to give Mrs. Macdonald a bouquet of flowers as she came off the train. Somehow, a slight error was made in transmitting the telegram. When the Prime Minister's wife arrived at Banff Station, she was presented with a hearty welcome and a 10-pound (4.5-kilogram) bag of flour.

ALTERNATE ROUTE THROUGH BANFF NATIONAL PARK
Highway 1A

Four miles (seven kilometers) west of Banff, Highway 1A takes a more leisurely route to Lake Louise. Several points of interest are marked along the way.

Coal Mining Comes to Banff
Bankhead Historical Site
Lake Minnewanka Road

The Canadian Geological Survey reported coal outcroppings east of Canmore and Banff in 1885. Because it was close to the Canadian Pacific Railway (CPR), the Canadian Anthracite Company began mining coal for the railroad in 1886. The CPR began its own mining operations in 1903. By 1910, nearly 500 people worked at the mines. The nearby community of Bankhead had grown to over 1,000 people. But in 1922, the mines closed and Bankhead was abandoned. Almost all the buildings were either torn down or moved to Banff, Canmore or Calgary. Today, the Bankhead Historical Site and interpretive exhibit can be found about two miles (three kilometers) north of the Trans–Canada Highway on Lake Minnewanka Road. A hiking trail on Cascade Mountain, the C Level Cirque Trail, begins near the interpretive exhibit and passes some of the remains of the defunct mine.

Silver City Booms and Busts
Highway 93, Castle Mountain

Near Castle Mountain, the village of Silver City had, perhaps, the shortest history of any town in the Canadian West.
Almost as soon as the railroad went through the area, rumors of
a silver find, probably spread by Canadian Pacific Railway
(CPR) officials, swept Alberta. Prospectors poured into the area,
and Silver City became a town of 3,000 people.

The town had actually got a start a few years before, when
John J. Healy of Fort Whoop-Up had done some prospecting at
nearby Copper Mountain. Healy named the camp Copper Mine,
but the railroad named the stop Silver City, probably because
they had a sister stop across the divide called Golden City. That
place, now known as Golden, British Columbia, survives to this
day.

Silver City was not so lucky. As many as five mines were started in the town, but none of them made money. Within two years,
Silver City's life as a town had played itself out. The prospectors
moved on in search of other rainbows. Many, in fact, went on to
Golden City. Even here, though, the CPR's rumors of gold turned
out to be inaccurate.

Only one resident remained at Silver City after the boom
ended. Joe Smith gave up the chase for gold and silver, and
stayed to hunt and trap in the area from the 1880s until the 1930s.
Smith was a good storyteller and popular with the park wardens,
who arrived when the area became a national park. The sympa-
thetic wardens turned a blind eye to Smith's cabin on park property, as well as his hunting and trapping. Smith lived in the park
until 1935, when, too old to fend for himself, he was taken to the
Lacombe Home at Midnapore. He died two years later.

Castle Mountain Named, Renamed and Named Again
Highway 93, Castle Mountain

The Palliser Expedition's Dr. James Hector first named this
mountain Castle in 1858. Despite the fact that the mountain
really looks like a castle, in 1946 it was renamed Mount Eisenhower in honor of Dwight D. Eisenhower, the commander of
Allied Forces in Europe during World War II. Eisenhower had

been expected to attend the ceremony officially renaming the mountain but according to rumor missed the occasion when he was delayed at a golf match.

After the official name of the mountain changed, however, most people continued to call it Castle Mountain, even after Eisenhower became president of the United States. As a result, in 1979, the name was officially changed back to Castle Mountain. Mount Eisenhower was applied to the southern tower and is still called by that name today.

Kicking Horse Names Pass
Highway 1, Kicking Horse Pass

The Palliser Expedition's James Hector explored several mountain passes between British Columbia and Alberta. He was looking for the best routes for wagon roads or, perhaps, even a railroad. Crossing the divide at what was then known as the Wapta Pass, Hector was kicked in the chest by a packhorse and knocked unconscious. Other members of the party thought he was dead. They dug a hole and were preparing to dump Hector in when the young geologist revived. Ever since, the nearby river and mountain pass have been known as the Kicking Horse.

In 1883, the route of the Canadian Pacific Railway (CPR) proceeded over the Kicking Horse Pass on the chosen southern route to the West Coast. Other passes were better suited for a railroad, but the southern route to British Columbia was deemed the best one for keeping the prairie provinces under Canadian control.

Lake Louise Discovered
Highway 93, Lake Louise

Early Banff outfitter Tom Wilson became the first white to see Lake Louise in 1882. While packing supplies for Canadian Pacific Railway survey crews, he heard an avalanche near the confluence of the Bow and Pipestone rivers. Wilson asked a Stoney Indian working with him where the noise would have come from. Snow Mountain and the Lake of Little Fishes, he was told.

The next day, Wilson had the Stoney take him to the lake. Wilson called the Lake of Little Fishes Emerald Lake, but the name didn't last. Two years later, it was renamed Louise, after the same Princess Louise Caroline Alberta for whom the future province would be named.

Columbia Icefields Discovered
Highway 93, Ice Fields Parkway

The discovery of the Columbia Icefields in 1898 can be seen as a measure of the difficulties facing early explorers in the Rocky Mountains. The icefields were undoubtedly known to Indians of the region for centuries. Still, it took 100 years of exploration before the first white men discovered the 150 square miles (389 square kilometers) of ice that lie along the Continental Divide. Two English alpinists, J. Norman Collie and Hugh Stutfield, discovered the glaciers after climbing the summit of Mount Athabasca. "A new world was spread at our feet," Collie wrote of the huge expanse of ice. On one side of the divide, glacial streams ran into the Columbia River and, on the other side, into the Athabasca and North Saskatchewan rivers.

First Tourist Travels the Banff–Jasper Highway

In the summer of 1912, Banff guide Major Fred Brewster escorted Samuel Prescott Fay over the unmapped trail between Lake Louise and Jasper. Another route had already been established by a group led by Mary T.S. Schaeffer when it traveled from Lake Louise to Maligne Lake in 1908. Schaeffer's group was the first to explore the Maligne Lake area, although the lake's existence had been known for many years.

Jasper National Park

When work began on the Grand Trunk Railway route over the mountains west of Edmonton, the federal government sought to emulate the success it had had with Banff National

Park. On September 14, 1907, the government created what was first called Forest Park. It contained 5,000 square miles (12,949 square kilometers) of land between the Continental Divide and the foothills.

Later, the park was reduced to 1,000 square miles (2,590 square kilometers) and then, in 1914, increased almost to its original size. Several other less drastic adjustments followed. In 1930, the question of park boundaries was finally settled. Today, the park covers 4,200 square miles (10,877 square kilometers). The name *Jasper* is in honor of an obscure Hudson's Bay Company employee named Jasper Hawes. Hawes established the first of what became a series of small fur posts operating intermittently in the area from 1813 until the 1880s.

Jasper National Park Named

Iroquois Indians began moving from eastern Canada to trap, hunt and guide for the North West Company sometime before 1800. Within a few years, the Iroquois were exploring the Rockies, looking for suitable mountain passes leading farther west. It was the Iroquois who led the first white fur traders into the area we know today as Jasper National Park. Among the earliest to enter the area after the Iroquois was the independent trapper Jasper Hawes.

Almost nothing is known of Jasper Hawes' life except for the years he spent in Alberta. He came from Missouri, was married to an Indian woman and had a large family when he moved into the mountains and built a log home near Brule Lake about 1801. Beginning around 1813, Hawes maintained a small post for the North West Company and later the Hudson's Bay Company. Although some trade was carried on at Jasper House, the post was always more a supply and stopping point for transmountain travelers than it was a trading post.

In 1807, David Thompson made the first of several trips over the mountains, crossing at Howse Pass north of Lake Louise. But in 1810, Thompson was prevented from using this pass by Peigan Indians who were mad at him for trading rifles to their enemies, the Kootenay. An Iroquois guide led Thompson through today's Jasper National Park north to the Athabasca River. The guide, known only as Thomas, then turned upriver and led Thompson over the Athabasca Pass in January 1911. Thompson thus avoided the angry Peigan.

For the next few years, Athabasca Pass became the primary route over the mountains to the Pacific. About 1825, however, Jasper Hawes decided to move to the West Coast. Instead of following the Athabasca and its pass west to the Columbia, Hawes traveled over the gentler Leather Pass to the Fraser River. He

and his family intended to follow the Fraser to the Pacific, but no one ever heard from them again. Whether they drowned or were killed in some other way no one ever knew. The post continued to be called Jasper House, however, and the name was eventually applied to a new post close to Jasper Lake and then to today's town of Jasper.

The Bungalows at Japser Park Lodge, 1920.

Yellowhead Pass Named for Iroquois Trapper
Highway 16

People began to call this pass the Yellowhead around 1825. At the time, one of the Iroquois who trapped in the region and worked for the Hudson's Bay Company had light-colored hair. He was called Tête Jaune, or Yellow Head, by the voyageurs. Tête Jaune kept a cache on the west side of the Leather Pass, and gradually people began to refer to the route as the pass to Tête Jaune's cache, or Tête Jaune's Pass, which in translation is the name we know it by today.

In 1827, Tête Jaune met a terrible end. He, his brother Baptiste, and their wives and children were all killed by Beaver Indians on the western side of his mountain pass.

Road to the Mountains
Highway 16

Until 1857, the highway to Jasper House, a supply and trading post for transmountain travel, was strictly a water route up the Athabasca River. In that year, however, Henry John Moberly, the factor at Jasper House, cut the first trail overland to Lac Ste. Anne. Here the new trail met an old one from Edmonton. Members of the Palliser Expedition led by Dr. James Hector were the first to use Moberly's trail. In 1862, the trail became the route taken by gold seekers, who became known as the Overlanders. The Overlanders were bound for British Columbia's Caribou diggings. Eventually, today's Yellowhead Highway developed from Moberly's old trail.

In 1916, road travel in Jasper National Park was greatly improved when the Grand Trunk Pacific and the Canadian Northern railways, each of which had built rail lines through the park, consolidated their route. After that, a single rail line traversed Jasper Park. Most of the abandoned rail beds were better than any of the existing roads, so they became the main highway through the park. Eventually, they would become part of the Yellowhead Highway system.

Roche Miette Named
Highway 16

A prominent landmark along the Athabasca River is Roche Miette. It was named for a clerk at Jasper House. According to the story, one afternoon Miette climbed to the summit and sat on the edge of the 2,000-foot (610-meter) precipice, dangling his feet over the sides. From that time on, it became known as Miette's Rock, or Roche Miette.

Last of the Snake Indians in Alberta
Highway 16, Snake Indian River

At one time, Shoshoni (or Snake) Indians ranged through much of southern Alberta (now they are found only farther south in the United States). By the early years of the nineteenth century, most of the Shoshoni were pushed south and west by the Blackfoot. The Shoshoni had horses, but they were at a disadvantage because they lacked the firearms of the northern Indians.

One small band of Shoshoni survived along the mountains, however. Around 1840, this group was camped near Jasper House. A larger band of Assiniboine was also camped nearby. The Assiniboine invited the Shoshoni into their camp for a feast under the pretense of celebrating a peace accord reached between the two peoples. When the Shoshoni arrived at the camp, however, all but three teenage girls were slaughtered by the larger group of Assiniboine. Fearing retaliation from the traders at Jasper House, the Indians retreated down the Athabasca River with their teenaged Shoshoni hostages.

At a point near today's Edson, the three girls escaped. Two of them built a crude raft, took to the Athabasca, and were never heard from again. The third, fearing the river, fended for herself in the wilderness. For more than a year, she lived alone in the forests. Eventually, an Iroquois hunter found strange tracks in the snow from her crudely made moccasins. Wondering who could have made such tracks, he followed them and captured the young Shoshoni woman. The Iroquois turned her over to Colin Fraser, the chief trader at Jasper House, and she worked at the post as a servant for several years. By then, the young woman was, as far as is known, the last of her tribe in Alberta. She later met and married a Shuswap man and moved to British Columbia.

First Homesteaders Come to Jasper
Highway 16, Jasper

In 1892, Suzette Jane Chalifoux, a metis woman from Edmonton, and John Lewis Swift, an American from Missouri, moved into the abandoned Hudson's Bay post at the north end of Jasper Lake. Here they established a small trading post. Two years later, the couple moved closer to the present town of Jasper and took up farming on Henry Flats. By the turn of the century, Chalifoux and Swift were raising cattle and horses, and they had 16 acres (6.5 hectares) under cultivation. Their crops included wheat, potatoes, turnips and barley. A few other settlers, mostly Iroquois and metis, had also begun to farm in the area.

When the government created Jasper National Park, it persuaded all the farmers except Chalifoux and Swift to move outside park boundaries. Unlike the others, Chalifoux and Swift had filed a homestead claim on their land, and they'd met the requirements for title. Besides, Swift and Chalifoux knew that surveyors' stakes from the first Canadian Pacific Railway survey of the area went right through their property. Even as the government was trying to remove them from the new park, the Grand Trunk Railway was negotiating with the couple for the right to cross their farm. The government tried to persuade Swift to give up title to the land by making him a game warden, but Swift wouldn't take the bait.

For years, a battle ensued between the homesteading couple and the federal government. In 1926, the government offered them $6,000 for their farm. The offer was declined. In 1935, however, Swift, now past 80, wanted to retire. He went to park officials and offered them the land for the $6,000 he had rejected in 1926, even though the land was worth more by that time.

It looked as if the problem had finally been solved, but when the Parks Department went to Ottawa for the money, the government wouldn't give it to them. Shortly thereafter, Swift received and accepted an offer of $8,000 from an Englishman named A.C. Wilby. Wilby turned the old farm into a dude ranch. On Wilby's death in 1951, the ranch was once more offered to the Canadian government, this time for $70,000.

Again, the government said it didn't have the money, so the ranch was sold to a Jasper contractor. Eleven years later, the government decided that it did, after all, want to buy the old Swift–Chalifoux property. After intense negotiations, it was able to acquire the property for $277,850, just $271,850 more than they could have bought it for 25 years earlier.

First Automobiles in Jasper National Park
Highway 16, Jasper

The Grand Trunk Pacific Railway brought the first automobile to Jasper Park in 1914. A little later that summer, a second car was brought to the park. Two days later, with the drivers enjoying a pleasant view or, perhaps, noting a passing bear, the only two automobiles on the 25 miles (40 kilometers) of road in Jasper National Park at that time had a head-on collision.

Banff–Jasper Highway
Highway 93

Roads in both Jasper and Banff were improved during the depression years of the 1930s, when relief projects brought road builders into the parks. The most important highway project was the Icefields Parkway section of the Banff–Jasper Highway. The southern section of the road was started in 1931, but because of the rugged terrain and the short working season, the highway wasn't opened until the summer of 1940. In the late 1950s, major improvements modernized and upgraded the highway further.

The two highest all-weather mountain passes in Canada, the Bow Pass (6,785 feet/2,068 meters) and the Sunwapta Pass (6.677 feet/2,035 meters), are along this stretch of road. The highest drivable pass in Canada is the Highwood Pass on Highway 40, south of the Trans–Canada. It reaches 7,238 feet (2,206 meters) above sea level, but it's closed to traffic throughout the winter.

Chronology of Alberta History

1730	Approximate date Alberta Indians acquired guns and horses.
1754	First European, Anthony Henday, arrives in Alberta.
1778	Peter Pond, the first white to settle in Alberta, builds fur post on Athabasca River.
1786	Second fur post in Alberta built at Fort McMurray.
1788	Fort Chipewyan built at Lake Athabasca.
1788	First North West Company post built on the Peace River, near today's Fort Vermilion.
1789	Alexander Mackenzie sets out from Fort Chipewyan and follows Mackenzie River to Arctic Ocean.
1792	Fort George becomes first fur post in Alberta on North Saskatchewan. Hudson's Bay Company's Buckingham House built same year.
1793	Alexander Mackenzie travels up the Peace River over the mountains to the ocean and becomes the first person to cross North America above Mexico.
1795	First Edmonton House established.
1799	Rocky Mountain House established.
1805	Fort Dunvegan established.
1807	David Thompson crosses Rocky Mountains.
1811	David Thompson follows Columbia River to Pacific.
1813	Fort Edmonton moved back to location inside today's city limits.
1821	Hudson's Bay Company and North West Company amalgamate.
1822	Bow River Expedition undertaken.
1823	John Rowand becomes chief factor at Edmonton House.
1824	First road cut in Alberta. Runs between Edmonton and Fort Assiniboine.
1832	New Fort Edmonton built. Includes John Rowand's famous Big House.
1838	First missionaries, Blanchet and Demers, visit Alberta.
1840	Reverend R.T. Rundle, Methodist missionary, comes to Alberta.

1841	Colonists bound for Oregon pass through Edmonton.
1842	Father Thibault comes to live at Edmonton.
1843	Thibault establishes mission at Lac Ste. Anne.
1846	Canadian artist Paul Kane first visits Fort Edmonton.
1852	Father Lacombe arrives in Alberta.
1854	John Rowand dies.
1857	Palliser Expedition arrives in Alberta.
1858	First prospectors arrive on North Saskatchewan.
1859	First Grey Nuns arrive at Lac Ste. Anne.
1861	Father Lacombe establishes St. Albert Mission.
1862	Overlanders pass through Alberta on way to Caribou gold fields.
1862	Missionary George McDougall arrives in Alberta.
1865	Cree and Blackfoot battle near Red Deer Lake.
1867	Canadian Confederation established.
1869	Red River Rebellion.
1869	Fort Whoop-Up established.
1869	Maskepatoon killed.
1870	Rupert's Land becomes part of Canada.
1872	Surveying of 49th parallel begins.
1874	North-West Mounted Police arrive in Alberta.
1875	Fort Calgary established.
1876	Indian Treaty No. 6 signed.
1876	Sioux seek refuge in Canada.
1877	Treaty No. 7 signed at Blackfoot Crossing.
1878	First official post office in Edmonton.
1879	Telegraph extended to Hay Lakes near Edmonton.
1879	The great buffalo herds are gone.
1880	First newspaper in Alberta, the *Edmonton Bulletin,* begins publication.
1882	North-West Territories divides into four districts, including the new District of Alberta.
1883	Alberta elects first representative to Territorial government.
1883	CPR reaches Alberta and crosses the province.
1883	First natural gas discovered at Alderson near Medicine Hat.
1883	*Calgary Herald* begins publication.
1885	Riel Rebellion.
1886	A narrow-gauge railroad, the Turkey Track, is built from Lethbridge to the main line of the CPR near Medicine Hat.

1887   Former whiskey trader D.W. Davis becomes first federal Member of Parliament from Alberta.

1887   Town of Cardston settled.

1890   Crowfoot, chief of the Blackfoot, dies at Blackfoot Crossing.

1891   Calgary and Edmonton Railway completed.

1896   Father Lacombe starts St. Paul des Metis colony.

1897   Klondike Gold Rush begins.

1897   Crowsnest Pass Railway started.

1899   Treaty No. 8 signed at Grouard and other northern points.

1903   Barr colonists arrive.

1903   Frank Slide.

1903   Billy Cochrane brings first automobile to Alberta.

1903   Homesteaders begin to arrive in the Peace River area.

1905   Alberta becomes a province of Canada. Edmonton becomes the provincial capital.

1905   The Canadian Northern Railway reaches Edmonton.

1907   First airplane flight in Alberta at Botha.

1908   University of Alberta established in Strathcona.

1909   United Farmers of Alberta established.

1911   CPR completes first of its large irrigation systems.

1912   Calgary's first Stampede.

1912   Edmonton and Strathcona amalgamate.

1914   Edmonton Equal Franchise League and the Calgary Council of Women petition legislature for right to vote for women.

1914   Turner Valley's Dingman Well #1 comes in.

1914   Start of World War I.

1915   Imposition of prohibition.

1916   Railroad reaches the Peace River area.

1916   Provincial franchise extended to women.

1916   First air mail delivery in Canada flown by Katherine Stinson between Calgary and Edmonton.

1917   Louise McKinney and Sister Roberta McAdams elected to Alberta Legislature, the first women in Alberta, Canada, and Great Britain to be elected to any legislative assembly.

1918   Federal franchise extended to women.

1918   Armistice signed in Europe.

1921   United Farmers of Alberta defeat Liberals. H. Greenfield becomes premier.

1921   Nellie McClung elected as liberal member of provincial legislature.

1922	First Alberta radio station started.
1923	Prohibition repealed.
1923	Alberta Wheat Pool organized.
1929	Women recognized as "persons" in Canadian law.
1929	Start of the Great Depression.
1931	Ottawa hands over control of natural resources to provinces.
1936	Number of farmers in the province reaches all time peak at 99,732.
1939	World War II begins.
1945	World War II ends.
1947	Imperial Oil's Leduc #1 comes in, and the oil era in Alberta begins.
1964	Great Canadian Oil Sands begin to develop Athabasca oil sands at Fort McMurray.

ACADIA VALLEY

Prairie Elevator Museum
Highway 41
Acadia Valley AB

This museum is housed in a former Alberta Wheat Pool Elevator. Displays describe how grain has been delivered, stored and shipped around the world from the Canadian prairies.

AIRDRIE

Nose Creek Valley Museum
Box 3351
Airdrie AB T4B 2B6
403-948-6685

Features aboriginal artifacts and antique cars, as well as agricultural, commercial, and household tools and memorabilia. There are also reproductions of a pioneer home, a blacksmith shop and a general store.

ALBERTA BEACH

Alberta Beach & District
Museum and Archives
Box 68
Alberta Beach AB TOE OAO
403-924-3678

ALIX

Alix Wagon Wheel Regional

Museum
Box 157
Alix AB TOC OBO
403-747-2462

Exhibits include pioneer and local history displays.

ALLIANCE

Alliance & District Museum
Society
Box 101
Alliance AB TOB OAO
403-879-3931

The museum is housed in what was originally the St. Agnes Roman Catholic Church. This museum includes a blacksmith shop and a log cabin furnished as it would have been in pioneer days.

ARROWWOOD

Arrowwood Restoration Society Museum
Box 238
Arrowwood AB TOL OBO
403-534-3924/534-3763

BANFF

Banff Park Museum
Box 160
Banff AB TOL OCO
403-762-1558

The Government of Canada

opened the Banff Park Museum—the oldest natural history museum in western Canada—in 1895. The current museum building was built in 1903 and restored in 1985. The museum features exhibits of the wildlife and natural history of the parks of western Canada.

Luxton Museum
Box 850
Banff AB TOL OCO
403-762-2388
This museum focuses on aboriginal peoples of the northern plains and Rocky Mountains. Displays range from quilt work to hunting equipment. Guided tours can be arranged.

Banff newspaper publisher Norman Luxton, one of the organizers of the original Banff Indian Days, opened the museum in 1952. Luxton came to Banff in the early years of the twentieth century. He started a weekly newspaper, using the name of Banff's former paper, the Crag & Canyon. *He also wrote and published several guide books for the Banff area.*

Walter Phillips Art Gallery
Box 1020
Banff AB TOL OCO
403-762-6281

Whyte Museum of the Canadian Rockies

Box 160
Banff AB TOL OCO
403-762-2291
The Whyte Museum focuses on the Canadian Rockies, particularly art and cultural history. Contemporary and historical art exhibitions are featured in the gallery. Also housed here are the Whyte Archives of the Canadian Rockies, the largest collection of archival material on these mountains in existence.

BARRHEAD

Barrhead & District Centennial Museum
Box 4122
Barrhead AB T7N 1A1
403-674-5203
The Barrhead Museum displays artifacts and photographs relating to the history of the area.

BEAVERLODGE

South Peace Centennial Museum
Box 493
Beaverlodge AB TOH OCO
403-354-8869
This museum focuses on pioneer life and agriculture. Fifteen display buildings house an assortment of artifacts ranging from antique dolls to farm machinery and antique cars. It's worth the stop.

Beaverlodge Hotel Museum
Box 389
Beaverlodge AB TOH OCO
403-354-2059
This mural-covered museum in one of Beaverlodge's oldest buildings. It houses an assortment of exhibits and artifacts.

BEISEKER

Beiseker Station Museum
Box 149
Beiseker AB TOM OGO
403-947-3774

BENTLEY

Bentley Museum
Box 620
Bentley AB TOC OJO
403-748-2132

BIG VALLEY

Big Valley Museum and Canadian Northern Railway Roundhouse Interpretive Centre
Box 40
Big Valley AB TOJ OGO
403-876-2593
The Big Valley Museum features railway exhibits, photographs and displays pertinent to local history. The Roundhouse Interpretive Centre, with a 1912 Canadian Northern roundhouse and explanatory signs, focuses on the workings of an early railroad roundhouse.

Canadian Northern Railway Society
Box 142
Big Valley AB TOJ OGO
403-876-2242

BLAIRMORE

Crowsnest Pass Ecomuseum
Box 1440
Blairemore AB TOK OEO
403-562-8831/564-4700

Frank Slide Interpretive Centre
c/o Alberta Community Development
Box 959
Blairmore AB TOK OEO
403-562-7388

Leitch Collieries
c/o Alberta Community Development
Box 959
Blairmore AB TOK OEO
403-562-7388

BONNYVILLE

Bonnyville & District Museum
Box 6995
Bonnyville AB T9N 2H4
403-826-4925

BOWDEN

Bowden Pioneer Museum
Box 576
Bowden AB TOM OKO
403-224-2122/224-3229

BRETON

Breton & District Historical
Museum
Box 696
Breton AB TOC OPO
403-696-2288/696-3404
*Exhibits focus on the history
of pioneer Black settlers of the
area who came to Alberta from
Oklahoma at the turn of the
century.*

BROCKET

Oldman River Cultural Centre
Box 70
Brocket AB TOK OHO
403-965-3939
*A small museum featuring
aboriginal artifacts.*

BROOKS

Brooks and District Museum
Box 2078
Brooks AB T1R 1C7
403-362-5073/362-6782

Brooks Aqueduct
Alberta Community Develop-
ment
Box 1522
Cochrane AB TOL OWO
403-653-5139/362-4451

BROWNVALE

Brownvale North Peace Agricultural Museum

Box 3
Brownvale AB TOH OLO
403-597-3950

CALGARY

Aero Space Museum of Calgary
Hangar #10
64 McTavish Place NE
Calgary AB T2E 7H1
403-250-3752
*Displays range from Cal-
gary's first airplane to contemporary aircraft.*

Alberta Science Centre Centennial Planetarium
Box 2100, Station M
Calgary AB T2P 2M5
403-221-3700

Arctic Institute of North
America
University of Calgary
2500 University Drive NW
Calgary AB T2N 1N4
403-220-7515

Beth Tzedec Heritage Collection
1325 Glenmore Trail SW
Calgary AB T2V 4Y8
403-255-8688
*Displays include artifacts
from Calgary's early Jewish
Community.*

Calgary Chinese Cultural Centre Collection
197 First Street SW
Calgary AB T2P 4M4
403-262-5071

Calgary Police Service Interpretive Centre and Museum
133 – 6 Avenue SE
Calgary AB T2G 4Z1
403-268-4565

Calgary Zoo, Botanical Gardens and Prehistoric Park
Box 3036, Station B
Calgary AB T2M 4R8
403-232-9300

The Canadian Western Natural Gas, Light, Heat and Power Museum
909 – 11 Avenue SW
Calgary AB
Focuses on the history of the Canadian Western Natural Gas Company and the development of natural gas in Alberta.

City of Calgary Archives
Box 2100, Station M
Calgary AB T2P 2M5
403-268-8180

Energeum
640 – 5 Avenue SW
Calgary AB T2P 3G4
403-297-4293

Fort Calgary Historic Park
Box 2100, Station M (#106)
Calgary AB T2P 2M5
403-290-1875

Glenbow Museum
130 – 9 Avenue SE
Calgary AB T2G 0P3

403-268-4100
The Glenbow is western Canada's largest museum. Its many exhibits and archival services offer comprehensive sources of information on the history of southern Alberta and the West. Displays, however, come from around the world. They range from Indian artifacts to contemporary art. In addition, the Glenbow has the largest collection of Canadiana in the country.

Grain Academy Museum
(Round-Up Centre, Stampede Park)
c/o Alberta Wheat Pool
Box 2700
Calgary AB T2P 2P5
403-263-4594
The focus of the display is the history of grain production. It includes a working model railway and grain elevator.

Heritage Park Historical Village
1900 Heritage Drive SW
Calgary AB T2V 2X3
403-259-1900
Heritage Park is Canada's largest historical village. It focuses on pre-1915 western Canada. Here you can walk down a re-created frontier street, ride on a steam-powered railroad or riverboat, visit a fur post, look through the more than 100 restored build-

ings or enjoy North America's only antique midway.

Leighton Foundation Collection
Site 31, Box 9, RR #8
Calgary AB T2J 2T9
403-931-3153

Locomotive & Railway Historical Society of Western Canada
4104, 2120 Southland Drive SW
Calgary AB T2V 4W3
403-281-4584

Museum of the Regiments
CFB Calgary
Calgary AB T3E 1T8
403-240-7674
This museum focuses on the history of Calgary's four military regiments. Exhibits include uniforms, weapons, medals, battle dioramas, photographs and video presentations.

Muttart Art Gallery
1221 – 2 Street SW
Calgary AB T2R 0W5
403-266-2764

Naval Museum of Alberta
1820 – 24 Street SW
Calgary AB T2T 0G6
403-242-0002

Nickle Arts Museum
The University of Alberta
2500 University Drive NW
Calgary AB T2N 1N4
403-220-7234

Olympic Hall of Fame and Museum
Canada Olympic Park, SS #1
Calgary AB T2M 4N3
403-247-5455

Petro-Canada Art Programme
Box 2844
Calgary AB T2P 3E3
403-296-6019

The Royal Canadian Naval Museum
1820 – 24 Street SW
Calgary AB
The museum houses naval displays and photographs from World War I, World War II and the Korean War, including the only three airplanes flown by the Canadian Navy during those wars. Guided tours are available.

Stampede Park and Exhibition Grounds
P.O. Box 1060 Station M
Calgary AB T2P 2K8
403-261-0101

Tsuu T'ina Museum
Box 135
3700 Anderson Road SW
Calgary AB T2W 3C4

Ukrainian Museum of Canada, Calgary Collection
404 Meredith Road NE
Calgary AB T2E 5A6
403-264-3437
Displays include Ukrainian

artifacts and clothing dating to the 1890s.

Calgary Walking Tour

A brochure for a self-guided walking tour of some of downtown Calgary's historic buildings is available at tourist information centers and the Alberta Historical Resources Foundation at 102 – 8th Avenue SE. There are also many restored buildings in the downtown area marked with brass plaques or signs recounting their history. A brochure outlining a driving tour of the Inglewood and Mount Royal residential areas of Calgary is also available. Buildings of particular interest include the Hunt House, Calgary's oldest building still on its original site at 890 – 9 Avenue SE, the Nellie McClung House at 803 – 15 Avenue SW and the Calgary Courthouse at 530 – 7 Avenue SW.

CAMROSE

Camrose & District Centennial Museum
Box 1622
Camrose AB T4V 1X6
403-672-3298
An exceptional local museum, the central museum building includes exhibits that range from household items to model railroads. There are 10

historical buildings on the site, including a log house, church, newspaper office, firehall and old schoolhouse. There's also a good collection of farm machinery, as well as a scale model of a steam threshing machine.

Camrose Railway Station Museum and Archives
Highway 13, Camrose
This refurbished 1911 Canadian Northern Railway station houses a railway library and archives focusing on Canadian Northern Railway history. Photographs and railway artifacts are on display.

CANMORE

Centennial Museum
Box 2131
Canmore AB TOL OMO
403-678-4868
This museum includes exhibits of Canmore's early mining history, a large doll collection, photographs and displays from the 1988 Winter Olympics. Guided tours and historical walks can be arranged.

CARDSTON

Court House Museum
Box 1830
Cardston AB TOK OKO
403-653-4322

Remington-Alberta Carriage Centre
Box 1649
Historic Sites and Archives Service
Alberta Community Development
Cardston AB TOK OKO
403-653-5139

CARSTAIRS

Roulston Museum
Box 1067
Carstairs AB TOM ONO
403-337-3710

CASTOR

Castor and District Museum
Box 864
Castor AB TOC OXO
403-882-3409

Housed in the old Canadian Pacific Railway station, the Castor Museum features exhibits from the early days of the community. It includes household, commercial, school and medical displays. The station master's residence is set up in the style of the period.

CLARESHOLM

Appaloosa Horse Club Senior Citizens Museum & Archives
Site 18, Box 1, RR #4
Edmonton AB T5E 5S7
403-973-3647

Claresholm Museum
Box 1000
Claresholm AB TOL OTO
403-625-3131

COCHRANE

Cochrane Ranch
Alberta Community Development
Box 1522
Cochrane AB TOL OWO
403-553-2731

Travelers interested in the early ranching history of Alberta may want to see the Bar U Historic Site near Longview, approximately an hour south of Cochrane on Highway 22. Fred Stinson started the Bar U Ranch with Montreal backers in 1882. Over the years, some of Alberta's most famous cattlemen worked on the ranch, including Tom Lynch, George Lane, John Ware and Montana cowboy Harry Longbaugh, who was known south of the border as the Sun Dance Kid.

Stockmen's Memorial Foundation
Box 459
Cochrane AB TOL OWO
403-932-2277

Western Heritage Centre
Box 1477
Cochrane AB TOL OWO
403-932-3514

Cochrane Historical Walking Tour

A pamphlet outlining an historical walking tour of Cochrane is available at the tourist information center in town. Be sure to stop at the Westlands Cowboy Bookstore, which has an excellent selection of books about aboriginal and western history. You can also get a good piece of Saskatoon Pie, and other kinds, too, at the Home Quarter Restaurant and Pie Shoppe on Main Street.

COLEMAN

Crowsnest Museum
Box 306
Coleman AB TOK OMO
403-563-5434

CROWSNEST PASS

Leitch Collieries Provincial Historic Site
Highway 3, north side
Located on Highway 3 in the Municipality of the Crowsnest Pass, Leitch Collieries preserves the ruins of this early coal processing operation.

CZAR

Prairie Panorama Museum

Highway 41, Czar
Czar, "the town where cowboys rein," is the home of the Prairie Panorama Museum. It features pioneer, homesteading, household and agricultural exhibits. There's also a large and unique salt and pepper shaker collection.

DeBOLT

DeBolt & District Pioneer Museum
c/o Box 447
DeBolt AB TOH 1BO
403-957-3957
A collection of buildings in Hubert Memorial Park in DeBolt house artifacts, machinery and memorabilia from the town's past.

DELBURNE

Anthony Henday Museum
Box 374
Delburne AB TOM OVO
403-749-2436
This museum is in the old Grand Trunk Pacific Railway station. Exhibits deal with homesteading, mining, early commerce and other memorabilia, including agricultural implements.

DELIA

Delia & District Dawson Historical Museum

Box 93
Delia AB TOJ OWO
403-364-3848/364-3836

DEWBERRY

Dewberry Valley Museum
c/o Hedley Dennill
Village of Dewberry
Box 30
Dewberry AB TOB 1GO
403-847-3053
Displays relate to the history of the area, and include aboriginal, fur trade and North-West Rebellion exhibits.

DICKSON

Dickson Store Museum
Box 54
Spruce View AB TOM 1VO
403-728-3355

DIDSBURY

Didsbury & District Museum
Box 1175
Didsbury AB TOM OWO
403-335-9295/335-9843

DONALDA

Donalda & District Museum
Box 40
Donalda AB TOH 1HO
403-883-2345/883-2100

Donalda Lamp Museum
Highway 53, Donalda
The Donalda Lamp Museum

is in the same building as the library and village office. It features an extensive collection of antique lamps, the oldest dating back to the 1600s. There's also a very large collection of salt and pepper shakers. The view of Meeting Creek Coulee is also worth the stop.

DRUMHELLER

Drumheller Dinosaur and
Fossil Museum
Box 2135
Drumheller AB TOJ OYO
403-823-2593

Homestead Antique Museum
Box 3154
Drumheller AB TOJ OYO
403-823-2600/823-9370

Royal Tyrrell Museum of
Palaeontology
Box 7500
Drumheller AB TOJ OYO
403-823-7707

EAST COULEE

Atlas Coal Mine
Box 203
Drumheller AB TOJ OYO
403-823-2220/823-2171

East Coulee School Museum &
Cultural Center
Box 539
East Coulee AB TOJ 1BO
403-822-3970

EDGERTON

Edgerton & District Museum
Box 64
Edgerton AB T0B 1K0
403-755-3963
Housed in a 1910 Railway Station, the museum exhibits a working windmill, farm machinery and an old school.

EDMONTON

Alberta Association of Registered Nurses Museum & Archives
11620 – 168 Street
Edmonton AB T5M 4A6
403-451-0043

Alberta Aviation Museum
11410 Kingsway Avenue
Edmonton AB T5G 0X4
403-453-1078

Alberta Railway Museum
Box 70014
Londonderry P.O.
Edmonton AB T5C 3R6
403-472-6229
The Alberta Railway Museum is set up as a railway terminal, with a yard, a station and an engine and car shop. The museum features the country's largest collection of steam locomotives outside the national museum. It's also home to the oldest railway car in Canada.

Calgary and Edmonton (C&E) Railway Museum
10447 – 86 Avenue
Edmonton AB T6E 2M4
403-433-9739
The C&E Museum is housed in a replica of the 1891 Calgary and Edmonton Railway Station. Historical photos, costumes, artifacts and memorabilia are on display.

Children's Educational Wildlife Museum
5304 – 97 Street
Edmonton AB T6E 5W5
403-436-4034

City of Edmonton Archives
Edmonton Parks and Recreation
Box 2359
Edmonton AB T5J 2R7
403-428-4761

Devonian Botanic Garden
University of Alberta
Edmonton AB T6G 2E9
403-987-3054

Edmonton Art Gallery
2 Sir Winston Churchill Square
Edmonton AB T5J 2C1
403-422-6223

Edmonton Police Museum and Archives
9620 – 103A Avenue
Edmonton AB T5H 0H7
403-421-2274

Exhibits focus on the history of law enforcement in Alberta.

Edmonton Public Schools Archives and Museum (Historic McKay Avenue School)
10425 – 99 Avenue
Edmonton AB T5K OE5
403-422-1970

This museum is housed in the old McKay Avenue School. The building, in addition to fulfilling its duties as a school for many years, also provided a meeting place for the first sitting of the Alberta Legislature in 1906. An educational archives and reading room are also located at the museum. As well, the oldest public schoolhouse in Alberta, the original McKay School built in 1881, stands nearby.

Edmonton Radial Railway Society
PO Box 45040
Lansdowne P.O.
Edmonton AB T6H 5Y1

Edmonton Space & Science Centre
11211 – 142 Street
Edmonton AB T5M 4A1
403-452-9100

Fort Edmonton Park
Box 2359
Edmonton AB T5J 2R7
403-496-8787

Girl Guides of Canada, Alberta Council, Archives and Museum
3 Floor, 11055 – 107 Street
Edmonton AB T5H 2Z6
403-424-5510

John Janzen Nature Centre
Box 2359
Edmonton AB T5J 2R7
403-496-2939

John Walter Museum
10125 97 Avenue
Edmonton AB T5K OB3
403-496-7275

Tour three homes of one of Edmonton's early entrepreneurs, John Walter. The first home was built in 1874.

Latitude 53 Gallery
Great West Saddlery Building
10137 104 Street
Edmonton AB T5J 1A3
403-423-5353

Loyal Edmonton Regiment Museum
Lancaster Park
CFB Edmonton
Edmonton AB T0A 2H0
403-456-2450, ext. 440

Muttart Conservatory
PO Box 2359
Edmonton AB T5J 2R7
403-496-6951

Old Strathcona Model & Toy Museum
8603 – 104 Street

Edmonton AB T6E 4G6
403-433-4512
*Cardboard models of
famous buildings, planes,
trains and ships, paper dolls
and an N-gauge model railroad are among the displays
found here.*

Provincial Archives of Alberta
12845 – 102 Avenue
Edmonton AB T5N 0M6
403-427-1750

Provincial Museum of Alberta
12845 – 102 Avenue
Edmonton AB T5N 0M6
403-453-9100
*The Provincial Museum fea-
tures exhibits, displays and
special programs of the human
and natural history of the
province. It has over 40,000
square feet (3,716 square
meters) of permanent exhibition space. There are regularly
scheduled children's programs
and special events. The provincial archives are in a separate
wing of the building. Alberta's
original Government House,
which was the official home of
the province's Lieutenant Gov-
ernors, is located nearby.*

Rutherford House
c/o Historic Sites & Archives
Service
8820 – 112 Street
Edmonton AB T6G 2P8
403-427-3995

Telephone Historical Centre
Box 4459
Edmonton AB T6E 4T5
403-441-2077

Ukrainian Canadian Archives
& Museum of Alberta
9543 – 110 Avenue
Edmonton AB T5H 1H3
403-424-7580

Ukrainian Catholic Women's
League of Canada Arts & Crafts
Museum
10825 – 97 Street
Edmonton AB T5H 2M4
403-424-7505

Ukrainian Cultural Heritage
Village
c/o Historic Sites and Archives
Service
8820 – 112 Street
Edmonton AB T6G 2P8
403-662-3640

Ukrainian Museum of Canada,
Alberta Branch
10611 – 110 Avenue
Edmonton AB T5H 1H7
403-474-3352/483-5932
*Exhibits include clothing,
Easter eggs, dolls, tapestries
and paintings.*

University of Alberta
Edmonton AB T6G 2E5
403-492-3111
Classics Museum
Clothing & Textiles Collection
Cryptogamic Herbarium

Department of Forest Science
Faculty of Dentistry Museum
Freshwater Invertebrate Collection
Laboratory for Vertebrate Paleontology
Marine Invertebrates and Malacology
Minerology/Petrology Museum
Museum of Zoology
Museums and Collections Services
Osteology Collections
Paleobotanical Collection
Paleontology Museum
Soil Science Collection
E.H. Strickland Entomological Museum
Vascular Plant Herbarium

Valley Zoo
Box 2359
Edmonton AB T5J 2R7
403-496-6911

Victoria Composite High School Museum and Archives
10210 – 108 Avenue
Edmonton AB T5H 1A8
403-426-3010 (ext. 2119)/434-8147

Historic Edmonton Buildings

Interesting historic buildings in Edmonton include the Strathcona Hotel, built in 1891, the Strathcona Library built in 1913, the Flatiron Building built in 1913, the Magrath Mansion built in 1912 and the Rossdale Brewery built in 1898.

EDSON

Red Brick Arts Centre and Museum
4818 – 7 Avenue
Edson AB T7E 1K8
403-723-3582

Galloway Station Museum
4818 7 Avenue
Edson AB T7E 1K8
403-723-5696/723-3582

ELK POINT

Fort George/Buckingham House Interpretive Centre
General Delivery
Elk Point AB T0A 1A0
403-724-2611

ETZIKOM

Heritage Museum of South-East Alberta
Box 563
Etzikom AB T0K 0W0
403-666-3737/666-3915/666-3792

FAIRVIEW

Historic Dunvegan
c/o Alberta Community Development
Historic Sites & Archives Service
Box 1334
Provincial Building
Fairview AB T0H 1L0
403-835-5244/835-7150

Fairview Agricultural Society
Museum
Box 1994
Fairview AB TOH 1L0
403-835-4044

FORESTBURG

Forestburg & District Museum
4707 – 50 Street
Forestburg AB TOB 1N0

FORT ASSINIBOINE

Fort Assiniboine Friendship
Club Museum
Box 28
Fort Assiniboine AB TOG 1A0
403-584-3825

FORT CHIPEWYAN

Fort Chipewyan Bicentennial
Museum
Box 203
Fort Chipewyan AB TOP 1B0
403-697-3844

FORT MACLEOD

Fort Museum
Box 776
Fort Macleod AB TOL 0Z0
403-553-4703

Head-Smashed-In Buffalo
Jump
c/o Alberta Community
Development
Box 1977
Fort Macleod AB TOL 0Z0

403-553-2731 or Calgary 403-
265-0048

FORT McMURRAY

Fort McMurray Oil Sands
Interpretive Centre
515 MacKenzie Boulevard
Fort McMurray AB T9H 4X3
403-743-7167

Heritage Park
1 Tolen Drive
Fort McMurray AB T9H 1G7
403-791-7575

FORT SASKATCHEWAN

Fort Saskatchewan Museum
10104 – 101 Street
Fort Saskatchewan AB T8L 1V9
403-998-1750

FORT VERMILION

Fort Vermilion Heritage
Museum
Box 1
Fort Vermilion AB TOH 1N0
403-927-4603/927-3416

GIBBONS

Sturgeon River Historical
Museum
Box 645
Gibbons AB TOA 1N0
403-923-3726

GIROUXVILLE

Girouxville Museum
c/o Village of Girouxville
Box 276
Girouxville AB TOH 1SO
403-323-4252

Located north of Highway 49 at Girouxville, this museum contains over 3,000 artifacts pertaining to pioneers, missionaries, native people and natural history of the area. There are also displays of local artwork.

GLEICHEN

Siksika Nation Museum of
Natural History
Box 249
Gleichen AB TOJ 1MO
403-734-3862

GRAND CENTRE

Tri-Town Museum
Box 11
Grand Centre AB TOA 1TO
403-594-4494

GRANDE PRAIRIE

Muskoseepi Park
Postal Bag 4000
Grande Prairie AB T8V 6V3
403-538-0300

Pioneer Museum Society of
Grande Prairie
Box 687
Grande Prairie AB T8V 3A8
403-532-5482

Visitors can learn some of the history of the area in this recreated pioneer village.

The Prairie Art Gallery
10209 99 Street
Grande Prairie AB T8V 2H3
403-532-8111

GRIMSHAW

Lac Cardinal Regional Pioneer
Village Museum
Box 325
Grimshaw AB TOH 1WO
403-332-2197/332-4753

GROUARD

Native Cultural Arts Museum
General Delivery
Grouard AB TOG 1CO
403-751-3915

Focusing on aboriginal culture, displays here range from artifacts and ceremonial furnishings to contemporary and traditional arts and crafts. Other exhibits feature the history of Grouard settlement.

HANNA

Hanna & District Pioneer
Museum
Box 365
Hanna AB TOJ 1RO
403-854-4244

This is one of my favorite restored villages. The buildings date from the early years of the century and include a school, ranch house, hospital, general store, railway station, church, blacksmith shop and jail cell. You can find them next to the town ballpark.

HIGH LEVEL

Mackenzie Crossroads Museum and Visitors Centre
Box 485
High Level AB T0H 1Z0
403-926-4811/926-2201
Housed in a log building, this museum features displays of a northern trading post, complete with merchandise and the attached living quarters of the trader. A tourist information area and interpretive center are also in the building and a highway rest area is provided on the grounds.

HIGH PRAIRIE

High Prairie & District Museum
Box 1442
High Prairie AB T0G 1E0
403-523-2601
Displays are of memorabilia and artifacts of local history. A Community Corner exhibits personal collections owned by local people.

HIGH RIVER

Museum of the Highwood

129 – 3 Avenue SW
High River AB T1V 1M9
403-652-7156

HINES CREEK

End of Steel Heritage Museum & Park
Box 686
Hines Creek AB T0H 2A0
403-494-3522
Northwest of Fairview on Highway 64, this local museum focuses on local history. Here you'll find railway artifacts, including a caboose, a trapper's cabin, pioneer homes, community and commercial buildings, a trail, a playground and a park. There are also old automobile and machinery exhibits.

HINTON

Alberta Forest Service Museum
Forest Technology School
1176 Switzer Drive
Hinton AB T7V 1V3
403-865-8211

HOLDEN

Holden Historical Society Museum and Masonic Lodge Gallery
Box 153
Holden AB T0B 2C0
403-688-3767
This museum focuses on homesteading and early village

displays, including a restored jail cell. The museum building was originally the town hall.

HUSSAR

Treacy's Antiques and Objects of Art
Highway 56, Hussar
This interesting operation combines a museum and store. Displays are of pioneer history and Indian artifacts.

INNISFAIL

Dr. George House
5713 – 51 Avenue
Innisfail AB T4G 1R4
403-227-1920/227-5447

Innisfail Historical Village
Box 6042
Innisfail AB T4G 1S7
403-227-2906/227-3847

IRRICANA

Pioneer Acres of Alberta
Box 58
Irricana AB TOM 1BO
403-953-4357

IRVINE

139 Prairie Memories Museum
Box 215
Irvine AB TOJ 1VO
403-834-3736
The Prairie Memories Museum is housed in the communi-

ty's old Government Immigration Building. The museum includes displays of household articles and farming tools from homesteading days. A number of town and school documents from the turn of the century are also on display. At the turn of the century, a sawmill operated at Irvine, milling timber from the Cypress Hills. The old Citizen's Lumber Company Building is currently being restored on a site next to the museum.

ISLAY

Morrison Museum of the Country School
Box 4
Islay AB TOB 2JO
403-744-2260/744-2271
This museum is housed in the old Morrison School, which was originally located five miles (eight kilometers) northwest of town. Displays concentrate on items that would have been found in country schools in the 1930s and 1940s.

JASPER

Jasper–Yellowhead Museum and Archives
Box 42
Jasper AB TOE 1EO
403-852-3013/852-5229

KINUSO

Kinosayo Museum
Box 267
Kinuso AB TOG 1KO
403-775-3774
Located at the Agricultural Complex, this museum focuses on the natural and human history of the area and region.

LA CRETE

La Crete Museum
Box 791
La Crete AB TOH 2HO
403-928-3744

LAC LA BICHE

Lac La Biche Mission
Box 1622
Lac La Biche AB TOA 2CO
403-623-3274

LACOMBE

Ellis Bird Farm
Box 2980
Lacombe AB TOC 1SO
403-346-2211

Michener House Museum
Box 2179
Lacombe AB TOC 1SO
403-782-3933
The Michener House, birth-place of former Governor General of Canada Roland Michener, has been restored and made into a museum at Lacombe. The house contains memorabilia of Michener's life, as well as exhibits and photographs of local history.

Lacombe Blacksmith Shop Museum
5020 – 49 Street
Lacombe AB T4L 1Y2
403-782-7333
A number of historic buildings in the commercial area of Lacombe have been restored including the old Lacombe Blacksmith Shop Museum.

LEDUC

Dr. Woods House Museum
Box 5201
Leduc AB T9E 6L6
403-986-1517
Located in the home of Robert Woods, an early Leduc doctor who lived here from 1927 to 1936, this museum focuses on the Woods family. It also includes displays and artifacts of Leduc's history. Restorations to return the house to its 1920s glory were underway at the time of writing.

LETHBRIDGE

Fort Whoop-Up Interpretive Centre
Box 1074
Lethbridge AB T1J 4A2
403-329-0444

Helen Schuler Coulee Centre
910 – 4 Avenue South
Lethbridge AB T1J 0P6
403-320-3064

Sir Alexander Galt Museum
City of Lethbridge
910 4 Avenue South
Lethbridge AB T1J 0P6
403-320-3898

Southern Alberta Art Gallery
601 – 3 Avenue South
Lethbridge AB T1J 0H4
403-327-8770

University of Lethbridge Art
Gallery
4401 University Drive
Lethbridge AB T1K 3M4
403-329-2690

LLOYDMINSTER

Barr Colony Heritage Cultural
Centre
5011 – 49 Avenue
Lloydminster AB/SK S9V 0T8
306-825-5655
*This museum is on the
Saskatchewan side of the border, so while the museum is
not technically in Alberta, half
the city where it's located is.
The center concentrates on the
history of the Barr colonists as
well as the local area. Exhibits
range from farm machinery
and antique cars to household
items and art.*

LOUGHEED

Iron Creek Museum
Box 249
Lougheed AB T0B 2V0
403-386-3934
*The Iron Creek Museum fea-
tures displays of leather and
shoemaking equipment, as
well as old farm machinery, a
prospector's cabin, two country
schoolhouses, a church and
other exhibits relating to the
early history of the area.*

MANNING

Battle River Pioneer Museum
Box 574
Manning AB T0H 2M0
403-836-2374/836-2180

MARKERVILLE

Historic Markerville Creamery
Museum
Box 837
Markerville AB T0M 1M0
403-728-3006/728-3450

Stephansson House
Summer Season: RR #1
Markerville AB T0M 1M0
403-728-3929
Year-round: c/o Reynolds-
Alberta Museum
Box 6360
Wetaskiwin AB T9A 2G1
403-361-1351

MEDICINE HAT

Clay Products Interpretive
Centre (Medalta)
Box 204
Medicine Hat AB T1A 7E9
403-529-1070

Echo Dale Historical Farm
Echo Dale Regional Park
c/o City of Medicine Hat
580 – 1 Street SE
Medicine Hat AB T1A 8E6
403-529-9393/527-2222

Medicine Hat Museum and
Art Gallery
1302 Bomford Crescent SW
Medicine Hat AB T1A 5E6
403-527-6266

Police Point Interpretive Centre
c/o Box 2491
Medicine Hat AB T1A 8G8
403-529-6225

MILLET

Millet & District Museum and
Exhibit Room
Box 178
Millet AB T0C 1Z0
403-387-5558
*Memorabilia from the village and area, including a
replica of a local barbershop,
can be found here. A restored
fire wagon sits out front.*

MIRROR

Mirror & District Museum
Box 246
Mirror AB T0B 3C0
403-788-3828/788-2126
*Exhibits of railway and pioneer artifacts, including replicas of a Canadian Northern
Railway station, a pioneer
kitchen and an early medical
clinic can be found here.*

MORLEY

Nakoda Institute
Box 120
Morley AB T0L 1N0
403-881-3949/881-3951
*This museum and lodge is
run by the Goodstoney Indian
Band. The lodge offers meeting
and hotel facilities. The Institute is a cultural and research
center. It includes a small
library and archives as well as
displays of Stoney artifacts and
native art.*

MORRIN

Morrin Historical Park
Highway 27, just off Highway
56 at Morrin
*A replica of a pioneer sod
house can be found in Morrin
Historical Park. The house
includes appropriate furnishings and an outdoor baking
oven. It was built in 1980 to*

mark the town's sixtieth anniversary.

MUNDARE

Basilian Fathers Museum
Box 379
Mundare AB TOB 3HO
403-764-3887
This museum houses a large collection Ukrainian religious and folk artifacts.

NAMPA

Nampa & District Historical Society Museum
Box 267
Nampa AB TOH 2RO
403-322-3741

NANTON

Nanton Lancaster Air Museum
Box 1051
Nanton AB TOL 1RO
403-646-2270
The Lancaster Society Air Museum focuses on World War II fighter planes. Its Lancaster bomber is one of less than 20 such planes that remain in existence from the thousands built during World War II. Southern Alberta was home to eight flying schools during the war, and two training planes are on display at the museum. Other exhibits include gun turrets, photographs, engines and a replica of a Vicker's Viking biplane.

NEERLANDIA

Neerlandia Historical Society
Box 130
Neerlandia AB TOG 1RO
403-674-6450

NORDEGG

Nordegg Historic Center
Nordegg Historical Society
c/o Municipal District of Clearwater No. 99
Box 550
Rocky Mountain House AB TOM 1TO
403-845-4444
The Nordegg Heritage Centre/Mine Site Interpretive Centre features photographs and memorabilia of the town during its coal mining days. Daily mine tours are scheduled throughout the summer.

OLDS

Mountain View Museum
Box 3882
Olds AB TOM 1PO
403-556-8464

OYEN

Crossroads Museum
Box 477
Oyen AB TOJ 2JO
403-664-3850/664-2330
Exhibits include those in a

blacksmith shop, a farm home from the early part of the century and the old Benton Community Hall. Displays range from household to medical and agricultural relics.

PARADISE VALLEY

Climb Through Time Museum
c/o Box 54
Paradise Valley AB T0B 3R0
403-745-2374

PATRICIA

Field Station of the Royal Tyrrell Museum of Palaeontology
Box 60
Patricia AB T0J 2K0
403-378-4342

PEACE RIVER

Peace River Centennial Museum & Archives
10302 99 Street
Peace River AB T8S 1K1
403-624-4261
   At the front of the museum, you'll find the original Twelve-Foot Davis grave marker. Inside, you'll find displays and exhibits from the area's history. Walking tours of Peace River start at the museum. Watch especially for the Twelve-Foot Davis statue, the murals and the Peace River train station.

PICTURE BUTTE

Prairie Acres Heritage Village & Farm Equipment Museum
Box 768
Picture Butte AB T0K 1V0
403-329-1201

PINCHER CREEK

Oldman River Antique Equipment and Threshing Club
Box 2496
Pincher Creek AB T0K 1W0
403-627-4369

Pincher Creek & District Museum
c/o Box 1226
Pincher Creek AB T0K 1W0
403-627-3684

PLAMONDON

Plamondon Museum at Plamondon
Highway 55, Plamondon
   The Plamondon Museum is housed in the community's first church, which was built in 1911. Displays focus on artifacts and history of the town.

PONOKA

Fort Ostell Museum
5320 – 54 Street
Ponoka AB T4J 1L8
403-783-5224/783-5968

RANFURLY

Ranfurly & District Museum
Box 162
Ranfurly AB TOB 3TO
403-658-2208/658-2107

RAYMOND

Raymond & District Museum
Box 1151
Raymond AB TOK 2SO
403-752-3496
Exhibits offer information on local history, and include household furnishings, textiles and agricultural tools.

RED DEER

Alberta Sports Hall of Fame and Museum
502, 4920 – 51 Street
Red Deer AB T4N 6K8
403-341-8614

Fort Normandeau Historic Site & Interpretive Centre
c/o 6300 45 Avenue
Red Deer AB T4N 3M4
403-347-7550
A replica of Fort Norman-deau stands at Fort Norman-deau Historic Park west of Red Deer. Built near the original fort's location, it includes an interpretive center, a variety of exhibits, audio-visual displays and guides wearing period costumes.

Heritage Ranch & Visitor Information Centre
Box 5008
Red Deer AB T4N 3T4
403-346-0180

Kerry Wood Nature Centre
6300 – 45 Avenue
Red Deer AB T4N 3M4
403-346-2010

Red Deer & District Museum
Box 800
Red Deer AB T4N 5H2
403-343-6844
The Red Deer & District Museum features displays, artifacts, local and traveling exhibitions, agricultural exhibits, and art and interpre-tive programs. The City of Red Deer Archives is also located here, and a guide for an histor-ical walking tour of the city is also available. Heritage Square, with a number of Red Deer's heritage buildings, is located in Rotary Recreation Park south of the museum. This is the best place to start an historic walking tour of the City of Red Deer.

REDCLIFF

Redcliff Museum
Box 758
Redcliff AB TOJ 2PO
403-548-3524/548-6260
Exhibits here include dis-plays from early industries,

farms, community and home life of the area.

REDWATER

Redwater Museum
Box 114
Redwater AB TOA 2WO
403-942-3552

RIMBEY

Rimbey Museum & Pas Ka
Poo Historical Park
c/o Murray Ormsberg
Box 641
Rimbey AB TOC 2JO
403-843-2084
    Home to a number of Rim-bey's historical buildings, including a trapper's cabin, a log home, the original Anglican Church and other buildings. There's also museum exhibits and a complete collection of International half-ton trucks.

ROCHFORT BRIDGE

Lac Ste. Anne Historical Society Pioneer Museum
Lac Ste. Anne Historical Society
Box 525
Sangudo AB TOE 2AO
403-785-2674/785-3467

ROCKY MOUNTAIN HOUSE

Rocky Mountain House
Museum
Box 1508
Rocky Mountain House AB
TOM 1TO
403-845-2332

Rocky Mountain House
National Historic Site
Box 2130
Rocky Mountain House AB
TOM 1TO
403-845-2412/845-3948

ROSEBUD

Rosebud Centennial Museum
c/o Rosebud Historical Society
Box 601
Rosebud AB TOJ 2TO
403-677-2284/677-2208/677-2256

ROWLEY

Yesteryear Artifacts Museum
General Delivery
Rowley AB TOJ 2XO
403-368-3816/368-2276
    This museum is in a refur-bished Canadian Northern Railway station, including a station master's quarters.

RYLEY

Ryley Museum
Highway 14, Ryley
    Features pioneer memorabil-ia. Also visit George's Shoe and Harness Shop. Billed as a work-ing museum, leather products are made and repaired with antique equipment and tools.

SADDLE LAKE

Saddle Lake Cultural Museum
Box 102
Saddle Lake AB T0A 3T0
403-726-3829

ST. ALBERT

Centre Vital Grandin Centre
5 St. Vital Avenue
St. Albert AB T8N 1K1
403-459-2116

Father Lacombe Chapel
c/o Historic Sites & Archives
8820 – 112 Street
Edmonton AB T6G 3P8
403-427-3995

Musée Héritage Museum
5 St. Anne Street
St. Albert AB T8N 3Z9
403-459-1528

ST. PAUL

Musée Historique de St. Paul
Historical Museum
4537 – 50 Avenue
St. Paul AB T0A 3A3
403-645-4800

SCANDIA

Eastern Irrigation District
(EID) Historical Park
General Delivery
Scandia AB T0J 2Z0
403-362-5010

SEBA BEACH

Seba Beach Heritage Museum
c/o 202, 9923 103 Street
Edmonton AB T5K 2J3
403-420-6704/797-3864

SEDGEWICK

Sedgewick Archives and
Gallery
Box 508
Sedgewick AB T0B 4C0
403-384-3741/384-3070
   *Features memorabilia from
the early days of the town,
photographs and a local
archives. It also occasionally
features displays by local
artists. It's located in the
town's old Bank of Montreal
building.*

SEXSMITH

Sexsmith Blacksmith Shop
Museum
Box 252
Sexsmith AB T0H 3C0
403-568-3681
   *Designated a Provincial
Historic Resource in 1986, this
working blacksmith shop,
with over 10,000 artifacts,
operated as a business until
1974. Built in 1916, the shop
also includes some history of
another sort—the local moon-
shine trade.*

SHERWOOD PARK

Strathcona County Agricultural & Heritage Museum
913 Ash Street
Sherwood Park AB
403-467-8189
This museum features a small exhibit of agricultural and local memorabilia.

SMOKY LAKE

Smoky Lake Museum
Box 302
Smoky Lake AB TOA 3CO
403-656-3503

Victoria Settlement
c/o Historic Sites & Archives
8820 – 112 Street
Edmonton AB T6G 2P8
403-656-2333

SPIRIT RIVER

Spirit River and District Museum
Box 221
Spirit River AB TOH 3GO
This museum features a post office, store, log cabin and country school, plus an assortment of artifacts and memorabilia dealing with the local area.

SPRUCE VIEW

Danish Canadian National Museum

c/o Box 92
Spruce View AB TOM 1VO
403-227-4917

STAVELY

Museum Society of Stavely and District
Box 389
Stavely AB TOL 1ZO

STETTLER

Stettler Town & Country Museum
Box 2188
Stettler AB TOC 2LO
403-742-4543/742-4291

STONY PLAIN

Multicultural Heritage Centre
Box 2188
Stony Plain AB T7Z 1X7
403-963-2777
This museum and art gallery focuses on early immigrants in Alberta.

Stony Plain & District Pioneer Museum
c/o RR #2
Stony Plain AB T7Z 1X2
403-963-6627

STROME

Sodbusters Archives & Museum
Box 151
Strome AB TOB 4HO
403-376-3688

This museum features displays and exhibits from the early days of settlement.

SUNDRE

Sundre Pioneer Village Museum
Box 314
Sundre AB TOM 1X0
403-638-3233/638-3855
The Sundre Pioneer Village features an old schoolhouse, a blacksmith shop, barn and Norwegian log cabin.

TABER

Taber & District Museum
Box 2734
Taber AB TOK 2G0
403-223-5708

THORHILD

Thorhild & District Museum
Box 274
Thorhild AB TOA 3J0
403-398-3672

THREE HILLS

Kneehill Historical Museum
Box 653
Three Hills AB TOM 2A0
403-443-2092/443-5970/443-5625

Tofield Museum
Highway 14, Tofield

Located in the local arena, the Tofield Museum has a small display of local memorabilia.

TROCHU

Saint Ann Ranch
Box 249
Trochu AB TOM 2C0
403-442-3924

Trochu and District Museum
Box 538
Trochu AB TOM 2C0
403-442-2334/442-3935/442-2141/442-2529

TWO HILLS

Two Hills & District Museum
Box 2
Two Hills AB TOB 4K0
403-657-2379

VALLEYVIEW

Valleyview & District Museum
Box 90
Valleyview AB TOH 3N0
403-524-3381

VEGREVILLE

Lakusta Heritage Foundation of Canada
c/o 203, 10348 – 176 Street
Edmonton AB T5S 1L3
403-478-7751/476-9925

Vegreville International Police
Museum
5029 – 45B Avenue
Vegreville AB T9C 1L6
403-632-2770

Vegreville Museum
5029 – 45B Avenue
Vegreville AB T9C 1L6
403-632-2192/632-2130/
632-4125

VERMILION

Vermilion Heritage Museum
Box 1205
Vermilion AB T0B 4M0
403-853-6211
   *Opened in 1991, the museum
is housed in the community's
former high school. The build-
ing has also been designated a
Provincial Historic Site by the
Alberta Historic Resources
Foundation.*

VETERAN

Veteran Museum Society
Box 534
Veteran AB T0C 2S0
403-575-2223

VIKING

Viking Historical Museum
Box 270
Viking AB T0B 4N0
403-336-3129/336-4931
   *Displays are of local and
area history.*

WAINWRIGHT

Wainwright & District Museum
Box 2294
Wainwright AB T0B 4P0
403-842-3115
   *Located in the old Canadi-
an Northern Railway station,
the museum features exhibits
of the area's homesteading
days, railroad memorabilia
and the history of Buffalo Park
and nearby Camp Wain-
wright.*

WANHAM

Grizzly Bear Prairie Museum
Box 68
Wanham AB T0H 3P0
403-694-3933

WATERTON PARK

Archaeological Displays in
Waterton Lakes Park
3 miles (5 km) from Waterton
townsite on Red Rock Canyon
Road
   *On the road to Red Rock
Canyon from Waterton townsite, the interpretive signs at
the Akaitapi Exhibit describe
archaeological discoveries in
the Waterton area. They also
explain how native people
used some of the resources
found in Waterton Lakes
Park.*

Waterton Natural History
Museum
Box 145
Waterton Park AB T0K 2M0
403-859-2624/859-2267

The Waterton Natural History Museum concentrates on the natural history of the area but also includes information about the human history of the park.

WESTLOCK

Westlock & District Historical
Museum
Box 2637
Westlock AB T0G 2L0
403-349-2887

WETASKIWIN

Alberta Central Railway
Museum
RR #2
Wetaskiwin AB T9A 1W9
403-352-2257/352-3202

Canada's Aviation Hall of
Fame
c/o Reynolds-Alberta Museum
Box 6360
Wetaskiwin AB T9A 2G1
403-361-1351

Reynolds–Alberta Museum
Box 6360
Wetaskiwin AB T9A 2G1
403-361-1351/352-5855

Reynolds Aviation Museum
4110 – 57 Street

Wetaskiwin AB T9A 2B6
403-352-5201

Reynolds Museum
4110 – 57 Street
Wetaskiwin AB T9A 2B6
403-352-5201/352-6201

Wetaskiwin & District Museum
5010 – 53 Avenue
Wetaskiwin AB T9A 0Y7
403-352-0227

WILLINGDON

Historical Village & Pioneer
Museum at Shandro
Box 102
Willingdon AB T0B 4R0
403-367-2452/2445

Useful Further Reading

Anderako, Mark. *Historic Trails of Alberta*. Edmonton: Lone Pine Publishing, 1985.

Bowen, Lynne. *Muddling Through: The Remarkable Story of the Barr Colonists*. Vancouver: Greystone, 1992.

Brado, Edward. *Cattle Kingdom: Early Ranching in Alberta*. Vancouver: Douglas & McIntyre, 1984.

Cashman, Tony. *The Edmonton Story*. Edmonton: Institute of Applied Art, 1956.

———. *A Picture History of Alberta*. Edmonton: Hurtig Publishers, 1979.

Dempsey, Hugh A. *Indians of Alberta*. Calgary: Glenbow Museum, 1988.

Fraser, Frances. *The Bear Who Stole the Chinook*. Vancouver: Douglas & McIntyre, 1990.

Fryer, Harold. *Alberta: the Pioneer Years*. Surrey: Stagecoach Publishing, 1977.

Gard, Robert E. *Johnny Chinook: Tall Tales and True from the Canadian West*. New York: Longmans, Green & Company, 1945.

Hallett, Mary, and Marilyn Davis. *Firing the Heather: The Life and Times of Nellie McClung*. Saskatoon: Fifth House, 1993.

Helgason, Gail. *The First Albertans: An Archaeological Search*. Edmonton: Lone Pine Publishing, 1987.

Howard, Joseph Kinsey. *Strange Empire*. New York: William Morrow and Co., 1952.

Hunt, William R. *Whiskey Peddler: Johnny Healy, North Frontier Trader*. Missoula: Mountain Publishing, 1993.

Innis, Harold A. *The Fur Trade In Canada*. New Haven: Yale University Press, 1930.

Jameson, Sheilagh. *Ranchers, Cowboys, and Characters: The Birth of Alberta's Western Heritage*. Calgary: Glenbow Museum, 1987.

Jones, David C. *Empire of Dust*. Edmonton: University of Alberta Press, 1987.

Kane, Paul. *Wanderings of an Artist....* Edmonton: Hurtig Publishers, 1968.

Luxton, Eleanor. *Banff: Canada's First National Park*. Banff: Summerthought Ltd., 1975.

MacEwan, Grant. *Between the Red and the Rockies*. Toronto: University of Toronto Press, 1952.

———. *Blazing the Old Cattle Trail*. Saskatoon: Modern Press, 1962.

———. *Coyote Music and Other Humorous Tales of the Early West*. Calgary: Rocky Mountain Books, 1993.

MacGregor, James G. *The Battle River Valley*. Saskatoon: Western Producer Prairie Books, 1976.

———. *Blankets & Beads: A History of the Saskatchewan River*. Edmonton: Institute of Applied Art, 1949.

———. *Edmonton: A History*. Edmonton: Hurtig Publishers, 1967.

———. *A History of Alberta*. Edmonton: Hurtig Publishers, 1972.

———. *The Land of Twelve-Foot Davis*. Edmonton: Institute of Applied Art, no date available.

Martin, John J. *The Rosebud Trail*. privately published, no city or date available.

McDougall, John. *Opening the Great West*. Calgary: Glenbow Alberta Institute, 1970.

Moberly, Henry John in collaboration with William B. Cameron. *When Fur Was King*. New York: Dutton, 1929.

Neering, Rosemary, and Michael Breuer. *Historic Alberta*. New York Oxford University Press, 1986.

Newman, Peter C. *Caesars of the Wilderness*. New York: Viking, 1987.

———. *Company of Adventurers*. New York: Viking 1985.

———. *Merchant Princes*. New York: Viking, 1991.

Palmer, Howard with Tamara Palmer. *Alberta: A New History*. Edmonton: Hurtig Publishers, 1990.

Palmer, Howard and Tamara Palmer, eds. *Peoples of Alberta: Portraits of Cultural Diversity*. Saskatoon: Western Producer Prairie Books, 1985.

Palmer, Howard. *Land of the Second Chance: A History of Ethnic Groups in Southern Alberta*. Lethbridge: The Lethbridge Herald, 1972.

Potrebenko, Helen. *No Streets of Gold: A Social History of Ukrainians in Alberta*. Vancouver: New Star, 1977.

Rasmussen, Linda, et al compilers. *A Harvest Yet To Reap: A History of Prairie Women*. Toronto: The Women's Press, 1976.

Russell, Andy. *The Canadian Cowboy: Stories of Cows, Cowboys, and Cayuses*. Toronto: McClelland Stewart, 1993.

———. *The Life of a River*. Toronto: McClelland and Stewart, 1987.

Sharp, Paul F. *Whoop-Up Country: the Canadian–American West*. St. Paul: University of Minnesota Press, 1955.

Silverman, Elaine. *The Last Best West: Women on the Alberta Frontier 1880-1930*. Montreal: Eden Press, 1984.

Stinson, Fred. *The Story of Calgary*. Saskatoon: Fifth House Publishers, 1994.

Tanner, Ogden. *The Canadians*. Alexandria, Virginia: Time–Life Books, 1977.

Willison, Gladys. *Land of the Chinook: Stories of Early Alberta*. Toronto: MacMillan, 1955.

294